KILIMANJARO AND BEYOND
(A Life-Changing Journey)

By

Barry Finlay

with

Chris Finlay

First published by Dog Ear Publishing
4010 W. 86th Street, Ste H
Indianapolis, IN 46268
www.dogearpublishing.net

ISBN: 978-145750-392-4

This book is printed on acid-free paper.

Printed in the United States of America

WHAT OTHERS ARE SAYING ABOUT KILIMANJARO AND BEYOND – A LIFE-CHANGING JOURNEY

"This book is a testament to all of us that dreams can come true with a little grit and determination. If you're the kind of person who can usually find any excuse to talk yourself out of a great idea, this book is the inspiration you need to get out of your comfort zone and make things happen. Kilimanjaro and Beyond is a very honest and detailed account of the trials and tribulations experienced while climbing Africa's highest peak. The most amazing part of this journey is that it wasn't just a selfish mission to stand at lofty heights but one which resulted in bringing clean water to hundreds of Tanzanian children. An inspiring read."

Helen Osler, author of *Cameras of Kilimanjaro*
Australia

"...honest, funny, very engaging and truly written from the heart."

Alysha Atma, Salem-News.com
Oregon, U.S.A.

"Finlay shares his story of self discovery and challenge against the backdrop of climbing Africa's highest peak: Kilimanjaro. His story is a descriptive illustration of the difficulties of climbing to high-altitude, and the lessons he learns along the way. Although not a climber's guide, one should always seek input from experts and professionals before embarking on an expedition, this book conveys Finlay's personal experience and connects to the reader with the smart use of a diary voice."

Meagan McGrath, Adventurer
Canada

"The book is a really warm and inspiring story, and I think highlights perfectly how a couple of regular people can really accomplish something amazing. It is a mini-memoir, comparing aspects of the author's childhood on the prairies with life in Africa and his reflections on the mountain."

Shannon Singh, Development Coordinator, Plan Canada

This book is dedicated to Keith
who battled to the end.

TABLE OF CONTENTS

Acknowledgements

CHRIS AND I would like to thank our families for the love and support given to us throughout our journey. Evelyn, Laura, Annika, Jaelyn, Trevor, Josée, Don and Marion have been unwavering in their support of our endeavors and for that we are deeply appreciative. We couldn't have done it without the knowledge that we had the support of our immediate and extended families every step of the way. Our friends and many we don't even know have been tremendously encouraging in offering moral support for our climb and our projects and significant time and money for our cause. We want to thank our editor, Kip Kirby, for correcting our spelling and grammatical errors, but more so for the (mostly) gentle prodding to get more out of us, which resulted in this being a better book. Kip was especially amazing towards the end of the book as she started her own journey through some very difficult times. Thank you to fellow climber, Peter Yates, for his camaraderie on the mountain and the newfound friendship that will undoubtedly endure from our experience together. To Francis, Shabaan, Ignace and the entire crew at Tusker Trail, thank you for making our trek up and down the mountain so enjoyable and safe and may their climbing continue to be uneventful. Finally, thank you to Plan Canada, Plan Tanzania and other child centered organizations everywhere for the work they do so that young people are given a better opportunity to achieve their own dreams and goals. The result will be a better world.

INTRODUCTION

IT IS JANUARY 16, 2009 at around noon local time, and my son Chris and I are sitting quietly propped up against a large rock. We are trying not to move too much as we enjoy a well-deserved sandwich, because every movement we make requires us to dig deep to draw a breath. The wind is howling and to our left, the sun is glistening off a glacier. We have climbed for seven days through a number of ecological zones, including steaming vibrant rainforests, moorland bursting with extraterrestrial-like trees, alpine desert where only the strongest, most determined of vegetation survives, and finally, to our current location where nothing grows. Perhaps the word "climbed" doesn't sufficiently describe it, as we have also scrambled, struggled, clung, slipped and slid. We've experienced extreme exhaustion and in the last few hours, the feeling of suffocation, as if someone was clamping a towel firmly over our noses and mouths.

I'm shivering, not so much from the cold or fatigue, but from the exhilaration of achievement and anticipation. But now it is decision time. We have made it to Stella Point on Mount Kilimanjaro, the highest peak on the African continent. Our destination is tantalizingly close, yet there are two factors that will determine what happens next: the weather and — more importantly — the state of our health. Where we go from here is in the hands of our guides. We await their decision.

To put it into perspective, for mountaineers, climbing the highest mountain on each of the seven continents (known as the seven summits) is a major feat. There are many mountains with high elevations that don't make it to the list of the seven summits because they are not the highest on their respective continents. For example, Mount Everest is the highest mountain in the world and the highest peak in Asia and therefore is on the list. But because K2, the second highest mountain in the world is also in Asia, it does not make the list. Although there are higher mountains that don't make the list, Mount Kilimanjaro ranks fourth among the so-called seven summits and at 19,340 feet (or 5,895 meters), reaching the top is no small feat.

Our guides tell us during our climb that about 40,000 people attempt to reach the summit of Kilimanjaro each year. This seems like a lot of people until you consider that almost 7 billion of us occupy this planet we call home. Relative to the number of people in the world, my son Chris and I could be considered two of a mere handful of climbers who have actually experienced the top of Mount Kilimanjaro. (Statistics on the number of climbers who actually make it to the top vary, although estimates place the success rate at somewhere between 50% and 85%.)

At age 60, my climb is the completion of the first part of a journey that has forever changed my life. But there is a second part to this incredible journey. Three days later, we will find ourselves bumping fists with a group of young Tanzanian children at their school in the dusty suburbs of Mwanza. We are standing in front of a small building with bricks piled nearby; bricks that are destined to one day give these children more space and a better facility for their education. The kids are smiling and laughing and seem to be enjoying our company. But amidst the laughter is an underlying reality. They have none of the clean water that we have for drinking and other daily activities that we take for granted. They are receiving an education that is severely limited by the size of their classrooms and the fact that many of them (especially the girls) have to walk miles to fetch water, which significantly reduces their availability for education. Chris and I had raised money to help the children before we embarked on our climb, and we are thrilled to have the opportunity to present them with a flag bearing the names of over 200 of our supporters. But it is obvious to us that there is so much more to be done.

You may be wondering what I was doing in the middle of Tanzania in the first place, or how I came to climb the fourth-ranked mountain on the list of the seven summits at an age in life where many people are safely thinking about their retirement years. It was a question I'd asked myself many times as well. When the whole adventure began four years earlier, I had never intended to set out on a journey to change my life! As far as I was concerned, my life was just fine the way it was. However, someone once said that life begins at the end of our comfort zone. I am not sure I unequivocally buy into that theory, since there are plenty of people who are completely satisfied living in their comfort zones. As it turned out, though, my comfort zone was not necessarily the best place for me to be, and I soon began to see that there were real rewards that came along with going beyond it.

It's human nature to find excuses for why we can't change ourselves. And I subscribed to them all. *I'm too busy. I'm too tired. I can't afford it. Change is too much work. I don't know where to start.* Change is a matter of choices and, yes, sacrifices, but as it turns out, those issues are the relatively easy ones to sort out! The difficult part is convincing yourself that you really *want* to make changes at all. Maybe this is why the last four years of my life have been such an incredible journey.

As I look back, I realize there were a number of converging personal events that set the stage for my lifestyle-altering adventure. Collectively they resulted in a commitment – completely unforeseen on my part — that I would attempt to conquer the mental and physical challenges necessary to climb a mountain. There was a routine visit to the family doctor that revealed elevated triglyceride levels, necessitating a health incentive on my part. There was a young personal trainer 38 years my junior, who showed me that even as I was approaching my sixties, I could overcome the limitations that my brain was placing on my body. Most of all, there was the inspiration that I later realized was all around me, capped by my lifelong and intense fascination with mountains.

Maybe it has something to do with being raised on the relatively-flat Canadian prairies that's always interested me in exploring the allure of the mountains and those who climb them. From the time I was 12 on a train ride through the Rocky Mountains, I have always been captivated by the sheer boldness and strength of the mountains. After watching a presentation by Laurie Skreslet, the first Canadian to reach the top of Mount Everest, I always came to admire the determination of climbers who undertake the preparations necessary to climb a mountain and then follow that up with the courage and commitment required to actually achieve their goal. Chris made me start thinking that maybe I could climb a mountain many years later when he mused about climbing Mount Kilimanjaro. I never dreamed then that we would ever undertake anything even faintly resembling what mountaineers like Skreslet had done.

In conjunction with our climb, Chris and I also discovered there was a need within us to try to give something back to the country that was allowing us and so many others to climb all over their mountain. We decided we wanted to give something back to the children of Tanzania. Its celebrated mountain came first for us, but we realized that attempting the climb would provide a good platform for raising money for a worthy cause. Meeting the children at two schools just after our climb was yet another event that would set me off on a new and tremendously satisfying path.

During our adventure, Chris and I each had unique individual experiences. Chris kept track of his in a journal and excerpts are included as annotations throughout the book. His perspective is different from mine, of course, but we hope you will find much to think about as you read our separate stories. We've chosen to address our journey in two parts. The first part deals with the change in lifestyle that led to the climb and describes the life altering climb itself. It describes how I took control of my life and improved myself physically and mentally. It describes adopting a healthier lifestyle so I can hopefully live a long life and embrace that second chance we're given called grandchildren. And the first section also describes Chris' own early life journey: the path that included a medical scare that led him to that first step up the mountain with his father and what it was like to stand at the top. It was not only the exhilaration of having done it, but the accomplishment of having climbed with another health issue - two tears in the meniscus of his knee!

The second part of the book discusses how, as ordinary people in our small way, we can make a difference in the lives of others if we have the desire to do so and with a little perseverance. The book tries to debunk some of the popular myths related to helping others, and it describes some of the tactics that have worked for me. And we attempt to demonstrate the power that one or two individuals can have by mobilizing friends, family and others to work together for a common cause.

With Chris' input, I decided to chronicle my life-changing experience facing off against a mountain that brings so many people to their knees – literally – because I think my story could provide inspiration for others who have retired, or grown older, or for whatever reason are at a crossroads. What I learned along the way is that it's NEVER too late to pursue a dream, even when the odds seem totally stacked against you. And from that, I hope there is inspiration for others who might be questioning their own abilities, their own fears and their own self-reliance!

We hope that you will enjoy our journey as much as we did, and that in some way it will encourage you to achieve your own dreams and aspirations and to help others with theirs.

PART I

HOW IT BEGINS
THE FIRST STEPS

CHAPTER 1

Dunia Ni Mapito (Life is a Transition)

THE SUN HAS barely popped up over the horizon, and Chris and I are sitting bleary-eyed on a regional jet, flying from Nairobi to the Kilimanjaro Airport in Moshi. It is January 6, 2009 and the pilot announces that we will be flying past Mount Kilimanjaro. We are both watching closely with eyes half open as we travel from Kenya into Tanzania, hoping that we can catch a glimpse of where we plan to be in a few days. Since the plane is not crowded, Chris has decided to sit on one side and I am directly on the other, giving us both the advantage of a window. There is a mountain in the distance on Chris' side early into the flight, but it is not what we expected to see and turns out to be a false sighting as the pilot announces it is Mount Meru. We settle back into our seats and continue to peer out the window.

Chris: I think the flight staff was trying to distribute the weight on the plane evenly, and that is what resulted in us sitting on either side. Maybe their concern was that we would fly in circles if we didn't cooperate.

There is a major battle raging between my body and mind right now. My body is succumbing to the dullness that settles in when there's been very little sleep in the previous 30 hours. My eyes are drooping. But my mind is resisting, fueled by the adrenalin rush that anticipation and excitement bring. My mind is willing my body to stay awake. Both receive a major boost as the barren expanse, occasionally interspersed with brownish shrubbery that we have been observing from our vantage point, starts to morph into lush vegetation rising from the ground. As the aircraft moves forward on its path to the airport, it is not the plane that is descending; it is the ground that is rising up towards us. I call Chris over to my side of the plane. From this height, the various green hues are slowly replaced by splashes of blue as the ground continues its march towards us and finally, we don't have to be told it is *our* mountain looming into view as the green has been completely replaced by a huge shape with blue-grey top and sides, which are dotted with mounds of frozen whiteness. One wispy cloud is drifting by the peak. The mountain is massive, both in width and height, rising rigidly from the ground in the middle of nowhere. It is Mount Kilimanjaro. We are flying at 18,000 feet or 5,486 meters, almost 2,000 feet LOWER than the top of the mountain we hope to be standing on in a few days! Chris looks at me and in four short words, he succinctly sums up what we are both thinking: "What have we done?"

Chris: Those four words still resonate in my mind to this day and the feeling that inspired them is something I know I won't be forgetting in this lifetime. It is one thing to talk about climbing a 19,000-plus foot mountain — it can be likened to talking about a billion dollars. You know it's a real thing, a real concept, but your life experiences can't really put it in perspective. All of a sudden, you are in a plane and you are BELOW the summit of the mountain, and you can't help but wonder what it is you have gotten yourself into. I have been on top of mountains before, but in hindsight they were hills, not mountains — and that is a big difference.

It has been a long ordeal getting to Africa from our home in Ottawa, Canada: 30 hours in total. Our route took us through London, England (where we had a 10-hour layover) to Nairobi (where we had a two-hour layover) and finally to the Kilimanjaro Airport at Moshi, Africa. Chris had been to London before but I hadn't, so we stored our luggage and caught the London tube downtown so he could show me around.

It was fairly typical London weather: rainy, cold (25 degrees Fahrenheit or minus 4 degrees Celcius) and generally miserable. We managed to see Buckingham Palace, Piccadilly Circus, Downing Street and the Tower of London in about 45 minutes, walking at full speed with our hands in our pockets and braced against the wind, cold and drizzle.

Chris: In case you're wondering how we accomplished so much in under an hour's time, the last time I was in London, I had a 12-hour layover at Heathrow, and believe me, you'd be surprised what you can do during a layover like that!

When we arrive in Nairobi, I notice some people in the airport with backpacks and wonder if we will be seeing them on the climb. (We don't see them again.) Neither Chris nor I had slept much on the plane during our long flight. Too much excitement! We did watch a few movies, though.

At the airport in Moshi, we are met by an elderly African gentleman who works for Tusker Trail, the company we've hired to guide our trek. Moshi means "smoke" in Swahili, and no one seems to know how it came by its name. We are told that the city has a population of around 145,000 and relies on glacial stream run-off from Kilimanjaro to irrigate its food supply. In just a few short days, we will see firsthand why this could become a serious issue in the future for the area's inhabitants.

As we drive from the airport to the hotel, my first impression of Africa confirms everything I have read. It's very dusty and very poor. That impression won't change over the next few days. There are people walking everywhere in different directions, and they all seem to have a purpose, although it's difficult to imagine where they are all going. The women are beautifully adorned in spite of the dust that surrounds them. They're dressed in flowing, vibrant caftans and we will notice that they always manage to look elegant in less than ideal conditions. We observe colored cloths wrapped around their caftans or covering their heads, protecting them from the dust as they work in the fields. We learn that the coverings are called khangas, which are pieces of cloth that are about three feet by five feet, making them ideal to use as a wrap. Each has a border with a central design in the middle. A Swahili proverb is imprinted on the border of the khangas. (My wife and I now proudly own two khangas bearing proverbs that are very relevant to the story that was unfolding in my life: "Dunia Ni Mapito" which translates to "Life is a transition" and "Kheri Huja Baada Ya Subira" which means "Success requires patience.")

When we check into the Keys Hotel, we find that our room is very small by North American standards – more like a dorm than typical hotel rooms we are accustomed to – but it's comfortable with two cots and a bathroom with a shower.

Chris: In some ways, it reminds me of hostels I've stayed in over the years.

After a short rest, Chris and I head out to the hotel patio. The sun is shining, and there are a series of poles bearing flags from various countries just across the road in front of the hotel. There are tall trees just beyond the flag poles. There is also a gap in the trees — which coincidentally enough is just to the right of the Canadian flag! — offering a stunningly-framed view of Mount Kilimanjaro. The sun is glistening off the glaciers, exaggerating the different shades of blue of the mountain in the distance. The details of the mountain are vague, but even from our vantage point it looks daunting, as it is by far the highest point in our line of vision proudly rising from the flat plains. We can see why it's the world's highest free-standing mountain. And in just a few more days, with luck, my son and I will be standing on its peak.

Chris: The view of the mountain is really impressive. During the drive in from the airport to the hotel, we had seen several different views of the mountain. What is really most noticeable is the fact that it is the ONLY mountain you can see. It rises up from the horizon and keeps rising, and then it drops off the other side to fade back into the horizon. In a lot of ways, it resembles a child's drawing of a mountain that you would see from a distance, but it is larger than life.

As we stare at the scene before us, it's like Mount Kilimanjaro is staring back with a smirk saying, "I'm here. Let's see what you've got."

I realize I am a long way from my roots.

CHAPTER 2

The Beginning

THE REAL STORY starts when I reached my mid-50s, but the determination to accomplish my goals was probably shaped long before, when I was growing up on a farm near a town called Rapid City, Manitoba, Canada (population of about 425). I firmly believe that a great deal of what we become is shaped by our upbringing. There are many who do not have an appropriate grounding and who are left to take control of their lives on their own. There are teenagers in Africa who are heads of their households because of HIV/AIDS, so they have little chance to have any grounding at all, let alone the opportunity to just be kids. By contrast, I was extremely fortunate to have been brought up in a good home with good family values.

I was to find out many years later that there are a number of factors that go into climbing a mountain and combining that activity with helping the less fortunate. Looking back, I realize that I was unknowingly preparing for this monumental feat during my formative years. I had to work for everything I wanted, which taught me that nothing worth having would come easily. I learned that success is something that is not owned; we have to earn it. From that came the willingness to accept a challenge and the perseverance to stick with it. I learned about the dedication and confidence it would later require to face the mental and physical challenges of a steep mountain climb and to carry out the second part of our adventure – to raise the funds necessary to help out some needy children. For some, these attributes are forged in the city. In my case, I credit my life on the farm for helping me to ultimately meet my goals.

Our town of Rapid City was not nestled in the Black Hills, nor could we look out on Mount Rushmore. That is Rapid City, South Dakota. Our town is in Canada, nestled on the banks of the far lesser-known Little Saskatchewan River. It is, however, known locally as the "Biggest Little City by a Dam Site." According to a book on Rapid City, aptly named "Our Past for the Future," the first settlers were brought into the area in the early 1870s. It was named in 1877 from the rapid waters of the river and it was called a "city" because of the optimism surrounding the settlement. Decisions related to the location of the railroad resulted in the settlement never growing much beyond its current population. The city of Brandon, with a population of close to 40,000, lies 25 miles to the south where…you guessed it, the railway actually settled.

I was the youngest of four brothers. Keith and Gene were the oldest – older than me by 12 and 11 years respectively. It has occurred to me that I may have been the result of poor planning on my parents' behalf. Of course, my next oldest brother, Melvin, who was six years older than me, might have had similar thoughts.

My dad was a farmer. The only days I can remember him taking off were Sundays. Sunday was a day of rest, except when he had to work because the crops had been delayed or the cows had to be milked. We didn't go to church that often, but I would certainly say it was a family with Christian beliefs and values. Rather than going to church, I can remember going for the odd Sunday drive. Of course, the stated purpose of the drive was to look at the countryside, but the ulterior motive for my dad was to look at the crops. However, the Sunday drive usually ended with a stop somewhere for a treat, so it was always a highlight when it did happen.

As they got older, Keith and Gene continued the farming tradition, and I am quite sure they would not have been happy doing anything else. Gene and his family still live on the farm that we grew up on. Keith unfortunately passed away in 2009, but his son carries on the farming tradition. Melvin is a recently retired Baptist Church minister. For me, and I think for Melvin, it was more a matter of "can't get off the farm fast enough."

Probably my fondest memories of growing up on the farm are the wide open spaces and everything they had to offer. There was never an issue with disappearing early in the morning as a kid on some exploration and reporting back at noon to wolf down a hearty farm meal, only to disappear again for the rest of the day. The farm was a cornucopia of sights and sounds. There was the smell of the spring rain as the cold of winter released its icy grip and gave birth to new greenery and flowers that would dot the landscape. The heat of summer could not only be felt, but it could actually be seen shimmering across the expanse of land. There were sun drenched wheat and barley stalks in the fall that created an ocean of grain with wave after wave rolling across the field in the wind. From nearly any vantage point in late fall, there was the sight of clouds of dust billowing up from the various machines arranged across the landscape harvesting the crops. There was the sight of the myriad of birds that migrate to the prairies, but especially the ever-present red-winged blackbird riding as one with a single cattail as it gently rocked like a pendulum in the breeze. The male blackbird drew attention to itself all day long with its song that starts out like a rusty gate and develops into a high-pitched warbling sound. Finally, there was the pristine sight of the snow in winter, untouched except for the odd rabbit or deer track. The winter sky, with the moon and stars unobstructed to the human eye and seemingly within reach, highlighted the whiteness of the snow. The farm on the prairies is an assault on the senses that is unlike any other.

Nevertheless, farming just didn't seem to be for me, so the perceived value of my contribution on the farm would vary, depending on who you talked to. I would say that I contributed a little more than my older brothers would probably give me credit for, but I guess it's not only beauty that's in the eye of the beholder! We were expected to drive a grain truck by the time we could reach the pedals, and we were out on the tractor in our early teens. One of the things that farmers are very proud of is the ability to cultivate the field in perfectly straight lines. Yet I couldn't do that if my life depended on it. I would aim for a tree at the opposite end of the field and still end up with cultivated furrows that looked like they had been done by someone heavily into the moonshine. My solution to the problem was to make sure I *never* cultivated the field perpendicular to the road so people driving by, and especially my brothers, wouldn't be able to tell if the furrows were straight or not. GPS systems are available on tractors now and probably would have solved my problem, but it wasn't even a consideration back then.

Life on the farm is one of long days and extremely hard work, and it is wrought with hardship. I can remember my dad putting in crops and then standing at the window watching hail stones wipe out the hundreds of hours of hard work that had gone into it. I knew I could never do that; I needed something more stable. My mother said farm life reminded her of a saying she'd seen embroidered on her mother's pillow shams: 'I slept and dreamt that life was beauty' while on the reverse it said, 'I woke and found that life was duty'.

In addition to the everyday challenges of running the farm, my parents had to face an additional challenge: the chimney for their wood stove became overheated, caught on fire and their house burned to the ground in 1943. It was reported to have been a very cold, windy and frosty day in February. For anyone familiar with Canadian prairie cold, you can imagine what the temperature could have been like. For those who aren't familiar, let's just say a typical temperature would be something like minus four degrees Fahrenheit (-20 degrees Centigrade). The wind would have made it much worse.

I hadn't been born yet but Melvin was still a baby, so my parents had to deal with a young family while losing everything. They stayed with neighbors until accommodation was ready for them. In Mom's words from her diary:

"We had a 12x14-foot wooden granary full of barley that could be made into a place to live. It was lined with gyproc, windows put in, linoleum bought for the floor, a stove put in, the cream separator set up (we were milking cows then and selling cream). We got moved in about the end of March and used the van outside for storage of clothes, etc.

The "van" was simply a "framework built on a set of sleighs with wooden walls about halfway up and heavy canvas for the rest of the walls and roof. It had a window in the front with a hole for the horse's reins for the driver, and a door in the back. Inside it had a little tin heater that burned wood and made it comfortable on the coldest days, and a bench seat on each side wall."

My three brothers ended up catching the measles, so there my parents were with three sick kids, in the dead of winter, living in quarters so small that they had to move the table outside at night so that the couch could be opened up for a bed. The table was brought back in each morning so they could have breakfast. The local community pitched in and helped build a new house for them, which they moved into in August. The farmer attitude is, "you get knocked down and you get back up." And that stuck with me.

Our family didn't have a lot of money, but we certainly didn't want for anything. My brothers and I had to save our money to buy anything special. I can remember saving my allowance to be able to buy a baseball glove. It was a long time coming, but it was certainly cherished when it finally did arrive. I think that work ethic was extremely valuable later in life for me and played a part in my being able to eventually achieve a major lifestyle change (as you will soon read more about).

As for discipline, I never heard either Mom or Dad raise their voice in anger. It was a rather strict upbringing, however, as I can remember being banned from watching Elvis Presley's *Jailhouse Rock* at the local weekly film showing because it was too violent. Imagine that! If you have seen *Jailhouse Rock* and compare it to — oh, I don't know, let's say everything in the theatres today, it will seem incredibly strict. Somehow I survived.

Even though they didn't raise their voices, our parents had this amazing ability to be able to look at us with a withering glance when we had done something wrong that made us want to undo whatever it was we had done. I think it was worse than being yelled at. When you are yelled at, it lasts until the person has exhausted their lung capacity and then you can forget about it. A withering glance lasts for hours. Dad was very supportive as long as we were in the right. If we did something really bad, we were expected to be accountable for our actions. When I was 16, I bought a motorcycle from the money I raised selling the steers I had so "lovingly" nurtured. One day an envelope appeared in the mailbox from the judicial court in Winnipeg. It was obviously not good news — and it was addressed to me. Dad stood over me and watched as I opened the envelope with shaky hands. It turned out to be a summons for something I had supposedly done with my motorcycle in Winnipeg. Now, Winnipeg was 150 miles away and fortunately for me, Dad knew I was nowhere near the city on the date the infraction allegedly took place. He went to bat for me and immediately cleared things up. It turned out some nefarious individual had altered his license plate so the numbers appeared to be the same as mine. I am sure to this day that, had I actually done what I was accused of doing, Dad would have let me pay the fine or go to jail or suffer whatever consequences were handed down just to make sure I would never do it again.

So it was that I had tremendous role models as I was growing up. The many life lessons I learned on the farm and the role models I had growing up would come into play on Mount Kilimanjaro in ways I could never have anticipated. I'm also convinced that the stories I heard about my family's house fire and how the community came together to help went a long way toward establishing another core value in me: a keen desire to help others.

My wife Evelyn and I were married in Rapid City and went on to have two wonderful boys. We have enjoyed every minute of watching Trevor and Christopher becoming young adults and pursuing their respective careers. They both found wonderful partners when Josée and Laura arrived on the scene. Chris and Laura have also presented us with two granddaughters, Annika and Jaelyn, so the family is growing considerably and, hopefully, passing on the same values that life on the farm gave to me. We moved from the prairies in 1976 to our current home in Ottawa, Ontario, Canada due to employment opportunities (I was an accountant with the federal government), but I still love to go back and remind myself of the way it was for me back in the day.

Of course, I could not have foreseen how my life on the farm and my subsequent career would somehow one day translate into a change in lifestyle, a trek up a mountain named Kili and the powerful desire to help others. But as I sit here on a patio in Africa, staring at the beautiful, terrifying land mass that we are about to attempt to conquer, it all comes together. I am sitting here because of everything that has come before.

Chris: My upbringing was obviously not on the farm but in the suburbs around Ottawa, though I will be the first to agree with my dad that the same values he learned on the farm and tried so hard to instill in me he did successfully. In my opinion, at least. I am also a firm believer in working for what you want, and the idea of things being given to me at my request is just ludicrous. If there is something you want to spend money on, go ahead. Save up and spend your money. It wasn't until much later in life that I started to understand the sort of hardships my parents went through, things like the 24+% mortgage rates that were prevalent during my youth.

I can't say I had a difficult youth, nor would I want to say that. Life was good, and my parents always strived to provide to me all of the opportunities that they felt I should have. Not all the cash to buy things with, but the opportunities to learn, to play sports and to grow. I moved out of my parents' home when I was 19 so that I could live downtown close to Ottawa University where I was enrolled in their commerce program pursuing an accounting degree (like father, like son!). Not because I had to, but because I had the opportunity to. I could have stayed at home as long as I wanted (which was effectively demonstrated by my older brother), but for me, the choice was an easy one. Time to spread my wings.

I worked hard through high school and university in order to save enough money to keep me in school. I then learned about the value of travel and the true learning experiences that could be gleaned from these adventures. Before I turned 21, I packed up a backpack full of camping gear, a sleeping bag and tent and headed off to Alaska for a month of backpacking and adventure. I encountered few obstacles and in general had a fabulous time. The spirit of adventure was in me from that day forth!

A year later, a friend offered me the opportunity to see South Africa firsthand, as he was headed back to the country he grew up in. This was a chance of a lifetime, since he had been there through the apartheid years and witnessed the transition of power that took place. It gave him a unique perspective, one that he didn't hesitate to share with me every chance he could.

Two years after that it was off to Southeast Asia for five weeks of self indulgence, excess, sun and sand. Less of an adventure, more of a vacation, though it would seem adventurous to some when you consider the meals of curried whole squid from the equivalent of a hotdog cart in Kuala Lumpur; the cockroaches outnumbering the passengers on the bus from Singapore to Bangkok, and the aromatic (to say the least!) durian or "king of fruits" that is apparently enjoyed by some. (If you have never tried it, you should as it is an experience you won't forget.)

The point of all of this is simply that I never felt the hardships of a broken home and learned from a young age that education is more than time in school. I was also taught that if you want something, you can have it as long as you are willing to work for it. These are all examples of the lessons my parents worked so hard to instill in me.

CHAPTER 3

How on Earth Did I End Up in Africa??

IT IS 3:00 am on January 9, 2009 at the Keys Hotel in Moshi, Tanzania and I am supposed to be sleeping. But I have had cold sweats and the more uneasy I become, the worse it gets. I have all kinds of things going through my mind. *What if I can't do this?* I have a bad cold. *What if the guides won't let me even start the climb? Am I too old to be trying this? What if I die from altitude sickness?* There are so many people thinking of us and supporting us and watching our every move through daily updates, not to mention the 200-plus people whose names are on the Canadian flag we are supposed to carry to the top of Mount Kilimanjaro! At least Chris will be able to carry it if I can't...

I am not prone to this kind of anxiety. Maybe it is the medication we are taking to help prevent altitude sickness. We are taking Diamox, which is used by climbers to accelerate acclimatization. There are many side effects attributable to Diamox that are discussed later. Anxiety is not one of them. *This is crazy*! I have overcome nervous situations before simply by telling myself that whatever it is that is bothering me will soon be over. Maybe I can use that strategy again. I really should be getting some sleep in preparation for the climb. *What am I doing in Africa, of all places? What if I really can't do this...?*

Chris seems to be sleeping soundly in the other bed in our small room. The room is comfortable enough. The fan has been off once or twice during the night because, as I am quickly discovering, the electricity is not very consistent in Africa, at least not in our hotel. The two previous weeks were very difficult. I really thought at one point I would have to cancel because of a head cold. I had a number of highs and lows as I thought I was improving, only to have the cold resurface. Some days I couldn't wait to get started; on others I was asking myself why I got us into this.

While I realize that my upbringing had mentally prepared me for many challenges, as I reflect back on how we arrived at this point in our lives, I also recognize it is a number of serendipitous events that ultimately converged and brought me here. Unknowingly, I probably took the first step on my incredible journey years ago in a darkened library auditorium. I was watching enthralled as Laurie Skreslet, the first Canadian to reach the top of Mount Everest, presented his experiences to a large audience in Ottawa, Canada. I sat and listened, absolutely fascinated by the multimedia presentation of his climb and his message that no task is too difficult if you really want it. Skreslet overcame constant stress, physical discomfort and danger to accomplish his goals. I was very impressed with his ability to overcome incredible odds to accomplish his dream. The seed may have been planted even earlier by a train ride with my aunt through the Canadian Rocky Mountains when I was 12. Growing up on the prairies, I would be challenged to say that I had observed much of a hill, let alone a mountain. The view from the dome car of the majestic mountains with their contrasting white snowy peaks superimposed on the clear blue sky left me with an impression that endured.

The next little jolt to my subconscious occurred one Sunday night in 1999 around the Finlay family dinner table. Chris had just returned from his trip to South Africa and he mentioned that he had had the opportunity to also climb Mount Kilimanjaro with some friends, but ultimately the trip fell through as people dropped out. He was musing about how he would like to make the climb some day. My wife Evelyn and I looked at each other because neither one of us knew anything about Mount Kilimanjaro, but we both immediately thought of mountain climbing involving ropes, ladders, crampons and impending death. I think we both fervently hoped that the only thing that would die would be the thought that Chris had raised!

Chris' comment seemed to drift away, but apparently only to the back of the mind where ideas sometimes seem to languish in a state of dormancy. Then one day, something will cause those ideas to sit up, leap forward, tap on the main part of the brain and say, "Hey, remember me!!??" I guess we assumed that since Chris had raised the thought, it would be one of those languishing ideas until he would actually do it one day. I never thought I would be a part of his scheme or actually be actively involved in causing it to resurface.

These were the first in a series of events that seemed to be lining up like the cars on a freight train whose destination would be a mountain. The next occurred in June 2006. I was due for my annual physical checkup, so off I went to visit our family doctor. What I heard was not the best news. The doctor advised me that my triglycerides were above normal. While I had no idea what that meant, all he really had to say was that high triglyceride levels can lead to heart attack and stroke. This was definitely not good news since heart disease runs in my family. I subsequently did more research and learned from an American Heart Association article that excess food that isn't burned for fuel is converted to triglycerides and stored in the body. Their website goes on to attribute high triglyceride levels to "being overweight/obese, physical inactivity, cigarette smoking, excess alcohol consumption and/or a diet very high in carbohydrates (60 percent or more of calories)". High triglycerides are obviously a lifestyle-related risk factor, and the main therapy to reduce triglyceride levels is to change that lifestyle. My doctor supported that view when he strongly suggested that reducing carbohydrates through diet and aerobic exercise should bring the levels down.

It was probably my career choice that was mainly responsible for a relatively sedentary lifestyle that brought me to this point where I would have to change. I was educated as an accountant and have had a wonderful career, mostly with the Canada Revenue Agency. I retired in 2004 after having spent my working life in various financial roles, including writing financial policy and having the responsibility for an operation to account for, analyze and report on the federal government's revenue. Following my career as a civil servant, I spent some time consulting with various federal government departments.

As life went on and the years passed by, my life became desk job by day and relaxation by night, often watching television or reading a book. I had played some baseball and golf over the years but, like most people who sit behind a desk for 30-plus years, at retirement my body was showing some of the signs of a sedentary lifestyle. I had gained weight and wasn't feeling all that energetic.

The thought of heart disease was probably the biggest factor in motivating me to take action. My father and brother had both had strokes. Now that I am at the stage where I have grandchildren, I want to be around to see what they become and to see milestones in their lives. I view grandchildren as a second chance. As most of us are, I was often at work when major milestones occurred with my own children, such as the first words or the first steps. While we may not see all the "firsts" for our grandchildren, we get to see them shortly after those events take place: we hear about them from the proud parents or see the video, so I want to be here for a long time to take full advantage of that.

Furthermore, I have always taken the words of our doctor seriously. We have known each other for a long time and he's approximately the same age as I am, so he can relate to some of the things that are happening to me. In fact, I have always been one to believe that all experts should know what they are doing, and I usually blindly follow their advice. My theory generally holds true, although it has been severely tested at times by certain experts, such as the contractor who hung our bathroom cabinet so high that we could not see in the mirror. (Okay, so maybe "experts" don't always know what they are doing.)

I took the doctor's advice seriously and stopped at a gym on my way home from my visit to his office, instantly becoming a member. I also signed up with a personal trainer to make sure I really did what I was supposed to do. While I'd joined fitness clubs previously, I really didn't know how to lift weights properly, and I was usually one of those in the top percentile whose attendance lasts about one quarter as long as their membership.

Any good article on fitness will encourage you to consult your family physician before undertaking physical activities. This becomes even more important as one ages. I had my doctor's tacit approval as he encouraged me to undertake some physical activity to deal with my triglyceride issue. However, I would certainly encourage everyone to consult with their doctor before starting on a fitness campaign or undertaking any serious physical activity.

CHAPTER 4

The Lifestyle Starts to Change

ONCE MY FIRST night in Moshi is over, I feel much better. My stomach is still a little uneasy, but nothing I can't live with. It led to a little euphoria, but my experience over many years has taught me that if something exciting has happened, it won't be too long until something will come along to bring me back to earth. By the same token, when something negative happens, it will usually be replaced by something positive over time. The moral is that we have to enjoy the good moments, but be prepared for what is coming next. We can also console ourselves with the knowledge that a bad time will eventually get better. In short, I try to keep my emotions in check and try to never allow myself to become too high or too low.

At one point during the afternoon, as we are sitting at the hotel on our first full day in Africa, Chris has gone back to the room for a few minutes and I am in the restaurant area contemplating the next few days and allowing myself to become more and more excited as the minutes tick by. There is one other person in the restaurant talking in French on his cellular phone. Because there is no other sound in the restaurant, it's impossible not to overhear his part of the conversation, and having had French language training for my job over the years, I am able to understand what he's saying. He is telling someone on the other end of the phone that it had been too dangerous for him to continue his trek up the mountain. He was forced to come down. That wasn't what I want to hear, and it is one of those moments when my exhilaration is quickly dampened by someone else's reality. Later that evening, we see people returning from their climb that are limping and groaning every time they walk up a few steps to their rooms at the hotel. But we put all that aside and focus on the trio who are excitedly grasping their climbing certificates, signifying a successful climb, and having a celebratory beer at a nearby table. It is the latter experience that we hope to have ourselves in a few days!

Long before the moment of sitting in the restaurant in Africa, I had embarked on a serious mission to change my lifestyle. I was about to enter the world of gymnasiums, trainers, sweat and satisfaction. As I walked into the gym on the first day of my quest, I couldn't help but compare the modern day gym to those I had been to in days past. Things had changed. It was not the dingy, smelly, sweatshop of old with the rusty sound of each rotation of the stationary bikes' pedals and the tiny changing rooms. Upon first entering the modern gym, I was struck by the music that no one listens to blaring from the speakers. I say no one listens because the second thing that became apparent is that everyone is plugged into iPods. They were oblivious to the raucous noise emanating from the loudspeakers. Then I noticed that the gym was full of beautiful people. There were toned and fit women in active wear that defined every contour of the female anatomy and the men with no necks and enormous muscular arms dangling from their sleeveless tops. It was apparent from my first impression that fashion and good looks are prerequisites for becoming fit. I decided I could address one of those by going shopping.

There was row upon row of gleaming equipment, all with pulleys and cables that surely must do something. There was the rhythmic slap, slap, slapping of running shoes hitting the treadmills, the sound of the weights being jockeyed around and the grunts and groans of the jockeys. Everyone seemed to be in a trance-like state, staring vacantly at the television monitors or working feverishly on their training routines. Eventually, I finally noticed that there were people of all shapes and sizes. There were people skipping, running, walking, pumping, pulling, pushing, sweating and…preening. The room was surrounded by mirrors, and there were people flexing and strutting and admiring their bodies from every conceivable angle. Now that I have been going to the gym for a few years, the same people that were admiring themselves then are still doing it! They never seem to work out. Could it be that I was away doing something else when God handed out the special physical attributes?

I remember driving to the gym for my first scheduled visit with my trainer and wondering what this experience was going to be like. I had seen personal trainers depicted on television, yelling at their poor victims and applying various instruments of torture to them. In the end, either they shaped up or finished their session curled up in the corner in the fetal position with their thumb in their mouth. I didn't want to be THAT guy!

It turned out my trainer was a 21-year-old woman. While she was pleasant enough to talk to in the few minutes we spent discussing my health goals and in our subsequent sessions discussing my progress, she was all business in the gym. There was no yelling and screaming in the gym. But there *was* a lot of grunting and groaning coming from me. She just had a quiet determination to help me reach my goals and improve the state of my fitness. I think personal trainers have to have an inherent knowledge of psychology because all I heard was encouragement in a determined tone of voice. It became apparent that it's so important to have the proper personality fit between you and your trainer. I was very fortunate to have had the trainer I had. Her attitude was more a matter of "I know you can do one more."

I learned a great deal about myself during the time I worked with her. Besides my improved fitness levels and a better understanding of the techniques involved, what I took away most from the training sessions was that when you think you have done everything you can do, you're wrong. You still have more to give! And a good trainer will get it out of you.

There were times, I think, when my trainer expected me to be able to do everything she could, in spite of the 38-year difference in our ages. On more than one occasion, I had to sit quietly in the locker room at the gym for a few minutes after a session, telling myself that I was not going to pass out or throw up. While I still feel like throwing up occasionally after a particularly grueling workout, it happens much less often and my recovery time has significantly improved.

Chris: This will probably be a story from the "too much information" file, but in seeing the progress that my father was having with the training, I decided to give it a go myself for reasons I'll get into later. On one of the last sessions I had with my trainer, who embodied many of the same characteristics of the trainer my father had, I had asked her to take it a bit easy on me due to a cold I was fighting off. I don't know about you, but when I have a cold, the last thing I feel like doing is exercising. Little did I know that she was in a particularly foul mood that day and I'm fairly certain she worked me harder as a result of my protests. I ended having to pull over to the side of the road in order to relieve my stomach of its contents in a (fortunately) empty church parking lot as rush hour traffic streamed by. I am fairly certain the last time I was that sick it was a result of too much alcohol, not exercise!

My sessions with my trainer reminded me of a story I once read when I was growing up. While I played a lot of sports, I was more a fan than an athlete. I would consume anything and everything to do with my sports heroes. I remember reading an article about a Hall of Fame football player by the name of Sam Huff, who played with the New York Giants in the '50s. In his article, he referred to getting older. Since he played every Sunday, he said that he noticed he would still be sore on Mondays after the game. As he got older, he still hurt on Tuesday, then on Wednesday and so on. He said he decided when the time came that he hurt all the way to the following Sunday, it would be time to retire. I have never forgotten his words, and there were times I definitely hurt from my last session with my trainer when I arrived for the next one. One day I arrived for my session and announced that I still felt some soreness from the last session. She said, "Are you hurt or are you injured?" I said that I wasn't injured so I guessed I was hurt. She said, "Good, let's see 30 sit-ups!"

I was asked to record everything I ate or drank, and I *did* record everything! I like the occasional beer and I would record it. I like my coffee and I would record it. If I had a muffin or doughnut, I would record it. Then I would suffer my trainer's wrath. "What's with all the beer?" she would ask if I'd had two or three that week. "Why are you drinking so much coffee?" if I had one or two cups a day during the week. We would go through my daily food intake for the week at the first session of the following week, and she would blast me on my shortcomings or give me a "gold star" if there happened to be some good days during the week.

Obviously recording daily food intake is an excellent reminder of how you are doing, and there are numerous websites to help track daily food intake and calculate calories, fat grams, protein, etc. I was surprised at what I saw when I first started to track my intake. While I thought I ate well, I found when I started measuring that my caloric intake in a week was substantially higher than my output for the week. No wonder I was gaining weight! The results were amazing once I started to track the calories. Now I check the nutrition labels on the food I eat to try to estimate the caloric intake for the day. I have learned to eat six small meals a day instead of three larger ones. That becomes a challenge sometimes when travelling, and it requires some planning and thought. My snacks are usually almonds or a piece of fruit, but if I don't have something, I find my energy level drops quickly. Nevertheless, the benefits of making the effort to ensure access to six small meals are many, including weight maintenance and stabilized energy levels throughout the day.

I did make one mistake during my weight loss process that I would not do again. Since the doctor suggested I reduce my carbohydrate intake, I thought eliminating it altogether would be even better. The weight dropped — but so did my energy level. Based on the difficulty I had just getting myself off the couch, I determined that a "no carbohydrate" diet was not going to work for me.

There were other extremely valuable lessons learned throughout this entire process. I had never really considered a personal trainer before. How difficult can lifting weights or working out be? Well, the answer is doing it right may not be that difficult but it is hugely important. Qualified personal trainers are extremely valuable, especially in the early stages of getting fit. To avoid injury and to maximize the benefits of training, it's important to know what you are doing. A personal trainer can help with that. From my personal experience there are two very good reasons why the average person doesn't last in the gym through a quarter of their membership. First, we don't see the immediate results we were hoping for. Secondly, we feel worse when we are going to the gym than we do when we are not. It became apparent to me that doing the wrong things at the gym or doing the right things improperly can result in both of the aforementioned issues. I realized that it had happened to me on previous occasions when I had taken out a membership at a gym. My trainer made sure that my nutrition and diet were correct to achieve maximum weight loss and nutritional gains and also provided the right series of exercises *and the right technique* to help me see measurable results in as short a time as possible. Trainers are not cheap but they are worth every penny, in my opinion, to establish the road to a change in lifestyle that will stay with us for the rest of our lives.

I discovered that what I was doing at the gym was important, but consistency is the key. It is essential to stick to the training plan. With my trainer and subsequently later on, I set small, achievable goals. While I didn't have my big goal of climbing the mountain in mind at the time, I found that setting small, achievable goals will lead to the bigger goal. There is nothing as motivational as knowing that you have achieved a goal. I always gave myself a small reward after each goal I earned. Sometimes it was just self congratulations, but other times it was more tangible like a trip to the ice cream shop. While enjoying the reward, I would think about the next goal and write it down.

I would ask my trainer a lot of questions as we worked. She was always very obliging in answering immediately or finding the answer for me. There were two questions that nagged at me, one of which she answered and the other for which she was unable to provide help. The first dealt with the settings on the various machines, including the treadmill, elliptical, rowing machine and others. Anyone who has used a cardio machine at a gym will have noticed that each has, at least for me, confusing settings. For example, there are settings for "fat burn" and "cardio." I quickly realized that the setting for fat burn required less exertion than the one for cardio. Huh!!?? I asked myself (and my trainer) why I couldn't set it at cardio and burn fat. I tried to follow along as she patiently explained that a higher percentage of effort goes toward burning fat at lower intensity levels. Nevertheless, she said, even though I would burn more fat by percentage when I was working at lower intensity levels, I would also burn fewer total calories and, therefore, less TOTAL fat. I decided I was sorry I asked and that always using the cardio level on the machine would provide the results I needed to reach my goal of reducing my weight and improving my cardio vascular conditioning.

The second question was a little more mundane. Why is it, I asked, that even though there are plenty of available empty lockers all around the change room, people who are coming or going and getting dressed or undressed always choose the lockers immediately next to yours? I defy anyone who has ever gone to the gym to tell me that that hasn't happened to them. It would take an in-depth study of human behavior to answer that one, and my trainer didn't have an answer.

I also learned the real value of mirrors. I mentioned the "preeners" earlier. I would see people watching themselves in the mirror and assume that they were simply admiring their physique. (I'm still convinced that some probably were.) But as I got more experienced in my own workouts, I realized that looking in the mirror helped me stay in alignment with my weights and ensured that my form was correct when using the machines. Before long, I became a "preener" as well.

And gradually, my fitness level started to improve. I began to look fitter and have more energy. I looked forward to the sessions at the gym with and without my trainer. I had learned how to use the equipment properly and it motivated me to continue.

There were two moments in my training regime when I really knew I was ready to move on to bigger fitness goals. The first involved my trainer and a swear word that's become part of the daily vernacular.

To put this into context, this word is so overused in today's popular culture that it's almost become laughable. I had never heard my trainer swear during the entire time I spent working with her — until one night near the end of our sessions together. She was putting me through her routine fitness test to measure my progress so she could increase my workout level. After the test, we always sat and assessed my performance. On this particular night, my test involved doing as many sit-ups, step-ups (stepping up and down on a raised platform) and push-ups as I could in one-minute intervals, with a little rest between each. I felt really good and believed I was sailing through the test, but there had been other tests when I thought I had done well, only to be met with her constructive criticism and tweaking of my training regimen. On this particular evening, I finished the last section of the test and waited patiently for her critique. My trainer was quiet for a few seconds studying the results and comparing them to my previous tests. She was so quiet that I began to think, uh, oh, there is a lot more work to do. Finally, she looked up with a big smile on her face and in the loudest voice I'd ever heard her use, she shouted, "THAT'S F**KING AWESOME!"

At that moment, I knew I was making real progress. Perhaps the time had come for even greater challenges. The train of converging events was warming up and getting ready to leave the station.

CHAPTER 5

Decisions, Decisions

I WAS NOTICING a definite improvement in my overall health. My energy level and stamina had increased significantly. I'd lost about 28 pounds; my cholesterol and blood pressure readings were in the "better than average" range. While I would still exhaust myself at the gym, my recovery time was much shorter. Was I a believer in exercise and diet now? Oh yeah! I was enjoying my workouts, and I even felt guilty if I missed a day at the gym. I was starting to do other things. In years past, every summer I would take my bicycle down from its rack and every fall I would put it back up, but rarely would it have many more, if any, miles on it in the fall than it did in the spring. But I was starting to put miles on it and finding other ways to exercise.

Around this time, I also came to the realization that my 60th birthday was looming. Hmmm…maybe it was time to think about marking a birthday milestone with something physically ambitious. I began to consider various ways to celebrate. Unbelievably, Kilimanjaro popped back into my head from that conversation around the dinner table so many years before.

I was still not convinced that climbing a mountain was something I could do. The thought really appealed to me because of the challenge, commitment and dedication required to do it, but I had a problem. Any videos I had seen of mountaineering and especially Laurie Skreslet's presentation of his ascent of Mount Everest, involved the ladders and rope that Evelyn and I had imagined when Chris raised the idea of climbing Mount Kilimanjaro. It isn't exactly that I don't like heights but I REALLY don't like ladders. As long as I can't see what's beneath me, I'm fine. It's being able to see through the rungs of a ladder to the ground below that petrifies me. Putting the Christmas lights up on our bungalow is scary enough for me. If climbing Mount Kilimanjaro required ropes and ladders, I would definitely be looking for another way to celebrate!

I researched the internet extensively and purchased some books on the subject. It appeared that people who climbed Mount Kilimanjaro were, for the most part, just like me. There seemed to be some common threads. They had never been to Africa, never climbed a mountain, and had no idea how altitude would affect them or what they were getting themselves into. But they all had a burning desire to take themselves out of their comfort zone to see what they could do.

This was encouraging. I researched companies that led hikes up Mount Kilimanjaro. I sent emails to people who had done it to seek their advice. While I asked a lot of questions, the one I really wanted the answer to was, "Is there a technical part to this climb that requires ropes and ladders?"

I received some interesting and varied responses. While the initial ones were a little discouraging, overall they helped me shape my decision — and they all educated me for the challenge I was about to undertake. They were becoming freight cars in my train of converging events. It was becoming obvious that the final decision was going to be mine. No one was going to make it for me. Here are excerpts from three of the early comments:

The first person said, "When we got to the last camp before the summit, we saw people in various guide groups on the 6-day trip…those who were coming down from the summit looked like zombies, and some of those going up decided at that point not to summit and go down. The only real challenge of the trek is the altitude. You move so damn slowly that the actual hiking is easy – it's just the elevation that gets you."

The second was even less encouraging. Their response was, "You do not want to use park toilets when 100% of the people on the mountain have diarrhea!" Finally, the third chimed in with, "I don't think I should tell you how I felt."

Oh, oh, there went whatever confidence I had started to gather. In fact, I found my resolve seriously wavering. Based on comments like these, my conclusion was that *if* I had the right attitude and was in decent shape and *if* I was willing to put up with some serious discomfort and potential pain, *if* I could go for more than a week without a shower, and *if* I was prepared to leave my dignity at the bottom of the mountain, I might make it to the summit — assuming also that luck, weather and good genes, were on my side. But how could I know if good genes were on my side? No one in my family had ever climbed a mountain that I knew of! I may have to rely solely on my improved physical conditioning to get through this.

I consulted Wikipedia for more information on making the trek. For those who don't know, Wikipedia's own description says that "its entries are written collaboratively by largely anonymous Internet users who write without pay. Anyone with Internet access can write and make changes to Wikipedia articles." The Wikipedia entry that I took to heart said "all climbers will suffer considerable discomfort, typically shortage of breath, hypothermia and headaches, and though most young, fit people can make the Uhuru summit, a substantial number of trekkers will abandon the attempt at a lower altitude." The "young, fit" part threw me for a loop. I should be able to qualify for the fit part given all my hard work at the gym and newly-healthy eating habits but the young part was beyond my control. I was somewhat encouraged by a reference later in the text to the oldest climber who'd successfully made the climb being "either 79 or 87 years of age." Oh, Wikipedia also mentioned that about 10 climbers and a similar number of porters die each year from altitude sickness. Porters!!?? How could *they* die? They do this for a living!

I discussed the possibility of climbing a mountain with friends and colleagues. Most of my younger friends and a handful of those around my age were encouraging. Sometimes, though, my proposal was met with absolute silence. I tried to read in their eyes what they were thinking. Sometimes I saw concern. Sometimes their eyes said, "Are you nuts?" A little later, my wife and I met Richard Tibandebage who works for the

Tanzania High Commission. I had contacted the High Commission to learn more about Tanzania and was introduced to Richard. He had read about our quest on our web page where I had mentioned that some of my friends thought perhaps I should have my head examined. Richard was born and raised in Tanzania and was well aware of what Mount Kilimanjaro had to offer. The first words out of his mouth were: "First, let me say that I am in the category of those who think you are nuts." (To this day I think Richard was only partially kidding but he was ultimately very supportive of our endeavors and has become a good friend of the family.)

The more people I talked to, the more positive the comments became, especially relating to the satisfaction of reaching the summit. Some of the more positive things said to me were:

"Would I do it again? No. But, it was the best experience of my life. There is never a day that goes by that I don't think *I have climbed Mount Kilimanjaro* I can do anything now."

"Age is not a factor. If anything, life experience will help you realize that the ordeal will not last forever. You just have to suck it up and get on with it."

It sounded like a challenge and definitely way outside my comfort zone! Which, after all, was what I'd been looking for . . . right?

When Evelyn and I first discussed the possibility of my climbing Mount Kilimanjaro she was very supportive but she wanted to read the information about it first. She seemed to be satisfied that a tour company would take every precaution to mitigate potential risks. She too realized that it was something that could potentially be done, although I had never even remotely tried anything like it before. Her sole comment was, "if you end up dying up there, I am not coming to get you!" I *think* her tongue was in her cheek when she said it. Here are Evelyn's words: "When Barry first mentioned he wanted to climb Kilimanjaro as a celebration of his 60th birthday, my immediate thought was: 'Isn't the celebration something we should do together?' After reflecting, I decided that if it was something he wanted to do, it was something he should do! I did not have to go with him, and I knew he would do his homework and find someone to lead the climb who could handle anything that arose, and that would set my mind at rest. The preparation for the climb was an education for both of us. We both learned to make better choices in our everyday lifestyle and began eating healthier." (Evelyn and a friend subsequently celebrated their own birthday milestones on a Caribbean cruise. She tells me I am not allowed to mention which birthday it was. But I can tell you that a few people accused me of being insane for choosing a mountain climb over a cruise!)

One of the most interesting comments came from Meagan McGrath, who has an incredible list of achievements. Meagan has climbed the highest mountains on each of the seven continents, including Mount Everest in 2007. In 2009, she completed a solo journey over 700 miles (1130 kilometers) on foot, unassisted and unsupported, from the coast of Antarctica to the South Pole, dragging 285 pounds of food, fuel and equipment in a sled for 60 days. At one point during her trek, she fell into a crevasse and sustained minor injuries in the process. Meagan's ultimate goal is to become the first Canadian to summit the world's highest 14 mountains — unguided and without oxygen.

I really admire Meagan's courage and determination to achieve these almost-superhuman goals. In response to my email just before Chris and I set out for our climb, Meagan offered a few tidbits of advice. The one that really stuck with me was, "I wish you and your son the very best of luck! Go slow - drink lots of water - eat lots of food - sleep well - and laugh lots!"

The next decision to be made was to find a climbing partner. Of course, Chris was the one who had planted the seed in my head so many years ago, so I approached him with the idea. At first, I don't think he thought I was serious. It took some time for him to make his decision, and I will let him comment on that. I knew that money would be an issue as he and his wife Laura had recently purchased a new house. More importantly, there was a new addition in the family. Chris and Laura's daughter Annika had just arrived on the scene, so it wasn't going to be easy for him to leave his wife and newborn baby behind to go on such a potentially dangerous adventure. I have to admit that I was torn in two different directions when I asked him. I really wanted to undertake the challenge of ascending Mount Kilimanjaro (and probably wouldn't have without Chris) yet I also did not want to put pressure on him to go. I put it out there for him to think about, knowing full well that his decision might be that he just couldn't do it. It took some time for Chris to arrive at his answer, but I was thrilled when he committed to the trek. Our unique father-son adventure was about to begin!

Chris: I really didn't think my dad was serious about climbing a mountain at first. After he asked me more than once, I realized I had better start giving it some consideration! The biggest hang-up was, of course, my family. Annika had been born in early November of 2007, which means she would have just turned one when we departed on the climb. With a new family come many new responsibilities, not the least of which is financial. Laura and I talked and talked and talked about this, as our first thought was that the two of us should go together with my father. We quickly realized that was not realistic. As much as we know our parents are here for us and able to help out watching Annika and our dog when we are in a jam, leaving them for the time it would take to climb the mountain just did not make sense for us.

The next conversations we had were about the possibility of my going with my father alone and leaving Laura with Annika. It would make the trip more affordable, but I was still hung up on leaving my daughter for almost three weeks while I headed out to challenge my body's limits. Additionally, I'd be leaving Laura alone with her career as a self-employed realtor, to care for a one-year-old child on her own and look after herself and the dog at the same time. That was a handful!

Fortunately, Laura's parents had rented a house in the south of France and were going to be away around the same time I was. This meant that all Laura had to do was go to France with her parents and she could have all the help she needed looking after

Annika and herself. What a hardship that would be! The other amazing part about this set of events was that it meant I would have some post-Tanzania decompression time in the land of wine and baguettes to look forward to before I reintegrated myself back into North American culture.

And the truth is, one of the main reasons I wanted to do this was the result of a medical scare. One day while playing soccer, I thought I had torn my shoulder joint. I played goalie for my soccer team and could throw a soccer ball halfway down the field with pinpoint accuracy — at least that is how I remember it. One day my shoulder started acting up on me and ultimately my entire right hand went numb. This lasted about 20 minutes until the feeling came back and with it, the pain. The pain would usually last 30 minutes and then it would pass.

Over time it got worse — it was coming and going every few hours, and I would endure a period of numbness and pain followed by just pain and then it would fade away. My first stop was to a friend who was a chiropractor, as she had some experience with shoulder issues. When she couldn't fix the problem, she quickly referred me to an acupuncturist. The acupuncturist tried and couldn't fix it, so he sent me to someone that applied active release therapy, which is basically a treatment that marries chiropractic with physio with massage with championship wrestling. The amount of strength involved in that was impressive! But ultimately it too was unsuccessful.

Massage was next, to no avail, followed by months of physiotherapy with no benefit. Then I pushed for an x-ray and learned I had a tumor in the bone of my right arm that was causing the pain (it was impacting the nerves all around it). It was another six weeks before I learned that the tumor I had was not a cancerous tumor. If you ever need an opportunity to rethink your life and get a better perspective, there is nothing better than being faced with your own mortality.

The treatment for this was a form of surgery performed by a specialist whose official title was something to the effect of "orthopedic oncologist specializing in the hand and upper arm." That is what was on his business card, anyway. As you can probably tell, an orthopedic oncologist is someone who deals with cancer-related maladies, and my case of a non-cancerous tumor was not going to be a priority. The coping mechanism to deal with the pain and numbness was taking a steady regimen of Advil, recommended because it's a non-steroidal anti-inflammatory and would help with the symptoms. Unfortunately, with the frequency that the pain and numbness were hitting me it meant taking an Advil at least every three hours. My schedule at night was to take one pill before bed, wake up in pain two and a half hours later, and take another, then wait half an hour for it to start working, sleep for two and a half hours, wake up in pain and do it all over again. Repeat. Repeat. Repeat.

Still, while that seems like a real hardship, there were some benefits. The first benefit was that it helped get me ready for having kids. Some kids sleep better than others but you never know what you'll end up with, so this was good practice. Secondly, when work was busy, this was a great opportunity to get a bit more stuff done at really strange hours when no one would interrupt me. I basically left my laptop running at the foot of my bed and would work with the hand that wasn't numb for a time until I was ready to sleep again. My favorite benefit, though, was when work wasn't busy; I would watch comedies on my laptop. Unfortunately, this sometimes caused me to wake my wife up if I was laughing too hard.

So far, my story has a happy ending, but it's also provided me with a new lease on life. I always remember being told when I was young that on your death bed you'll never look back at life and say "Gee, if only I had spent more time at the office." Now I just do a better job now of emulating that spirit. I also came home from the doctor's office after being told I had a bone tumor and they couldn't tell me how serious it was but it might be cancer, and opening the bottle of Scotch that I had been saving "for a rainy day." I no longer save anything for a rainy day, and I spend as much time with my daughters and wife as I can (my second daughter was born in November of 2009). I also go out of my way to tackle challenges if it's something I feel I can't afford NOT to do, like climbing a mountain.

When Chris agreed to make the Kili climb with me, Evelyn commented, "I felt better about not being able to go with Barry. I knew that they would look after and challenge each other."

The only decision remaining was the timing of our trip. We chose January for two reasons. Tanzania lies just south of the equator and is subject to hot, dry months and rainy seasons. The main rainy season is known as the season of "long rains" and generally lasts from March through May. The humidity is very high then, and the temperatures reach low to mid-30 degrees Celsius (35 degrees Celsius equals 95 degrees Fahrenheit). The long, dry season normally follows the season of "long rains" and runs from June through October. Then there is another rainy season called the season of "short rain" in November and December, which is followed by drier weather in January and February. We chose to leave in early January with hopes that the weather conditions would hold true and the rainy season would indeed be over by the time we arrived.

The second deciding factor was that we would be back before tax season began and my accountant son became completely unavailable. Accountants!!

CHAPTER 6

How Much Training Is Enough?

IT IS NOW just before 11 a.m. in the morning on our first full day in Africa, and we are sitting in a shady area among the trees beside the hotel waiting for our guides to arrive. As I write this and think back, I realize that the ravages of jet lag and the seven-hour time difference did not really affect us. We were tired from the long flight but we just adapted to the new time. I guess we simply had too many other things to think about.

There are a few mosquitoes buzzing around, and my thoughts turn immediately to malaria. Good thing the doctor recommended Malarone to ward off the threat of mosquito bites turning from minor annoyances into something far more serious. In very unlike-Africa fashion, our guides Francis and Shabaan arrive at precisely 11:00. Incredibly, Francis has been climbing for 11 years. Christopher asks how many times he has climbed Mount Kilimanjaro and Francis replies, "How many times have you gone to *your* office?!" Shabaan has a friendly face and a jovial nature. It is obvious he enjoys kidding the clients, while Francis is the more reserved of the two. He states the facts and makes sure we understand completely what we will be facing.

We receive our orientation and medical tests, which involve recording our blood pressure, heart rate and the level of oxygen in our blood stream, all numbers which will be used later as a baseline for comparison when we are on the mountain. The guides show us the medical equipment that will be going with us. The comfort of knowing we will have it with us is only surpassed by the discomfort of knowing we might have to use it. The guides certainly seem well prepared. Then they want to see everything that we will be taking with us on the climb. We have 15 minutes to spread our clothing and equipment out on our beds so they can check everything. They want to make sure we have the proper weight of clothing, that it's wicking material and won't retain moisture, that we have the right quantity of energy bars, water containers and other necessities. Tusker Trail provided us with a detailed list so it wasn't difficult to make sure we had what we needed, but apparently there are people who have to leave things behind or have to go into town to purchase more. We passed the test. I am starting to feel good about the climb again and really looking forward to getting started!

Chris: The medical tests my dad mentions above include the use of a little device called an oximeter. This device indirectly measures the oxygen dissolved in the blood stream. The value that it produces is, at normal ranges, in the realm of 95-100% although values as low as 90% are still quite common. It is non-invasive: it just clips onto the end of your fingertip and it also measures heart rate at the same time. My research has shown that if your readings are below 88% in the United States, you can get Medicare to pay for oxygen for you. A reading below 80% means you are susceptible to hypoxia, which is a condition whereby the body is deprived of oxygen and ultimately can result in fatal complications. Had I known that little tidbit of information, I would have been a bit more concerned about some of our later readings on the climb, but perhaps it's better this way. Throughout this book, I will be reporting on our resting heart rates and oxygen levels at daily intervals – once before we start climbing for the day and again after the climb. The accountant in me compelled me to record all of this information in my journal, and so I will include excerpts.

A resting heart rate is just the measure of the number of beats your heart pumps in a minute – beats per minute, or bpm.

This varies depending on your body's need for oxygen. The oximeter also measures this at the same time as it checks the level of oxygen in your bloodstream. A typical healthy resting heart rate for an individual would be in the range of 60-80bpm. Tour de France cyclist Lance Armstrong reportedly has a resting heart rate of 32bpm while other elite cyclists report bpms as low as the mid-20's.

We needed to set a baseline before we began the climb, so we had our first readings done during this orientation. Being the competitive duo that we were, my dad and I immediately began comparing our results. Our baseline readings before we started the climb were an oxygen reading of 86% for me (which was apparently okay, though I guess I could have qualified in the U.S. for some paid oxygen!) and a resting heart rate of 66bpm, while my dad registered an oxygen rate of 96% and a resting heart rate of 85bpm. Healthy enough to continue on!

It was June 2008 when I decided I didn't want the training to end just because the money for hiring a personal trainer was running out. There had been a noticeable lifestyle change that made me want to stay fit. I was motivated by the thought of climbing the mountain, and when I thought about it later, I realized that inspiration was all around me. I wanted to have a successful climb, but success to me would be giving it my best effort. There are so many factors beyond the climber's control that can limit the results, so the best one can hope for is that you've prepared yourself well enough to take care of all the things within your control and be satisfied with the result.

Chris and I made a pact very early in the process. We agreed that if one of us fell sick or was injured, the other one would go on and take the flag to the top. Practically speaking, I am not sure this was logical. If one of us had to be removed from the mountain due to altitude sickness and the prognosis wasn't good, I am not sure the other would have been continuing the climb. I guess the pact should have been, "If one of us is sick or injured, the other one will continue…depending on the nature of the sickness or injury."

So my training continued. I kept up my routine at the gym, and I performed some physical activity every day in the months leading up to the climb. The climb was six months away, but there was still a lot of preparation to do. Ottawa is one of the most beautiful cities in the world, I think, but it does not offer the best training opportunities for someone planning to climb one of the world's tallest mountains. It is the nation's capital; and it does boast miles of green space with biking and hiking trails. Because it is situated between Montreal and Toronto, Canada's two largest cities, it seems to be often overlooked by tourists, so the trails are relatively uncrowded. The fall colors are absolutely stunning and there's something for everyone: the canal, the many museums, Parliament buildings, the art gallery, and professional sporting events. Just to the north of Ottawa lie the Gatineau Hills. As described by someone's entry in Wikipedia, the "geology of Gatineau Park, which encompasses these foothills, is related to the Eardley Escarpment, which is a fault line that lies along the southern edge of the hills." This escarpment makes the park an attractive location for rock climbers and hikers, offering a beautiful view of the relatively flat fields below which extend to the Ottawa River.

There is nothing that I have found that compares with a bike ride or walk along the Rideau Canal in Ottawa, and Gatineau Park is truly a beautiful place to hike. However, for someone who is training to climb a mountain, there is one concern. The average elevation in Ottawa is 305 feet (93 meters). In Gatineau Park, the elevation gain of its signature Wolfe Trail is 1,312 feet or 400 meters. In a few months, we would be climbing to an elevation of 19,340 feet or 5,895 meters. Training in our home town for the elevation we were about to be facing was going to be a challenge!

I decided the best I could do was to make sure my cardiovascular conditioning was the best it could be. I bought a heart rate monitor watch to track my heart rate while doing various exercises. Being goal-oriented, I continued to set little achievable goals as a way to keep me motivated and track my progress. I combined this with my other goal of doing something physical every single day, but I was careful to follow the advice of my trainer to give certain muscle groups a rest while challenging others.

In discussions with my trainer about mountain climbing just before I stopped working with her, she pointed out that strength and core training would be extremely important for success. The core involves the muscles of the abdomen and back and are the set that stabilize, align and move the trunk of the body. We would be carrying heavy backpacks up the mountain, so training the core muscles would correct postural imbalances that could lead to injuries. Proper training of those muscles could make the backpack seem a little lighter while carrying it for up to 12.5 miles (20 kilometers) a day. The biggest benefit of core training is to develop fitness that's essential to both daily living and regular activities, but in our case, Chris and I would be going beyond "regular activities" so it became that much more important. It was crucial to have the strength and endurance to hike long distances for nine long days, so strength training also continued to be part of my physical regimen.

There's a myriad of good books, fitness magazines and internet sites on core and strength training. If you can't afford a trainer to help get you started, it helps to find a good article you like and follow it consistently. I can also attest to the need to vary exercises from time to time. The body gets used to doing the same thing over and over, so it's good to change your program every six to eight weeks.

During the summer of 2008, I would spend three days in the gym varying upper and lower body weight training with core strengthening and cardio activities. On off days, I would go for a hike or bike ride or just for a walk, keeping my upcoming confrontation with Mount Kilimanjaro firmly in mind. Of course, I also managed to squeeze in a few games of golf during that time.

The main source of training during this time involved hiking. There were more than a few times when Evelyn would drive me to a parking lot at the head of a hiking trail and read her book until I returned 30 - 90 minutes later Evelyn was unable to hike due to osteoarthritis. One of her knees had been replaced, but the other one had yet to be done. She always said that when she'd been able to walk, I wasn't particularly interested…unless I had a golf club in my hand. When I finally became interested, she couldn't walk easily.

Sometimes friends accompanied me on the hikes, and they were invaluable. It makes the hike go that much faster if you have a hiking partner. Hiking on your own can get boring, so finding a partner who is willing to help you train is all the better. No matter what a person is thinking about on the hiking trail, thoughts will eventually turn to the fatigue that the body is experiencing. Exercising with someone helps take the mind off how you're feeling and time passes more quickly. Also, on the trails I was doing, there were occasional bear sightings. I always kept the old adage in mind: If you come across a bear on the hiking trail, just be sure to run faster than your hiking partner and you'll be fine!

Some days I hiked up to 9.5 miles (15 kilometers) and biked about 12.5 miles (20 kilometers) on others. My hiking trails were as steep as Ottawa's geographical landscape allowed. I attempted to do each one a little bit faster each time to add new levels of difficulty.

As fall approached and we were only three months away from the climb, my focus shifted to my legs. I still did cardio and weights, but now I looked for stairs to climb. There are 284 steps behind the Canadian Parliament Buildings in our home town, and I began climbing them at lunch time.

During the winter, I continued to go to the gym regularly but I also went snowshoeing. In Canada, we have three choices in winter: We can stay in the house and wish winter would go away. (However, in spite of the warnings about global warming, winter is guaranteed for at least five months, so that is a long time to hibernate.) We can join those people called snowbirds who head south to warmer climates for the winter. Or we can embrace winter and take part in the many activities available to us, such as skating, skiing, and snowshoeing. In fact, winter is so lengthy in our part of the country, many of us do it all; wish it would go away, go south **and** embrace it. *Chris: The idea of going south to embrace it sounds good to me!*

This brings me to the second of the two moments when I knew I was as ready as I was ever going to be. The first was when my trainer expressed her satisfaction with my training through her little obscenity. The second was during the winter of 2008, just a few weeks before our climb. I was navigating the steps in our office tower before I went home at night and realized I was doing this with less and less difficulty. The goal I'd set for myself was to climb up and down 50 flights of steps without stopping before I turned 60 on December 11. On December 8, I accomplished my goal – a thrilling moment and one that showed me I was as ready as I could hope to be. Of course, there were still times when my confidence level rose and fell at least as many times as the steps I was climbing. But as our departure date loomed, I knew I'd done all I could possibly do to make myself ready for the adventure of a lifetime.

I'll add just one more thing before ending this chapter on training. There is a saying in mountain climbing that going up is optional, but coming down is mandatory. When I got to Mount Kilimanjaro, I learned rather painfully doing the mandatory part of the climb that I should have practiced going <u>down</u> hills a lot more in my training. With a little thought there are ways when you are training to start at the top of a hill and find a different, flatter route back to your starting point. For example, I could have started at the top of the steps behind the Parliament Buildings and followed a flatter route to my starting point to train my legs for descending the mountain but the thought really never crossed my mind. My entire focus was on climbing up. The thought of the pain that would be endured coming down never occurred to me. On the mountain, I did not have any pain going up. Coming down was a totally different story. There will be more about that later. I should have done my ankles, calves, shins and knees a huge favor. I should have found some hills and started at the top as part of my training routine and I should have done it often. My lower body would have been very thankful for it, especially once we were staring Mount Kili in the face.

CHAPTER 6, PART 2

How Much Training Is Enough at 30?

Chris: I had to take a slightly different approach to training than my father since I was neither retired nor on a paid contract. With a full-time job and a young family, my training was often done at strange hours, which meant getting up and going to the gym, coming home to shower and then waking up the rest of the house. My strange times were VERY early morning, and I came to be very thankful for the hour at which the local gym opened for business. I never managed to be the first one there, but let's just say there was never a line to use any of the equipment!

I had spent my entire life playing what I affectionately refer to as leg sports: soccer for pretty well my entire life, as well as cross-country skiing, downhill skiing and rugby in high school. Most recently I had taken up both squash and Ultimate Frisbee. Every one of those activities resulted in a heavy workout to my quadriceps (the muscles in the front of your thighs) and hamstrings (the muscles on the backs of your thighs). They also contributed to my having been given the award for "best legs" in my high school graduating class. I'm fairly certain it was the short rugby shorts that sealed the deal on that though . . .

Back when I was hiking in the hills of South Africa in 1999, I experienced something rather unusual. I woke up in the middle of the night unable to bend or straighten my left leg. I was pretty tired at the time so I worked through the pain as best I could and decided I would have to wait and see what came of this once the morning came around. When morning came, I had some mobility back — not all, but enough that I could hobble back to the trailhead that was to be our destination that day. Coincidentally, my travel companion Justin and I had picked up walking sticks along our hike just the day before to ease some of the burden of the walk. I'm not a big guy, but I had a good 20–30 pounds on Justin and I'm fairly certain that if it weren't for that walking stick he would have been carrying me back down the hill we were on.

Time passed and the pain subsided. I decided to try my hand at running in late 1999 and learned that even though pain subsides, it can come back. We have a wonderful health care system in Canada but it can be even better when you know someone who knows someone. I decided to have my knee looked at by a specialist and was lucky enough to know someone who knew an orthopedic surgeon. I was in to see him a few days later and was diagnosed with having "loose joints." They told me there wasn't much that could be done, other than to take it easy. No problem, I thought. My orthopedic surgeon even went so far as to compliment me on the muscle tone of my legs when I asked him if strengthening my legs would help the situation.

More time passed and my soccer career was ended by an injury that took six months to diagnose and another eight to have corrected. Once I was fixed up, I decided to try Ultimate Frisbee with my good friends and former roommates James and Caroline. At the end of the first season in August 2008, we had our playoffs and after playing in two back-to-back games, the worst happened: my left knee finally gave out. Now I was in trouble.

Multiple trips to various specialists resulted in an MRI which revealed a tear in the meniscus of my left knee. And a second one.

By no means am I an expert or a doctor (let alone an expert doctor), but I learned that the meniscus is the soft tissue in the knee that allows the femur (thigh bone) to sit on top of the fibula and tibia (the bones in your lower leg) and allows your leg to bend at the knee and glide smoothly. Meniscus tears can occur in two places— the inner part and the outer part of the knee. Because of the nature of the meniscus (it is effectively cartilage – like what your nose is made out of), blood flow within it is fairly limited, so if there is a tear in the inner portion of it, it won't get much blood flow. This means it can't heal without surgery. Help comes in the form of surgery which in Canada has at least a one year wait from the time of diagnosis. We were to begin the climb three months from the time of this diagnosis.

Fortunately, this is where my early-morning training came into play. My regimen at the gym had ramped up by this time to five days a week, so I had my weekends with my family. Laura is a realtor and invariably had to work on Saturdays. So I would load Annika into the stroller and we would walk for hours at a time. We'd go shopping eight kilometers away; we would go see friends on the other side of the suburb we lived in; we would just walk and spend time together with me pushing Annika in the stroller. My doctor had been good enough to set me up with a brace for my knee to allow me the stability to do this.

The five days at the gym would always include at least 20 minutes on a cardio machine of some sort with three of the days spent working leg muscles heavily (but carefully) and the other two days focused on upper body strengthening with light leg exercises. I would often throw in 30 minutes on the stair climber on days when I felt particularly energetic.

In addition to my time at the gym, I was also spending some time with Wii Fit strictly as a means to monitor my progress, improve my balance and keep tabs on my body mass index (BMI). Wii Fit isn't a precise science, of course, and not always indicative of true fitness level, but it was a fun diversion and it gave me an excuse to play video games!

I stuck to the basics in exercise and focused a great deal on my form during my workouts. With a bad knee and 100 pounds sitting on your shoulders, you have to really concentrate on how you position your squats or you could end up in a heap on the floor with 100 pounds sitting on your head. Lunges had traditionally been one of my LEAST favorite things to do when it came to exercising, but I quickly learned to love walking lunges as I traversed the gym time and time again. The calf raises were my favorite "ego boosters" because I was able to raise a much greater amount of weight than I would have thought possible.

Often people who knew me at the gym would stop me as I was working out to either suggest more leg exercises, get some insights on what my workout schedule was like, or sometimes just to encourage my work effort and ask how the knee was holding up. My black knee brace and I became a familiar sight around the gym.

The important points to take from all of this are similar to what my father has previously written with a few addendums and reiterations. First, consult your doctor before you begin. You can do most anything you put your mind to; however if your doctor has some warnings for you, remember to heed them. Doctors have been trained in their profession a lot longer than you have been training to climb a mountain or for any other activity, so they just might have something useful to say.

Secondly, don't take aches and pains for granted. They're coming from somewhere and if you don't look after them, you're more likely to make them worse through poor form in exercising or just continuing to aggravate something minor until it becomes a major issue. Either way, the damage could set you back months.

Finally, I know of people who have climbed Mount Kilimanjaro with little or no training whatsoever, so I know it can be done if a person is reasonably active beforehand. For my own purposes though, the idea of spending thousands of dollars on a trip across the globe and putting blind faith into your ability to do it with absolutely no training seems ridiculous. If nothing else, just challenging yourself to do one more repetition on the weight machine, one more minute on the cardio machine, one more walking lunge with 25 pounds in each hand is more security and a better test than just crossing your fingers and hoping all goes well.

CHAPTER 7

Doctor's Orders

WASTING AWAY AGAIN in Moshi, Tanzaniiiia . . . Okay, with apologies to Jimmy Buffett, Moshi isn't exactly Margaritaville, and the lost shaker of salt he refers to in the song definitely isn't here. But we are whiling away the hours in a beautiful setting with butterflies flying around... mostly in my stomach. After we meet with our guides for our orientation, the rest of the day is spent relaxing and mentally preparing for the arduous days ahead. We have a clear view of Mount Kilimanjaro all day from the open-air restaurant area, and it reminds me in some small way of the astronauts who must have stared at the moon prior to their journey. It's hard to imagine that in a few short days and with some good luck, we will have fulfilled our dream and will be standing on the top of that very mountain. I am really getting excited.

In the afternoon, we meet a delightful group from Australia who are working on an orphanage in Moshi. They have brought two kids from the orphanage for a swim in the pool at the Keys Hotel. Orphans are a sad reality in Africa because of HIV/AIDS. Many households are run by the oldest child, simply because the parents have succumbed to the disease. It reminds us that the work the Australians and others are doing — and projects like ours to bring clean water and classrooms to Tanzania — are desperately needed.

One of the kids holds up eight fingers when we ask how old he is. We think he might be four. The kids go off to enjoy the pool. The water in the pool does not look too inviting, but then again, we do get spoiled in North America. It is an exciting time for the kids, and we commend the Australians for their initiative. We exchange business cards with the promise of having a beer together when we return from the mountain.

Tomorrow, the adventure REALLY begins!

Long before we left, Chris and I were advised by our family doctor to visit a doctor specializing in travel before embarking on our expedition. I had my first visit on November 28, 2008. As it turned out, he had climbed Mount Kilimanjaro "when he was young and foolish" some 20 years before. The visit with him absolutely made my head spin. One of the first things he said was that we shouldn't even put a finger in Tanzania's Lake Victoria because of the high pollution rate. We were going to be visiting Lake Victoria, so that was good advice. Then over the next few minutes at a rate of speed that seemed to equate to playing a 33-1/3 rpm vinyl record at 78 rpm, he discussed the medication I would need. The rpm (revolutions per minute) and vinyl record reference is for people who are about the same age as I am. For the younger crowd, let's just say he talked really fast.

Chris: I think the speed Dad is referring to would have been like watching a television show in fast forward – that should clear it up for those of us who weren't around to enjoy the sound quality of a vinyl record.

What I heard was this: "Take diarrhea pills in two doses two weeks before leaving then one week before take Diamox as needed but it is highly recommended to take it during the whole climb put diarrhea medication in the fridge don't drop it only have sex with a latex condom don't drink the water! don't eat the lettuce! don't have ice cubes in your drink! if you get diarrhea and it has blood in it do this but if it doesn't do that…." Whoa! Wait a minute! Breathe, doctor, breathe!! (And what was that about a *condom*?)

Fortunately, the doctor wrote everything down, so I went home, studied the information and resorted to my old friend the Internet to sort everything out. It translated to the following: Take Dukarol, which is an oral medication to prevent cholera. In case your stomach becomes upset, make sure you have some Gravol. If the Gravol doesn't work and you still get diarrhea, you should have some Imodium, which will treat short bouts not caused by bacteria. If it gets really, really bad, then take Cipro, which is an antibiotic used to treat infections that are caused by certain bacteria. Finally, in the event it gets worse than "really, really bad," make sure you have an extra pair of pants with you. (Okay, so I made this last one up, but after what I heard and read, it seemed like a good idea!) Obviously, diarrhea was going to be a major issue lurking in the shadows during our climb.

We were also vaccinated for yellow fever. The yellow fever vaccination wasn't mandatory for Tanzania at the time. However, we were told that policies could change quickly (possibly even when we were still on the plane flying to Africa, so we decided it was better to be safe. We were also vaccinated for typhoid and meningococcal meningitis and both of us had previously been vaccinated with Twinrix®, the only combination vaccine that protects against both hepatitis A and B. It also provides long-term protection for at least 15 years when all scheduled doses are administered. But wait, we weren't finished! We were also advised by the travel doctor to take with us the following medications: Malarone for the prevention of malaria, Gastrolyte to aid in rehydration, Diamox to prevent altitude sickness, and Clotrimaderm, an antifungal cream.

The latter was to rub on any body parts that became raw. The doctor seemed to be especially concerned about raw nipples from constantly wearing the backpack. Yikes! If I wasn't feeling anxiety about all the other stuff we had to take with us, the mention of raw nipples was enough to ratchet up my anxiety meter several notches. I suspect that there's been a technological improvement in the design of backpacks from the day that the doctor made his climb because I did not have a hint of raw nipples. However, I bought and carried everything he suggested, even the antifungal cream. I didn't want to think about having *anything* scraped raw, but if it happened, I would have my antifungal cream to take care of it. We also carried moleskin for blisters, and Chris had a small first aid kit just in case.

As it turned out, the only medication we did take on the mountain during our trek to the top was preventative rather than corrective: Diamox and Malarone. That changed after the summit, but more about that later.

I realize I'm making a bit of fun at the expense of the travel doctor here, but still, I was thankful to learn everything he had to tell us. I had seen hints of all the potentially-required medication in my research; but when it was all explained at once, it became clear that this was serious business. If something did start to go wrong, it would be important to be as prepared as possible. You can't kid yourself into thinking that you can be prepared for every eventuality, but I highly recommend a visit to a doctor who specializes in foreign travel. Forewarned is forearmed, as they say.

Chris: Ah yes, the travel medicine. This was an area that had me laughing. I have this habit of reading instructions before I put things together (much to my wife's surprise as this habit doesn't seem to be common among males) and this also includes reading the information and possible side effects of medication.

The whole point of taking the Diamox was to prevent acute mountain sickness. We'll get into what acute mountain sickness is later on, but for fun I've put together a little chart that compares some of the symptoms of acute mountain sickness with some of the side effects of Diamox:

Acute Mountain Sickness Symptoms	Diamox Possible Side Effects
Lack of appetite	Decreased appetite
Fatigue or weakness	Weakness, fatigue
Dizziness or light-headedness	Dizziness
Nausea, vomiting, diarrhea	Nausea, vomiting, diarrhea
Insomnia	Headache or confusion
Swelling of hands, feet and face	Unusual bleeding or bruising
Pins and needles	Tingling or tremors in hands and feet
Shortness of breath upon exertion	Difficulty breathing, closing of throat

This isn't an exhaustive list of the symptoms of acute mountain sickness, of course, nor is it a comprehensive list of the possible side effects of the medication meant to prevent acute mountain sickness. However, as I review the list, I have to wonder if I should have even taken the medication or just rolled the dice. In most cases, I think I'd rather have the acute mountain sickness! Given the choice between being short of breath on exertion or having my throat close on me, I think I like my chances with the former rather than the latter. Chances are after walking for eight hours a day for a week, I'd have been feeling short of breath, anyway! I also prefer that my hands swell up rather than experience "unusual bleeding or bruising," but again, maybe it's just me. Either way, I couldn't help but laugh. Please remember though, I am neither an expert nor a doctor, and certainly not an expert doctor. No matter how unnecessary it seems, you should always seek professional help before assessing your medical needs.

CHAPTER 8

The Company You Keep

THEY SAY YOU can choose your friends, but your family is forever. I guess that is true. In my case, I didn't have to look for a friend on the mountain as Chris was pretty much my first and only choice as a climbing companion. However, we expected to meet many more people that we would be climbing with when we got to Africa. It turned out we were wrong.

Just before Christmas, we were advised by Tusker Trail, the company that we had chosen to lead our climb, that there would only be the two of us on the mountain with the guides and porters, unless someone else signed up before the actual climb date. We had thought that would be highly unlikely and were just getting used to the idea of hiking together as a twosome. We were even discussing what we could possibly talk about for nine days on a mountain when I received an email from a fellow named Peter Yates who lived in London, Ontario. Peter had seen our web page and thought he would ask if he could join us on our journey. He said he was 50 years old and was physically active. Chris and I talked about it and finally decided we would ask the people at Tusker Trail to make the decision. I said to Peter, "If it is okay with Tusker, it's okay with us." Peter called a few days later to tell me that Tusker had said that if it was okay with us, it was okay with them. I think he sensed a little trepidation on my part at this last minute change as he made a point of telling me he wasn't a complete jerk.

Chris: As I remember the story, he told my father he wasn't an asshole, but perhaps Dad was trying to sanitize it a little.

Peter also mentioned that he had spent the first 11 years of his life in Nairobi, Kenya and that his grandpa used to tell him as he sat on his knee that Father Christmas would come over Mount Kilimanjaro on December 25 with gifts for all the boys and girls. He said that climbing Mount Kilimanjaro had been a lifelong dream for him.

How could we resist that? Besides, Peter did seem like a good guy so we decided to increase our little group by a third. It turned out to be a great decision. We liked Peter as soon as we met him in Africa. We ended up sharing a lot of laughs and commiserations about our aches and pains as we made the climb up Mount Kilimanjaro.

But a much more important and difficult decision had been the choice of the tour company that we were going to entrust with our lives on the mountain. We had done our research carefully; assessing companies that we thought might do the job professionally. The main criterion for me initially was safety. The words from Tusker Trail's website were reassuring: "If all you're looking for is a cheap price, then you should book with a volume-based outfit. But if you want a spectacular experience with expert guides whose key focus is your safety all the way to the summit, and to expose you to Kilimanjaro's habitat, then Tusker's your sure bet."

They went on to say, "Tusker Trail's founder, Eddie Frank, was born and raised in Africa, and has climbed Kilimanjaro 40 times over the past 33 years. He knows Kilimanjaro exceedingly well. Since his first climb in 1977, he has built Tusker Trail's reputation as the most experienced and qualified trekking company on Kilimanjaro."

We continued to do our research. We spoke with people who had used Tusker, and we were satisfied. We made contact with Tusker's representatives, and again, we were satisfied. We liked the idea that they would do medical tests twice a day, and we really liked the idea that they were very experienced. They weren't cheap by comparison to other companies we researched, but we suspected there was a reason for that before we left – a suspicion that was later confirmed to us on more than one occasion. We decided to hire Tusker as our tour guides.

Shortly before our final ascent, one of our guides told me that Tusker's motto is "safety first, summit second." Our lead guide was trained as a First Responder. They bring along a safety porter who followed us every step of the way carrying a Gamow bag, a stretcher and two bottles of oxygen. (A Gamow bag is a nylon bag that surrounds a patient to simulate altitude up to 7,000 feet, thereby relieving symptoms and severe reactions of altitude sickness)

Just how wisely we had chosen our tour company became obvious while we were on the mountain. There were climbers who were not receiving medical tests as we were or eating as well as we did or receiving the same acclimatization as we were. In fact, we met some climbers who were very disgruntled about their experience. However, one of the biggest issues was the completely inadequate clothing that some of the porters were wearing. We saw porters climbing with sandals instead of proper foot gear.

According to the Kilimanjaro Porters Assistance Project (KPAP), of which Tusker Trail is a partner, the working conditions on the mountain can be deplorable. As described on its website, KPAP was registered as a Tanzanian non-governmental organization in 2003. It is an initiative of the International Mountain Explorers Connection, a nonprofit organization based out of Boulder, Colorado. KPAP's mission is to improve the working conditions of the porters on Kilimanjaro.

The porters' job is incredibly hard and treacherous work. It is exhausting and dangerous. They must carry their clients' supplies (except what the climber needs for the day) as well as their own gear, usually on their head. Their luggage is supposed to weigh 20 kilograms (about 44 pounds) but it can weigh up to 30 kilograms (66 pounds). They will work for as little as 4500 Tanzanian shillings per day, which is about $4.50 and they are susceptible to altitude sickness, injury and even death while trying to make a living for their families on the mountain.

Climbing companies can be unscrupulous. We learned that

the ones charging less will then base their profits on volume. We saw guides allowing their clients to drink from a stream that was undoubtedly polluted. We spoke with one climber who said she was not feeling well and her guide was making her go back down the mountain without offering any kind of medical treatment. While it is sad to say, companies that base their profit on volume apparently sometimes rush the climb or don't bother to check the seriousness of a client's ailments. At the first sign of difficulty, their clients are deemed incapable of finishing the trek, allowing the guides and porters to turn around and go back down the mountain to start again with another tour group.

Chris: We crossed back over the stream that my dad is referring to later that day and I saw firsthand a porter with one of the other companies relieving himself into it, upstream from where the guides were allowing their clients to drink.

The corollary of that situation is the client who is desperately ill but because the guides have no medical training or do not administer medical tests, the client is left untended. This can very quickly lead to a serious situation and even death.

We are certainly not suggesting that Tusker Trail is the only company that should be considered because we can't compare them with other equally-reputable companies. However, we can say that we were very happy with our choice and would definitely recommend them. In order to be a partner with the Kilimanjaro Porters Assistance Project, a company must prove its reliability and reputation. After seeing how hard the porters work for their meager salaries, we believe climbers such as ourselves have a responsibility to ensure that porters are treated humanely and properly.

Chris: I would say that Tusker is easily one of the more expensive outfits on the mountain, but as with most things in life, you get what you pay for. As you read the rest of this book, keep track of the little things that our guides and porters did for us — the quality of the food, the number of porters, the availability of water, etc. There really is not enough that can be said in favor of the work this group of men did for us to ensure our safety, comfort and complete satisfaction along the climb.

CHAPTER 9

A Funny Thing Happened on the Way to the Mountain...

LIFE BECAME PRETTY interesting in the days leading up to our climb. Some of the incidents that occurred were amusing at the time, and some are humorous now that we have the benefit of hindsight. Some were not funny at the time and still aren't funny, but they were part of the journey and are worth telling.

In the early days of my training, I had lost about 28 pounds as a result of my diet and hadn't really gained much muscle. I was down from 186 at my heaviest to around 158 pounds. I considered the process to be one of tearing my body apart and putting it back together again. Before I started the process of rebuilding myself out of scarecrow status, I shaved off the moustache that had been part of my face for over 25 years. I noticed people looking at me strangely, and I was (vainly) thinking that that they were probably admiring my new body. I was proud that people were noticing, but I was wondering why no one was really saying anything. Then one day Evelyn mentioned to me that people were pulling her aside and whispering in her ear, "Is Barry sick?" I had lost a lot of weight in my face and that, combined with the sudden disappearance of my moustache (which people couldn't quite place) was concerning them. In fact, a friend of mine who was obviously concerned and didn't quite know how to approach the subject, blurted out in a moment of unbridled insensitivity, "My wife and I think you look really old." Fortunately, I was stunned into silence. What is the moral of this story? Well, there really isn't one, unless it's not to cut off your facial hair at the same time you lose weight.

Chris put a scare into me in November 2008. As he mentioned earlier, he had injured his knee playing Ultimate Frisbee in the summer of 2008, and I noticed that it was causing him quite a bit of discomfort when we were on our hikes. He had the knee tested in November and found out there were two tears in his meniscus. Since the meniscus is the tissue that provides structural integrity to the knee when it undergoes torque, this was not good. Imagine how much torque there is on the knee when navigating steep mountain terrain, and even worse, how much additional torque there is coming *down*. I knew this bad news would test my son's resolve to the max.

Chris: Let me tell you, there was torque. Fortunately, there was much more resolve than torque. Or perhaps it was just pure stubbornness.

In August, Chris, his dog Tundra, and I were hiking in the Gatineau Hills. It had been raining quite a bit prior to our hike. We came upon a wet bog area where there were two places to cross. We could go a little further and cross on a log, or we could try to wade through the bog. There was a young man watching two women with whom he was hiking. For whatever reason, the three of them had chosen to attempt to cross through the bog. The young man had made it, but the girls were stuck up to their knees. He was standing there laughing at them, and seemed quite prepared to leave them there. Chris was raised to be chivalrous, so he decided to lay down a log and help pull the young women out of the mud. (I am sure the fact they were cute damsels in distress had nothing to do with his rather questionable decision.) Tundra bounded out enthusiastically to greet them and immediately sank up to her belly in the mud. I could see this had all the makings of a total disaster. First the young ladies . . . now the dog . . .

Chris took one step on the log, then two. Sure enough, down *he* went up to his knees in mud. Somehow, the women got themselves out of the mud with the help of the log Chris had thrown in, and Chris managed to struggle his way out. Chris emptied out his waterlogged, mud-covered boots, and we all went our separate ways. They thanked him for his efforts, and I had to listen to his complaints about how much mud he had in his boots and on his socks for the rest of the hike.

Chris: It did seem like a foolproof plan, but apparently it wasn't. The mud was well past my knees, and then my knee hit something under the mud and scraped it up pretty badly. Fortunately it was my good knee. And contrary to what my father just wrote, my complaints were quite limited – I knew the more I dwelled on it, the less merciful he would be on me when this book was written. Rather than typing more, I should really just be deleting his last two paragraphs!

Our local church, Barrhaven United, became a prominent factor leading up to our climb. Reverend Dianne Cardin, the minister at the time, became very interested and supportive of our endeavors. She asked me to deliver a presentation to the congregation about our upcoming Mount Kilimanjaro adventure, as well as our efforts to help the kids in Africa. I made the presentation on October 26, 2008 and entitled it, "*Even Ordinary People Can Make a Difference.*" It was well received. The Sunday before our departure, Reverend Cardin called Evelyn and me forward at the service to give me the blessings of the Church. She also said that she felt especially concerned for Evelyn as she would be the one left behind, wondering what was happening. I was moved by this little ceremony and felt good that I had the blessings of the Church with me. (Dianne has since become a friend and huge supporter and active participant in our fundraising activities.)

Chris and I determined that we had two choices to obtain visas for entering Tanzania. It was obviously necessary to get visas as official authorization allowing us to enter the country. We could purchase our visas in advance at a local embassy or High Commission office, or obtain them at the Tanzanian airport once we arrived. We found out it would be a little cheaper to purchase the visas before leaving and it would save us a little time once we got there. Now remember, Chris and I are accountants. Did I mention the word "*cheaper*"? You can probably imagine which option we took.

We applied for our visas on November 17, which involved filling in an application and submitting our passports. By December 11 we had heard nothing, and my phone calls to the Tanzania High Commission went unreturned. The pressure was mounting. We had visions of the day of our departure arriving with no passports or visas. The visas we could do without until we got there; not so the passports. Finally the phone call arrived from the High Commission in late December advising us that the passports were ready. Our relief was palpable.

Around Christmas in 2008, Evelyn developed a bad head cold and as usual, I couldn't avoid it. I was taking everything I could think of to try to get rid of it because I knew I would need all the air I could get on the mountain. Finally I went to a clinic between Christmas and New Year's. I just had to rid myself of this cold before leaving or consider canceling the trip. I was thinking about everything I had gone through and accomplished to get to this point — as well as the effect it might have on Chris if I cancelled. Believe me, canceling was the *last* thing I wanted to do.

I sat in the clinic waiting for a doctor to see me. Finally, I was ushered into a room where the doctor's assistant was very pleasant in asking me questions about my cold. I told her I needed something to get rid of it before leaving for Africa in a few days. I was encouraged by the conversation. Then the doctor came in, and the conversation with her went something like this:

Doctor: "What is your problem?"
Me: "I have a head cold. I can't breathe. I will be climbing Mount Kilimanjaro in a few days where the oxygen level is 50% of what we normally breathe. I need something to get rid of this."
Doctor: "There is nothing I can do. It is a virus that will have to take its course."

Me: "I guess I have to keep it in my head then. If it goes into my lungs, I won't be able to go."
Doctor: "It won't stay in your head. It will go into your lungs and you will have a cough for weeks. Have a nice day."
Me to her: "Thank you!"
Me muttering under my breath: "Nice day this!"

I would like to thank my musician son Trevor for introducing me to such an appropriate comeback (even though it was under my breath) in his song "Hurry Up!" that he wrote and performed on his 2001 CD, *Bumpy Roads*. Audience participation is normally encouraged when he performs the song as people are asked to flip their favorite gesture (i.e. one finger salute) as they shout the line. As I was silently muttering the phrase, I was also mentally flipping the gesture.

Throughout the next few days I wrestled with the infection. Even if I'd wanted to, there was no way to forget about it. There were constant reminders about the dangers of having a cold or illness if you are about to climb a mountain. I could hear my breathing with every small activity I undertook. My trepidation grew when we received our planning packages from Tusker Trail. There is a section on "Your Health" which states, "If you experience a cold or flu in the 2 weeks prior to your climb, we advise that you consider postponing your climb. This can be potentially dangerous." Oh great! That was the last thing I wanted to hear.

There was one more thing to do before leaving for our rendezvous with Mount Kili, head cold or not. We are true Canadians, who consider hockey to be a form of religion. Chris and his wife Laura and I had tickets to see the World Junior Hockey Championships in Ottawa during Christmas. The tickets entitled us to a number of games to see the best young hockey players under the age of 20 compete for the world title. I managed to get to every game in which Canadian players were involved, but I stayed away from a few games in the hopes of getting rid of my cold. I was downing all the cold medication I could get my hands and sleeping as much as I could. Nothing seemed to be helping. I thought long and hard about what I should do. Finally, laying everything on the line, I decided to get on the plane for Tanzania and deal with the consequences.

Evelyn felt miserable about having passed on her cold to me. Her comment was, "I felt absolutely awful about that and Barry was very discouraged about having trained for two years and then catching my cold and possibly not being able to climb the mountain. I was very relieved six days before the departure date when he came out of the bedroom and said, 'I have decided that I am just going to go for it. I will do what I can and that is all I can do!' Decision made, he was going!"

If I was limited because of my cold, at least I would have made the effort. And maybe, just maybe, the cold would be gone by the time we arrived in Africa.

The train of converging events was completely assembled. Now we only had to await January 6, the date of departure. And when it came, I boarded the plane carrying my cold with me, not knowing that it would later become a factor in my climb.

Oh, I should also mention that Canada beat Sweden in the final of the World Junior Hockey Championships to win the gold medal for the fifth straight year!

Chris: It's probably worth mentioning that the Swedish and Russian Junior Hockey Teams were in the airport with us on our departure date. Unfortunately, we didn't get an opportunity to congratulate them on their silver and bronze medal finishes, respectively.

The last observation from the airport is one of my favorite moments from the trip, and it happened before leaving Ottawa. As we were sitting in the lounge waiting for the flight to board, I saw a gentleman wearing a t-shirt that had the word "Mzungu" written on it. I always try to learn a few words of the native language before I visit a country. In this case, the language of Tanzania was Swahili, and a good friend of mine who had spent a lot of time in Africa was teaching me some phrases to help me get by. One of the words he had taught me was the word

"Mzungu" which translates roughly into "white person" or "European." Now picture a tourist-y looking person who is as white as copy paper wearing a t-shirt that identifies him as a white person — you can't help but wonder whether he knew that's what it said or whether he just wanted a t-shirt from somewhere exotic. Needless to say, I knew I had to find one for myself.

PART II

GUIDES, PORTERS AND A MOUNTAIN

CHAPTER 10

Day One - Mti. Mkubwa

IT IS A beautiful and exciting day! This is the day we have been looking forward to for almost two years, and it's finally here. There is some apprehension and a lot of excitement. We are anxious to get going. A truck is supposed to come by to pick us up. Tusker has given us the bags we are going to be using. We are told to put everything in them that we won't need for the day. Everything else goes in our backpacks.

Yesterday morning we met our fellow climber, Peter Yates, in the outdoor restaurant at the Keys Hotel. We hit it off immediately. We had breakfast together and shared a few laughs. Peter is carrying his 35mm camera which has a huge lens. We know he will be able to take some great photos, but we speculate that it might be a little heavy in his backpack after six or eight hours of hiking. (Later, our suspicions would be confirmed as we overheard some minor grumbling on the mountainside about how heavy his backpack was.) I had seen an IMAX film about a Mount Kilimanjaro trek and thought at the time about the men whose job it is to lug the cameras up and down the mountain. It would turn out that neither Peter's camera nor the cameras carried for documentaries could compare with the workload the porters undertake on a daily basis.

Peter had advised us before we left that he had a torn ligament in his calf, so he was limping slightly when we met him. I notice he's still limping this morning. We make quite the group: Peter with his torn ligament, Chris with his torn meniscus, and me with a head cold. The chances of all three of us making it to the top seem pretty slim.

We are told to relax and wait for our "limousine" to arrive. After a significant wait (this is Africa, remember) a light-colored six-wheel vehicle huffs and puffs its way into the hotel parking lot and our climbing gear is loaded up inside. We have a driver and someone riding shotgun in the front. Francis, Shabaan, Peter, Chris and I are in the back. We didn't know how many porters we would have, but there are a number of them piling into the back of a truck behind us. Shabaan tells us that we will be traveling for six hours to reach our starting point. We can expect two hours of "good paved road," then two hours of "bumpy road" and finally, two hours of "no road" at all. We ask at one point if we are on the "no road" yet. The answer with a smile is, "No, man, this is the bumpy road." I can see that we have a lot to learn yet!

We are headed for the trailhead of the Lemosho route. We had been given our choice of six possible routes to the top of Mount Kilimanjaro. There are many sources describing the various routes, and I am sure any reputable hiking company will offer assistance in choosing the best one to take. Chris and I had spent a great deal of time studying the different routes, trying to decide which one would be best for us. Here is a compilation of what we studied, and why we chose the one we did.

The Marangu Route: This is considered to be the easiest route on Mount Kilimanjaro. It is commonly known as "the Tourist Route" or the "Coca-Cola Route." This route is the most popular trail up the mountain, and it's the only one that offers sleeping huts. Beverages like Coca-Cola are served along the way. (Hence its nickname "the Coca-Cola Route.") In Mount Kilimanjaro terms, Marangu is considered to be a relatively short, friendly hike, measuring a mere 22 miles to the summit. So you'd expect the overall climbing success rate to be amazingly high, right? Wrong! Because it's reputed to be the easiest route, it also attracts the most inexperienced, least-prepared climbers. As a result, Marangu's success rate for those making it to the top is a sad 35%. Reports are that it's not really that much easier than any other route, but the thought of soft drinks and huts along the way up encourages those who want the thrill of the climb without doing the hard preparation work in advance. Personally, I found it to be a little counter-intuitive to think that the easiest route could have one of the lowest success rates, but when one thinks about it, it absolutely makes sense. The faster you ascend a mountain, the more trouble you're likely to run into.

The Machame Route: This is commonly known as "the Whiskey Route." Machame is considered a more difficult route than Marangu because there are no sleeping huts or soft drinks for climbers. Machame is the second most popular route on the mountain and has a higher success rate than its easier counterpart. Perhaps the reason for this is that it takes people longer to ascend using this route.

Chris: Contrary to its nickname, I do not believe whiskey is served on the way up the Machame Route. If it had been, I might have reconsidered my approach.

The Rongai Route: This route is not particularly popular as it is the only route that approaches Kilimanjaro from the north, near the Kenyan border. Because of that, the cost of getting to this route is higher, and bandits have occasionally been reported at the trailhead. The benefit of following Rongai's route is that the climb to the top is gradual and steady. According to various sources, it offers the best opportunity to see wildlife through the remote wilderness areas since it's the trail least traveled. We definitely considered the pros and cons of this route, but its cost factor — and the notion of possible trailhead bandits! — were a major deterrent for us.

The Shira Route: This route offers a certain uniqueness about it as the first section of the trail is not hiked but generally driven. It is possible to hike the trail, but you will be on the track used by four-wheel drive vehicles. It's considered to be a difficult route that begins in the west at Shira Gate. The gate is located at 11,500 feet, which is a hefty altitude gain for someone who just the night before slept at a modest altitude of 2,500 feet in Moshi. Also, climbers using the Shira ascent miss out on the hike through Kilimanjaro's ecological rainforest, which to me is a good reason for *not* choosing this route. Our guides told us that the mountain is littered with folks turning back who have driven to the gate but couldn't complete the climb because they just weren't ready for the higher altitude.

The Lemosho Route: This climb is nearly identical to the Shira route, but with one significant difference. The first section of the trail is hiked through the rainforest. Rather than being dropped off at Shira Gate, Lemosho users trek through the forest on the first day and exit the rainforest on the second day. Because of this, the Lemosho Route usually takes seven to eight days to complete. Lemosho is considered to be a more difficult route, but because the climb takes a day or two longer, there is more time for acclimatization. It seemed to offer the best chance for success, and hiking through the rainforest was important to Chris and me. Unfortunately, we later discovered for ourselves that there is a downside to Lemosho. Because it is the third most popular route, it has a lot of garbage strewn about from other hikers and guides. Lemosho can also be the wettest route, which we didn't have to endure but obviously, that can be very unappealing.

The Umbwe Route: This is the most difficult climb on Mount Kilimanjaro. It is said that you can actually stand on the trail in places and kiss the trail at the same time. Umbwe is the least used, most untrafficked route on the whole mountain. While it isn't considered a technical climb by mountaineering standards, it is so steep that it offers little chance for acclimatization. Therefore, its success rate is very low. Chris and I quickly decided — no thanks!

A climber's decision on which route to follow is a personal one. It must be based on time, money, climbing ability, what's most important to see, weather, and terrain. I congratulate anyone who successfully completes the route they choose! In our case, we finally chose the Lemosho Route because it appeared to have an optimum chance for success. And Chris and I wanted to *experience* the mountain. The rainforest was particularly appealing to us. Even then, we had a choice of 12 days (which consisted of nine actual climbing days) or 13 days (which meant

10 climbing days). We opted for nine climbing days because we wanted to visit the schools after our climb. Most companies also offer safaris that can be tacked onto the end of the climb, but we were limited by time, so we passed on the opportunity. (We met a number of people who had done it, though, and said it was a wonderful experience.)

And so this is how Chris and I find ourselves jouncing along in the back of a truck on our way to the Lemosho Route to start our trek up Mount Kilimanjaro. More of the Tanzanian landscape is visible as we head for the mountain. The ground is fairly barren, with only odd tufts of limited vegetation that survives in the desert-like soil. There is the occasional tree that seems out of place with its much shorter companions. There is smoke arising in the distance from the communal fires that are used for boiling water and cooking.

Just before we start on the "bumpy" part of the road, we stop at a tiny village so our porters can pick up some supplies. We have a short break, giving us a chance to sit outside a ramshackle shack and take a few pictures. Peter uses his rusty understanding of Swahili to ask a young man if we can take his picture. He obliges and Peter gives him a few coins. Some kids go by herding gaunt-looking goats, and a number of women pass, dressed in their beautiful wraps balancing packages on their heads. Every vehicle that passes, including the bikes, raise a cloud of dust. Bicycles are obviously the most common means of conveyance, next to walking. Most of the cars we see are old and belching smoke as they rumble along. There are young men with their heads sticking under the hoods of their cars, trying to fix something or other. We see an adult man washing his car, which seems to be the epitome of an exercise in futility, given the hopelessly dusty conditions. Everywhere we look is a beehive of activity. A boy hangs off to the side watching us; every time we make eye contact, he gestures to us, hoping for some coins. I had read that begging is acceptable in Africa, but if you give money to one, you have to be prepared to give to all so we have to ignore his request.

As we sit in the African sunshine, I ponder my own childhood upbringing on my family's farm and the many opportunities I'd had. I wonder if the kids we see walking around are too busy with the responsibility of looking after siblings or fetching water to have the opportunities for an education or for any family fun. Growing up on the farm as I did builds character, toughness and determination, and I am sure these kids had that in abundance. But I couldn't help but wonder to myself if they had time to just enjoy being kids.

I am reminded by the multitude of bikes going by of my own experience learning how to ride. I remember that thanks to two of my brothers, I had to learn quickly or die trying. They had placed me on the seat and pointed me downhill towards a granary. After my inevitable crash, they asked why I hadn't applied the brakes. However, the term "brakes" and how to use them were completely new concepts to me since they had conveniently neglected to tell me that a bike had any brakes. A few years later, I found myself in similar straits on a warm summer day. I was careening around the yard on my bicycle, focusing on training for what I hoped at that time was my future career as a motorcycle racer. My dream evaporated in a headlong collision with a piece of farm machinery that had been parked in a rather unfortunate place (for me anyway). It was one point for the farm implement and 0 points for me (unless points were awarded for style) that particular day, but neither of us suffered permanent damage.

Sitting there outside the hut, waiting to begin the biggest physical challenge of my life on Mount Kilimanjaro, I watch the chickens scratching in the dust for something to keep them alive for another day. This reminds me of something that had become part of our family folklore one day on the farm when a chicken was, unfortunately, knocked cold by a rock thrown by one of my playmates. By the time Mom came out to see what was going on, the evidence had become circumstantial as the victim had somehow arisen from the dead and staggered away, leaving behind a couple of feathers.

Perhaps it was the warm African sun and the sights and sounds of the bustling activity in that tiny location that contributed to my daydreaming. It's odd what we think about from time to time or what triggers a memory in our minds. As we sat waiting to move on, I bizarrely remembered a Pyrex pie plate that was mysteriously spirited out of the Finlay family house and shot nearly dead centre with a BB gun by someone with amazing marksmen skill. While the perpetrator has never admitted guilt, the pie plate has been awarded to me since I was the owner of the gun.

Watching the African children and seeing their meager surroundings, I'm struck by how little they have and the challenges they face. There was always food on the table and clean water available in abundance when I grew up. I had parents who could provide for me. I had the good fortune to be able to have an education. Seeing these kids in the African sun was a stark reminder of just how much where we are born can affect our lives forever – a point that will soon enough become even clearer to me when Chris and I travel to Mwanza after our climb.

I am brought out of my reverie and back to the present by the signal that we have other mountains to climb, so to speak. It is time to move on. Peter had bought some pieces of sugarcane that we share along the way. It has the texture of hard celery and is very sweet and refreshing as we bump along on our way to our destination. Peter is taking photos and asks if it would be possible to lower the canvas sides of the truck so we can have a better view. The response is, "No, no…can't do that!" But something changes when we hit the final "no road" section of the driving part of our journey. The truck stops, and the driver piles out to put down the sides. We start up again in clouds of dirt and grime, and I think I can speak for the three of us when I say that we are all suddenly realizing that our next shower is nine long days away.

The "no road" has apparently had very little recent activity. We hit a few muddy spots on our way. In a couple of areas, the truck goes around the mud onto the hillside, and we are leaning at a severe angle as the truck slides sideways. Our guides are relaxed and are very proudly telling us that some days, only the Tusker truck can make it through the mud. When we look back, the truck behind us with the porters is also going around the mud and is dangerously tilted to near the tipping point. We can hear shouts of Swahili, either encouraging the driver or perhaps admonishing him to be more careful. We really can't tell, but the shouting is very enthusiastic.

As we pass through the Londorossi Gate on the west side of Kilimanjaro, we notice a number of Africans sitting idly by. While being a porter is very difficult work, it *is* work and many African men would welcome the opportunity to do it. These men are hoping that one of the climbing companies will offer them employment, so every day they sit in the hot sun and wait. We don't know what their success rate for finding employment is, but since the job of a porter seems to be in high demand, it is doubtful that their chances are very good.

We have to stand in line at the gate so that we can sign in. There is a strict policy of recording passport numbers upon entering and leaving. The numbers are apparently cross-checked so the authorities can be assured that no one is left on the mountain. We don't have to carry our passports on us, but we do have to have our passport number. We won't see the people again that we are standing in line with as they are on their way to a safari. It is interesting to see solar power adjacent to the building housing the gate — as well as a satellite dish behind the building. It is an indication that Tanzania is indeed a country of contrasts.

The porters are required to load their packs and weigh them. There are restrictions on the amount of weight they are allowed to carry. We have the impression that once out of sight, some of the packs are repacked and adjusted to suit the porters (or the various companies they work for).

Chris: I would even speculate that some porters would be sent back down the mountain after their check-in and the contents of their packs would be redistributed amongst the remaining porters, but I have no evidence of that.

There is a sign at the gate listing the rules as to what one should and shouldn't do on the mountain. Just as I was starting to think my head cold would not be an issue, I'm confronted with another reminder. The second line on the sign announces, "If you have a sore throat, cold or breathing problem, do not go beyond 3,000 metres A.S.L. (9,842 feet above sea level)." That would take me only just beyond our next campsite. I tell myself, let's start out and see what happens. Rule number 6 on the sign is interesting. It reads, "Do not push yourself to go if your body is exhausted or if you have extreme." Extreme? Extreme WHAT?! I guess I will find out soon enough what "extreme" is.

Finally we arrive at the trailhead at 7,392 feet. We are each given a snack of fruit and bread and some time to put on sun-screen and ready ourselves. There are a number of people milling about, including our porters and other climbers and their porters, who all are working on preparing the supplies to start the trek. The area is extremely lush and rich. We are obviously in the rainforest. I can feel some apprehension now. It's really starting to dawn on me that *this is it*. We're really doing this. I walk over to look at the trail that we will soon be hiking on. It doesn't look to be too bad, I think; it seems to have about the same steepness as the Wolfe Trail that we had been practicing on. But trust me, this thought would soon change!

It is time to begin. We start off. Francis is in the lead, hands in pockets, slowly putting one foot in front of the other. Peter follows, then me, Chris and Shabaan. There is a sixth member of our little group that none of us expected. His name, we find out, is Ignace and his job is to follow us every step of the way, no matter how far we go, carrying two oxygen bottles, a portable stretcher and the portable hyperbaric chamber. Comforting? Yes—and no.

There is a Swahili expression we will hear on the mountain over and over again. It is *"pole, pole"* (pronounced "polay") and it means *slowly, slowly*. We are sauntering along uphill, but it is slow! I turn around to Chris and comment that *now* we know what they mean by *pole, pole*! We manage to pass a small group of climbers that left ahead of us so our pace can't be that slow. Just a few minutes later, though, I find myself puffing like a steam engine! It is about 91 degrees Fahrenheit (33 degrees Celsius), we are in the middle of the rainforest, there is no wind, and the slope has become much steeper. It is potentially embar-rassing because I am thinking that everyone is going to be able to hear my breathing. My mouth is open and every breath I take seems to be magnified and ringing in my ears. When we arrive at the campsite about two and a half hours later, I ask my fellow climbers if they had heard me breathing. They replied no, that all they could hear was themselves.

One very important piece of clothing recommended to us by Tusker and again by the guides was our gaiters. Gaiters are pieces of canvas-like material that fit over the top of the boots and bottom of the pant legs. In Chris' case, that would be the bottom of the legs since he wore shorts for the first few days of the climb. Gaiters serve a variety of purposes, including keeping dirt and small stones from entering your boots. However, in the rainforest, an important purpose was to keep the razor-sharp leaves from cutting and scraping our legs. We will wear the gaiters every day of our climb as a precaution.

Chris: Another benefit of the gaiters I actually learned hiking on a small island off the coast of Malaysia. I didn't have the gaiters with me, but I was wearing my typical shorts and boots combo. On this hike, the terrain was very lush and very much a rainforest and some of the tree inhabitants were actually a type of leech. These little buggers would wait for something warm-blooded to pass by underneath the leaves of the tree, and they would let go of their perch and drop onto people. By the end of the hike, I had quite a collection of them just inside the tops of my boots — not an experience I recommend. Gaiters would have prevented this, but this shouldn't be an issue on Kilimanjaro for anyone that wants to follow in our footsteps. Small islands off the coast of Malaysia? They're another matter.

I don't think I can get enough of the rainforest. Evelyn and I had once visited the rainforest in Costa Rica. It was amazing and about as far removed from the Canadian prairies as one can get. We even saw poisonous frogs in Costa Rica, which we wouldn't be seeing in Africa. Being able to hike through the rainforest is one of the main reasons we chose the Lemosho Route for our climb. The sights and sounds are beyond compare. There is a feeling of underlying danger, because you know that surrounding you, unseen amidst the vegetation, are the creatures that call the rainforest home. The danger is real as sadly, at the time of writing this book, there is an article in the paper about a young mother and her one-year-old daughter from New York being trampled to death by a lone elephant that charged out of the brush. The family was hiking near Mount Kenya when the elephant emerged from the brush at full speed without warning. Wildlife experts are quoted as saying that the elephant, being alone, probably felt quite threatened. My heart goes out to the family.

We don't see elephants, but we do see paths where they had crossed our trail. The indigenous flora is simply breathtaking. Bearded lichens with their threadlike sinewy strands hanging like well, beards, are common and giant ferns are everywhere. The sun peeks through the thick vegetation periodically and sun and shadows alternate along the path. The sun bounces off the leaves and highlights the different shades of green, the blues, yellows, oranges and browns. It is a complete palette of color as we make our way through sun and shade.

When we arrive at our first campsite, the three of us look at each other and can't help but laugh. We had reached our first campsite after six hours of riding and two and a half hours of hiking. As we enter the campsite, we receive high fives from Shabaan for a job well done. We are exhilarated by our first day's accomplishment, and some of the apprehension has worn off. We have eight or nine more days on the mountain ahead of us. And we are filthy. Peter's t-shirt, which was white when we started, is now a dull grey color with its coating of dirt and grime. Chris and I are wearing darker clothing so it isn't as obvious to us, but we can see the dirt on each other's faces. We even have dirt on our teeth. It actually brings more childhood memories flooding back. The last time I had been this dirty was after spending a day trying to cultivate straight lines in the field as I was growing up so many years ago. It feels good.

This is our first experience of what our campsite would be like. There are a few other climbers in camp at the same time as us, but dominating the scene is a Tusker flag that will become the marker for our destination each day. It is another beehive of activity as the porters rush around performing their various functions. The area is awash in color, contrasting with the greenery surrounding it. The Tusker tents are orange and green, others are blue and white and still others are brown. Chris and I have one tent and Peter the other. The guides and porters share tents. There is a portable toilet for the three of us and a mess tent where our food will be served. There is a small table in the mess tent and folding chairs for each of us. A kerosene heater and lamp are brought in to provide light and heat for us in the evening. It is a little bit of luxury in the middle of nowhere, in sharp contrast to the dirt and grime that is covering us. Even that is taken care of to some extent when a basin of water is brought for us to use to freshen up.

Peter, who was climbing with his torn calf muscle, would later describe the first day like this. "… I had to do it on my tiptoes, because it was all uphill. Whenever you put your heel down, you overextend your calf muscle. I had to do it on my tiptoes to try and get through it. It was so flippin' painful, I managed to get to the first camp and I was just trying to show that I was okay, because our guides were constantly monitoring us."

Indeed, we soon discover there will be a ritual every morning and night that we will have to get used to. One of the guides joins us in the mess tent where we have our pulse and oxygen levels in our bloodstream measured via the oximeter. The guides also listen to my lungs with a stethoscope because of my cough. They tell me that if they hear any noise, I will have 12 hours to either improve or go back. Everyone will be tested with the stethoscope from time to time.

We appreciate the safety measure of these twice-daily measurements. It will prove to be invaluable. As we later became accustomed to the process, we would even try to play games with the oximeter by taking turns to be measured first. The two of us who were not being measured would try to go into a Zen state to bring our heart rates down. I am not sure that it worked or that anyone was fooled by it (in fact, I am sure we were not the first to try it!), but it was fun trying.

We also find that it's time to learn about leaving our dignity at the foot of the mountain. The oximeter is not the only thing we will have to endure twice daily. We will also be asked a series of questions that go like this:

How is your appetite?
Did you pee recently?
Did you have a bowel movement in the last 24 hours?
Do you have a cough?
Are you having difficulty breathing?
How did you sleep?
Are you taking Diamox (altitude medication)?
Are you taking Malorone (malaria prevention)?

The questions are designed to assess how we are adapting to changes in altitude. Responding to the questions felt a lot like having to go through security at the airport. Nobody likes to do it, but if it prevents something serious from occurring, it is well worth the little bit of discomfort.

All of us pass our medical tests with flying colors this first night. In fact, the guides tell us that all three of us are above average. I assume they mean "for our respective ages." It makes me feel that the hard work I have done in preparation for this climb is going to pay off, but I also sense there will be a lot more tests to endure before I can say that for certain.

Chris: Day One for me proved to be an amazing experience. We may have only climbed (hiked, really) for a grand total of two to three hours, but it still was an exhausting day having spent the six hours in the back of the truck and experiencing the exhilaration of starting our journey. That exhilaration is one of the most incredible feelings I have ever known and a feeling that also proved to be exhausting! It presents quite the conundrum when the excitement is such a large part of what tires you out. Day One really made the whole experience all of a sudden very real, where it had been still pretty surreal up to that point. I couldn't wait to start on Day Two!

This was the beginning of the real score keeping. My oxygen level was 95% as compared to my father's 93%, while my pulse was 77bpm as compared to Dad's 91. That makes me more rested and more oxygenated than him . . . not that I'm competitive or anything.

Another thing I have learned from various travels is to keep track of the types of foods I am eating on the trip. Before we left for the trip, we were at the hotel and a few times I had ordered a meal of "beef bits and fries." However, surprisingly the food on the mountain would prove to be far, far better. This first night we had a dinner of Nile perch, potato, vegetable curry of some sort, zucchini soup (which would knock your socks off!) and oranges and bananas. Keep in mind that all the food was prepared on the mountain itself by our team of porters. Among the porters was one gentleman who was the designated chef, while another was the designated waiter. They were both a lot of fun, and if our chef ever wanted to open a restaurant back home, I have no doubt that it would be an overwhelming success!

At bedtime (9:30pm, Tanzanian time) the temperature was a whopping 48°F (9°F).

There is one more thing to do before going to sleep and that is to call home. As part of our fundraising efforts, which will be addressed in the last part of this book, we agreed to provide daily updates on our climb to a local internet site in Ottawa. In order to help us do that, a local service club organization, the Lions Club, provided us with a satellite phone so we could call Evelyn with updates that she could post on the website.

The satellite phone reception had been disappointing thus far, but somehow Evelyn was able to get enough from our conversation that first night to post something for us. She said that whatever she didn't understand, she would try to create or make up. As it turned out, her accounts were amazingly accurate throughout our trip, and she received many compliments from people following her writing.

And now, it is time to try to get some sleep. Tomorrow will be Day Two on Mount Kilimanjaro. Another big day — and unknown challenges that lie ahead.

CHAPTER 11

Day Two - Shira Plateau

"TWENDE!" "LET'S GO!" And with that we start out this morning around 8:30 a.m. continuing through the lushness of the rainforest. Once again it is *"pole, pole"* as we make our way, uphill all the way, by the ferns and through the vegetation. We will soon find out that "uphill" is the order of the day. There are places enroute where the vegetation has grown over the path. We start off very slowly as we are expecting a hike of about six to eight hours. It isn't long before we hear some noise behind us. The porters have torn down the camp and are heading for the next one to set up. They pass us by with calls of "Jambo", which is Swahili for "Hello" as they go. This becomes a daily ritual.

We will occasionally catch up to groups of porters as they sit having a break and in some cases a smoke, but they will quickly pass us again. We catch the occasional whiff of marijuana when we pass some of the porters. I guess it is a matter of "whatever gets you through" but I am a little shocked. First, I am shocked that they are able to smoke and still have the lung capacity to climb. Secondly, I am shocked that they are smoking *marijuana*. Without overreacting, I certainly don't want my life in the hands of someone whose judgment is impaired. However, I didn't recognize any of the porters who are puffing away and when you think about it, it is not *our* lives that are jeopardized. Our lives are in our hands and those of our guides.

Chris: I agree that the smell was coming from porters from other companies, not ours. The porters on the mountain, regardless of who they work for, have an amazing sense of camaraderie. They always seemed to congregate together at the various break points and seeing that level of co-operation was a really reassuring thing to witness.

Earlier, just before daybreak, I remember noticing a strange noise emanating from deep inside the rainforest that managed to infiltrate my sleep. I had wondered what it was. Slowly awakening from what would be my last decent sleep for some time, I tried to recall what it was the guides had warned us about. Oh yes, it's the Colubus monkeys that are letting us know they own this part of the forest and we are only visitors. Their sound is a fairly high pitched, frantic sound, like they are having trouble catching their breath. It is doubtful they are having the same difficulty we were as we came up through the rainforest yesterday, but the sound seems oddly appropriate. As I was waking up, it sounded like there were hundreds of them deep in the forest. It's unlikely we'll actually see any of the monkeys because they are very shy, but they certainly let us know they were there, safely hidden from our view. Oh well, I guess it was time to get up anyway.

Chris: It was, after all, 5:30 in the morning Tanzanian time. It was also still 48°F (9°C). Our oxygen levels hadn't changed since last night so we were in good shape. Our resting heart rates changed, though. Mine went down a bit but Dad's increased by 4bpm. I figured either Dad's cold was affecting him more than we had hoped it would, or he was a bit on edge at that moment. Maybe the cold was causing the edginess. I had no concern over his ability to keep going at this point though, as I knew that his body would be healing itself when he slept.

Exiting the tent, we saw our 18 porters bustling around, doing their various activities or waiting until we packed up so they could start tearing down the tents. They'll be carrying our tents, our food, the garbage and everything else that goes with the expedition; they also have to carry our personal belongings that we won't be using that day. We are fortunate to have this porter-hiker ratio as it is normally around 2-1.

Five of our crew are considered to be "senior" porters with special duties. Ignace carries the security pack, and Benson is, of course, our waiter. The other three are in charge of the tents, cooking and the toilet respectively. We were told that porters hike up the mountain every three days with fresh supplies and take the garbage back down with them. They follow a different, shorter route up and down the mountain. We can't help but marvel at their strength and ability to deal with the altitude on a daily basis. We assume the altitude is just something they get used to, but later we find out that this isn't necessarily the case.

Day Two is a clear, warm day but the sun is shrouded by the canopy of the rainforest. Everywhere we look, there is lush vegetation. Everyone is in a good mood as we prepare for what lies ahead. We can't see where we are going yet because of the surrounding ferns and trees. We don't know what to expect!

Benson or one of the other porters brings us "warm water for washing" and water to fill our Camelbaks and water bottles. He explains to us that warm water for washing is "maji ya kunawa" and water for drinking is "maji ya kunywa." Miraculously, Chris remembers that throughout the remainder of our climb and to this day! I refer to our water containment systems throughout the book as Camelbaks because that is what we had and called them. There are other brand names for sale that may be equally as good. Camelbaks are water containers that fit in our backpack with a hose running over the shoulder so that we can drink easily. They are very convenient and a necessity. We also carry water bottles, energy bars and our myriad of medications. Every day we will be reminded to carry our rain gear because the weather on the mountain can change at a moment's notice. We dress in layers, so the weight of our backpack varies throughout the day as we add or remove items. As for boots, I learned from my research that I should buy the best quality I could afford and make sure they were well broken in before starting the hike, which I did. I also bought ones with an aggressive tread to handle the rocks and the extreme slopes we'd be climbing. Slipping on the rocks has serious consequences and, of course, blisters are the last thing you want — they would take the enjoyment out of your climb very quickly!

Chris: Breakfast this morning is spectacular again. It consists of porridge and toast, along with papaya and avocado. There are always lots of beverage mixes, such as instant coffee, hot chocolate, tea and other drinks. At every opportunity, our guides advise us to drink lots of water to stay hydrated. As we get higher on the mountain and closer to the summit, our guides have told us that our meals will become pretty starchy and carbohydrate-rich which will help to satisfy our nutritional needs and exertion efforts.

We had had a choice to hire a porter who would carry our day packs for us. Did we do it? Of course not! We were there to climb a mountain! We figured carrying a pack was part of the experience. But we were increasingly thankful that we had trained so well carrying our practice packs. It helped us stay comfortable with their weight.

After about 90 minutes of strenuous uphill climbing, we break out of the rainforest into a huge zone known as alpine heath. It is a pretty abrupt transition. One minute the vegetation begins to thin out, and the next we start to experience the vast openness that we will be seeing for the next few days. We are told that Kilimanjaro was formed about 750,000 years ago. I had not known until Francis told us, that it consists of three large cones: Shira, Kibo and Mawenzi. Eventually the Shira cone collapsed and became extinct, forming a volcanic crater known as the Shira Caldera.

Looking back towards Moshi, we can see the top of the rainforest that we just left. As we sit down for lunch, admiring the view, we see our first white-necked raven. It is a huge bird, about three times the size of our North American crows, and we will be seeing many more of them in the days to come. They are predominantly black with some white on the bill, and their name obviously comes from the white splashed across the back of their neck. They are definitely scavengers, based on the size of their bills, but we will joke later on when we see them flying overhead that they are actually buzzards in disguise, just waiting for one of us to keel over! When we stop for our break, Chris checks his thermometer, which is registering a very pleasant 55°F (13°C).

And it's here that we catch our first glimpse of Kibo, the summit of Kilimanjaro. It is a massive hump with stark white glaciers outlined against the clear blue sky. It is difficult to know the route we will follow to actually get there. All we can tell at this point is how immense Kilimanjaro really is as we look *down* onto Moshi, *across* the vast plateau and *up* at Kibo. It is at moments like these when we have mixed emotions. There is the sheer exhilaration of standing on the mountain that only two days before we had observed from a distance. But there is also some trepidation as we can now see up close the challenge that lies ahead.

Chris: Trepidation is a really good word for what we were feeling, but the fact that we had such a good look at the summit at this time was also an incredibly good feeling. Seeing where we were headed made us feel very excited, but WOW! Did it look to be a long ways away!

We are surrounded by a high altitude desert plain filled with lava rock from Kibo's last eruption. It is very tough slogging through here. It's a long steep hike and mostly uphill. It is a beautiful area, though, as we see colorful flora. Our guides tell us that Kilimanjaro has a mixture of zones and vegetation because of its close proximity to the equator and the Indian Ocean. Additionally, because of its sheer size, there are dramatic changes in temperature, solar radiation and climate from the bottom to the top. We observe grasses on the mountainside mixed with yellow and silver flowered plants.

After lunch, when our energy starts to sag a bit, Shabaan tries to teach us the "Song of Kilimanjaro" in Swahili. Shabaan explains that the song starts with a greeting and welcome to the tourists. The chorus lists each of the campsites we will be reaching, and each is followed by "Hakuna Matata" which loosely translates to "No problem." It is a wonderful song, but we are slow learners. We blame it on the altitude. We do understand that the song is basically saying that we will be able to reach each of our campsites without difficulty as we gain altitude. We love their optimism and hope it's well-founded!

Actually, the altitude hasn't affected us that much to this point. I joke with the others that nothing has changed for me as I couldn't breathe before, and I still can't. We are ever watchful of the altitude change and there are two milestones in the back of my mind. The first was at 10,000 feet, the altitude we were warned by the sign at the gate not to go beyond with a cold. The next is at 16,000 feet, which is an altitude at which many people will start to be seriously affected. In fact, *anyone* who goes to 16,000 feet without proper acclimatization will be affected in some way, and our travel doctor told us that humans can't live above that level for any length of time without oxygen. We have made it past the first milestone as we are standing at approximately 3,600 meters above sea level or 11,810 feet. So far, so good (I think). The proof will in tonight's medical tests! The second milestone will just have to wait as we make our way slowly, but relentlessly towards it.

During the hike across the plateau and after our miserable attempt at singing in Swahili, I have time to think about my motivation for being on this mountain and the inspiration for continuing. It is true there were a number of converging events that brought me here. But it isn't something someone just decides to do one day out of the blue. There are still times when the goal seems to be too far away or too difficult to achieve. It is those times that the need for inspiration becomes more acute.

Chris: I found that a great deal of inspiration came from thinking about my young family back home. I drew a great deal of motivation and drive from thinking about when my daughter is older and begins to understand what Mount Kilimanjaro is and what an accomplishment it is to have been to the top of it and *then to be able to talk to her about my experiences on the mountain. The thought has crossed my mind of someday doing this climb again with my kids, the same way I did it with my father. This thought reoccurred to me regularly on the mountain and was a great way to keep myself moving day in and day out. As I write this, I can see the changes in my oldest daughter and I can really see that she is starting to get a sense of distance, and how far away things are, like her uncles who are spread across the globe. All of this makes my dream of taking the girls there with me some day seem all the more tangible.*

Somewhere along the way, we have passed into a moorland zone where precipitation must be much scarcer. The vegetation has morphed into tufts of grass. We have dropped down a bit in altitude as we reach Shira Camp at 11,500 feet. The surroundings are pretty sparse at this campsite. We made it in about six hours, and there is tea and popcorn waiting for us in the mess tent similar to what we had enjoyed the previous day. There was also a healthy helping of peanuts and chicken wings. We quickly learn that rituals are an inherent part of mountain life and snacks will be part of our camp ritual.

We relax outside in the balmy 64 degree Fahrenheit late afternoon air, although the wind is whistling around our campsite and making it feel much cooler. Now that we are here and reflect back on the day, I feel tired but there is an anticipation building in preparation for tomorrow. There is no thought in my mind of going back because of my cold or for any other reason – just curiosity at what tomorrow may bring. I am grateful for my travelling companions and consider myself fortunate to be able to do this with my son. No matter what happens next, the accomplishment to date will be something I will always remember!

Chris: Dinner arrived shortly after and once again our "chef" is to be congratulated. Could it be as we sit on the mountainside that we are actually eating better than we would be at home? I am not sure I would have had an appetizer of leek and potato soup at home today (though it is one of my favorite dishes!) but that is what we had. Then we had our medical evaluations. I was pleased to see that Dad's heart rate had improved considerably from this morning and mine was remaining constant. Our oxygen levels were still not being impacted much by the altitude as they were pretty consistent.

We are sitting in our mess tent in the evening sharing some laughs about our day and generally in good spirits. Peter regales us with a story about ordering a half chicken, potato and vegetable at a grill in downtown Moshi earlier in the week. The bill came to 17,000 shillings (about $17). The young guide who had accompanied Peter to the restaurant told him not to pay that amount because it was too expensive. After some negotiation, Peter was satisfied with paying 9,000 shillings. Benson told us *he* would probably have paid about 5,000 shillings for such a meal. That is pretty typical of life for tourists in Moshi. It is "buyers beware," and tourists must negotiate for anything they want. Like many other countries, tourists are fair game for price gouging. Anyone not prepared to barter and negotiate will pay whatever the locals can get.

I make my daily satellite phone call home early in the evening. Tonight the reception is excellent, as if I were just in the next room. We are on a plateau with very few high rocks near us, so this probably helps somehow, although I don't quite understand why high rocks would impede a satellite phone.

Benson spends quite a bit of time in the mess tent talking with us. He is trying to learn English and is very deliberate with his conversation. He is 25 years old and tells us he doesn't want a girlfriend until he has saved enough money to finish his education. He needs $500 and tells us it will take him about two years working as a porter to be able to save the money. He makes about $10 U.S. per day and helps support his family. He writes out the words to "Song of Kilimanjaro" for us in the hopes that our singing will improve. It doesn't.

After the question and answer ritual and the medical tests, it is early to bed again tonight. Chris has brought his own sleeping bag from home, but mine is a rented bag and liner from

Tusker Trail. We've also been provided with a "mattress" which is about two inches thick and deflects some of the discomfort of the rock-hard ground. The arrangements are quite comfortable, considering Chris and I are sharing a tent. The sleeping bag is warm enough, although I soon learn it is wise to wear a toque on my head during the night to keep the heat in. Believe it or not, this is the first time I have camped in about 25 years. So I keep an eye on my son who has had considerable backpacking experience. I am trying not to embarrass him too much with my complete lack of the simplest camping techniques, such as properly rolling up the sleeping bag. I am not sure that it is working.

I go to sleep tonight, as I will every night while on this adventure, thinking about the people at home. I think especially about my brother Keith, who was admitted to hospital with a very low blood platelet count in late December just before our departure. This, combined with his years of fighting leukemia, meant that I wasn't sure when I left what would happen to him. Demonstrating his usual sense of humor, Keith had relayed the message to us through his family that he was sorry his stay in the hospital would prevent him from joining us on the mountain, as if that had ever been a possibility! I was grateful for his brave attempt at humor. His situation is resting heavily in my thoughts.

CHAPTER 12

Day Three - Moir Camp

AS WE WAKE up this morning and look out the tent opening, there is our destination right in front of us, but seemingly out of reach. What a spectacular view!

Peter and Chris are both gimpy today (their respective injuries are taking their toll) so they are traveling at my speed. Not that I wish them any discomfort, but I am quite sure I would have been the slow one had they both been completely healthy. So far, we all seem to have been quite comfortable with the speed we are hiking. It might be a good time to remind you about the 10-year and 32- year age differences between them and me.

Chris: Even this early on I started to wonder whether we were going to be able to make it to the top. My knee is hurting, and I had the thought of not being able to make it pass through my head on more than one occasion. When you see a break in the trees or a break in the clouds and you realize just how far the top of the mountain is, you can't help but wonder. Of course, my knee made me think long and hard about my chances for success as the constant up and down really takes its toll. Then there was my father — he had worked really hard to get this far, but again, the wonder of how his age will impact him inevitably wormed its way into my head. It is cold this morning at 32°F or 0°C, including a fair dusting of frost on the ground (and this is only Day Three!). It helped that we were welcomed to the mess (dining) tent with a breakfast of millet, toast, fruit and Spanish omelets. Admittedly, the omelet had gotten a bit cold by the time it made its way to us, but that didn't stop any of us from voraciously devouring it. Our morning stats revealed resting heart rates of 87bpm for me and 93bpm for Dad, while our oxygen concentration was at 93% for me and 89% for Dad. The heart rate is going up; the oxygen levels are going in the opposite direction. It was bound to happen sooner or later!

The scenery on today's hike is absolutely spectacular: volcanic rock plateaus alternating with sheer cliffs. We spend most of the day hiking across the Shira Plateau. There are enormous caves and Chris climbs inside one and completely blends in with the surroundings, creating a "Where's Waldo?" moment. We are surrounded by lobelia plants, which resemble cactus but with very soft leaves. We start talking among ourselves about Kilimanjaro and the last time it erupted. Francis gleefully tells us that it erupted about 3,000 years ago so it is due to erupt again at any minute. I laugh, hoping he's wrong. Actually, the only information that I was able to find indicated that the date of the last major eruption is unknown, which means it probably happened before recorded history. Frankly, I think a volcanic eruption is the last of our worries. However, we do see the obsidian (dark natural glass) that has been formed by the cooling molten lava, and we are surrounded by volcanic rock, both reminders to us that an explosive event occurred here at least one time in history.

Chris: This part of the climb was one of my favorites. I have hiked in rainforest before, and while that certainly does not diminish the beauty of it there on Kilimanjaro, it was something I'd seen in some facet before. This area, however, was fascinating. Prior to this, I had never been to an area where there were volcanoes and remnants of eruptions, and while this is probably breaking some sort of law of nature (and/or the law of the mountain), I made sure to stoop down and grab a piece of obsidian to bring home to show to my wife and daughter. The landscape was incredible, with the jagged rocks and caves. Caves consistently inspire awe and wonder in me every single time I see one.

One thing that is becoming very apparent is that we will spend a lot of our hike looking at the back of the feet of the person in front of us. Peter took a bit of a fall at one point, but his pride was hurt more than anything. We kid him about losing his balance when the weight of his enormous camera shifted in his backpack. But all three of us slip or lose our balance occasionally. Even the guides will occasionally slip on the loose shale. The sound of a foot sliding on the gravel surface will bring calls of "Hey, are you okay?" from someone, depending how serious it sounds; if it sounds more serious, it's a concerned chorus from all of us. Ignace is ever watchful from his location at the back of our little group, ready to spring into action with his medical supplies, if necessary. It is very rocky with loose gravel, and one of us could easily twist an ankle. Shabaan has taken to calling me "Papa," so I occasionally hear, "Are you okay, Papa?" ring out. Our guides are great at stopping for photo opportunities so we don't miss anything.

We stop for lunch at Fisher Camp. It has been a steady uphill climb to this camp over and around rocks. This is just a rest stop as we prepare for moving on to Moir Camp.

Chris: Lunch is pretty standard fare — if you were at home. It includes carrots, zucchini, green peppers, and chicken noodle soup. Once again I find that I seem to eat better on this trip than normal meals back home, not to mention the fact that I'm consuming about twice as many calories per meal as usual. I don't think gaining weight will be a problem as we are easily burning off the calories we are taking in. That caloric deficiency that leads to weight loss that Dad was talking about earlier will be easily in favor of calories burned on this trip!

We stop to observe some bones along the way. Francis and Shabaan quiz us as to what we think they might be. No one comes up with the correct answer because it turns out they are the last thing we would expect them to be. They are elephant bones, and they remain a mystery to the experts as to why an elephant would have ventured to this altitude. Elephants don't typically journey to these heights. There are various theories, but none that seems to satisfactorily explain the reason for the bones' existence at that location.

We arrive at Moir Camp at 13,159 feet after about six and a half hours of hiking. Our porters made it from Fisher Camp, where we had lunch, to our camp at Moir in 45 minutes. It took us an hour and a half. We all have a good laugh at Benson's expense as he comes into the mess tent wearing a frilly apron. We kid him about it, and he proudly tells us he has two. He poses for pictures with the one he has on. No matter how much we kid him about it, he seems very proud to be wearing it. I think it was given to him by a previous climber, so who are we to argue? Our teasing falls completely flat anyway!

Chris: I think that the ability to tease our waiter speaks volumes to the kind of camaraderie we developed with our fellow climbers, porters and guides. Being able to make him feel like one of us and make us feel like one of them was a great moment that won't soon be forgotten!

We meet some people at our campsite that drove up the Shira plateau to the campsite here, so they missed the splendor of the rainforest, but more importantly, they also missed the first 3,000 feet of altitude acclimatization. Acclimatization can have a major impact on a climber's success rate, but it's their choice. All we can do is we wish them well as they continue to ascend.

We are now at an altitude where the clouds are blowing by us periodically. We literally have our heads in the clouds. It is an incredible feeling — like being in fog, although the clouds lift from time to time to give us a view of our surroundings. One could equate it to being in the middle of a fairy tale, but the clouds do add a layer of cold and dampness so we put on extra clothing. In my case, it is a Merino wool top, followed by my fleece jacket, followed by my rain jacket. It is important to stay warm and dry.

There is some shortness of breath as we have moved higher. I notice that my breath is coming in shorter spurts; and I spend the day breathing in through my mouth and out through my nose. There are times, when the climb is noticeably steeper, that the breathing becomes just that much shallower. Not enough to be alarmed about, though.

Chris: The temperature at 7:30 p.m. is 36°F (2°C). Coming from a cold climate at home, we probably adapt to these temperatures a little more quickly. After all, winter was in full rage in Ottawa, Canada when we left. Nevertheless, we sit shivering in the mess tent until Benson brings us a heater that quickly helps warm the interior. No matter what time of day you are reading this, I have a feeling your taste buds will water when you find out that we had pumpkin soup, along with spaghetti in meat sauce and a bit of curry (most foods we are served have a hint of curry, in fact), chapatti (which is like a pancake) and pineapple. I wish I could have gotten the recipe for that soup! As our medical conditions are checked, we report in with consistent resting heart rates again, and Dad's oxygen concentrations are the same but mine are affected yet again. They have dropped to 82% from 95% two days ago. All in all, we are very healthy still, even though the oxygen levels continue to drop.

While in the mess tent, I flip through the one book I brought with me, which is *Kilimanjaro: The Trekking Guide to Africa's Highest Mountain* by Henry Stedman. It is an excellent guide for anyone contemplating climbing Kilimanjaro; I've referred to it many times before arriving here and continue to do so throughout my journey. When Shabaan and Benson enter the tent, I show them some of the photos in the book, and they both recognize a guide who is pictured. The story they tell us in their broken English is not totally clear to me, but I have no difficulty in understanding that the guide is now paralyzed from an experience he had on the mountain. I'm uncertain as to whether it was a direct result of Acute Mountain Sickness (AMS) or whether the guide slipped and fell because of AMS. But one thing is sadly clear: he is now paralyzed. Once again, we are reminded (as if we needed to be) that serious events can occur on the face of a mountain.

AMS is what mountaineers fear most. It can strike anyone at any time at any higher altitude, but normally does not occur below about 8,000 feet (2,500 meters). We are well within that range now. Before leaving, I had read an excellent article by the International Society for Mountain Medicine called "An Altitude Tutorial" that describes what happens at altitude. I wanted to understand attitude sickness and reading the article gave me a sobering perspective. The article mentioned certain physiological changes that occur in every person who reaches upper altitudes:

Hyperventilation (in which breathing becomes faster or shallower, or both)
Shortness of breath during exertion
Changed breathing pattern at night
Awakening frequently at night
Increased urination

All of these things happened to me to some extent at about 13,000 feet, and they would all become much more noticeable later. Apparently, we breathe faster and more deeply so that our body can try to replenish the oxygen supply it is starting to miss. Breathing harder is a natural attempt by the body to keep up, and it's important not to become alarmed when this occurs. I find that by stopping for a few seconds, my breathing comes back to normal.

However, things can quickly get out of hand. The article refers to a zone of tolerance in which the body adapts to the change in altitude. This explains a mountaineering axiom that says the climber climbs high and sleeps low. It is important to climb higher during the day and sleep at a lower altitude than you reached throughout the day. The ridges and valleys of Kilimanjaro have accommodated that nicely so far, but we are told that later in the hike, we will be taken on acclimatization hikes after we reach our campsite. That thought is a little depressing as going for a hike *after* a day of hiking doesn't seem to be something to look forward to.

The zone of tolerance stays with a climber as he continues up the mountain and his body has time to adapt. As long as the movement is at the proper pace, most people will stay within the zone of tolerance and acclimatize to the altitude sufficiently. They may experience the symptoms I've mentioned or others, but not to the extent where it becomes a severe a problem. It is only when the body reaches the outer limits of its zone of tolerance that serious problems occur.

Chris: Interestingly enough, as I read through the notes I took while on the hike, I can see the impact of the altitude on my thoughts. For example, many of the lines I wrote in my journal go from full sentences to very brief points. Also, I even wrote down on this day that I'm feeling forgetful and that things are taking longer to process through my brain. I didn't expect that I would notice these items as I began the trip. I just figured that they would happen and in hindsight I would realize they had happened; but in actuality, I was recognizing and noting them as I climbed.

The altitude tutorial article I'd read mentions that the "exact mechanisms of AMS are not completely understood, but the symptoms are thought to be due to swelling of brain tissue…" This swelling causes headaches and can occur along with loss of appetite, nausea, or vomiting, fatigue or weakness, dizziness or light-headedness, and difficulty sleeping. This is why our guides ask us the questions they do every morning and every night. In spite of our futile (and foolish) attempts to outsmart the oximeter, we are always honest with the answers we give to the questions. This is serious business!

Chris: Some of our foolish attempts to outsmart the oximeter included holding our breath to lower our pulse (which you can only do for so long when you are struggling with oxygen levels and exerting yourself on the climb) and trying to think peaceful, relaxing thoughts. It is funny in hindsight to see the games we tried to play with the technology that consistently was smarter than we were!

There are two types of very serious altitude sickness; High Altitude Cerebral Edema (HACE) and High Altitude Pulmonary Edema (HAPE). HACE occurs when the brain swells and ceases to function properly. The symptoms can increase rapidly and can be fatal in a matter of hours to one or two days. HAPE is fluid on the lungs and can also be fatal. Both can be treated by immediate descent, rest, fluids and analgesics. The Gamow bag that Ignace is carrying is for severe cases; the oxygen is for milder cases.

It seems that there's really no explaining altitude sickness or who it will affect. Francis told us the story of the previous group they took up the mountain. It was a family of seven plus a friend. All seven started showing signs of AMS at 10,000 feet and remained ill for the entire climb. The good news is that they made it to the summit, but with a great deal of discomfort all the way up. The friend did not suffer any ill effects. We also had a porter sent back down the mountain on our climb because of altitude-related illness. We aren't exactly certain when that occurred, which is why I mention it now. There is no shred of doubt that altitude sickness is the wild card in our adventure if a trained and experienced porter who climbs Kilimanjaro for a living is required to descend!

The seriousness of what we are trying to do is very apparent, and it drives home the need to climb with guides who are well trained and experienced and who won't take unnecessary risks. Our research helps explain some of the things that have occurred to date and that we will face as we go higher. If we develop mild forms of AMS, we know that our guides will treat us for it. If it becomes more severe, they will also know how to deal with it. Our lives are literally in their hands. Reaching the summit is important to us, but if we don't make it, we can always try again. Being dead wouldn't afford us that luxury.

CHAPTER 13

Day Four - Barranco

THE ANSWERS TO two of the medical questions last night and this morning were "yes" and "no." The first question had been, "Are you coughing?" and the second was, "Did you sleep well?" I'm not really thinking about the cough any more. It is there. Constantly. It doesn't seem to be getting any better, but it doesn't seem to be getting any worse, either. Still, I am always a little anxious when the stethoscope comes out.

As for sleeping, it's been hard to get much sleep on the mountain. In addition to the issues I mentioned related to altitude and sleep, there are a lot of things to think about as we start to drift off. I rehash the day's experiences. I try to imagine what tomorrow will be like. I wonder if we are actually going to reach our goal.

The Canadian flag that I carry in my backpack slipped into my subconscious during one of my fitful sleep periods last night. There are over 200 donor names resting on the flag, names that will hopefully ride with us to the peak and then be presented to school officials in Mwanza when we visit in a few days. I dreamt that Chris and I were holding the flag at the top of the mountain. That was the good news. Then a huge gust of wind whipped the flag out of our hands and down the mountainside. I believe I woke up right away rather than spending time going back down the mountain to chase it, or worse yet, throwing myself off the mountain in a fit of despair! Nevertheless, the damage had been done, and it was a while before I could get back to sleep.

And then there is the issue of breathing in such extreme altitude. This is why our travel doctor had recommended we start taking Diamox *before* we began our climb. Over the years, I've experienced sleep apnea when my breathing stopped for a few seconds at night. It's a scary feeling. My apnea is mild so I really feel for people who have severe cases. The thought of having an episode of apnea on the mountain is more than I care to think about. Diamox seems to help speed up breathing, especially at night. Diamox can be used as a corrective measure in case of more severe AMS, so the doctor had suggested that we only take half a pill at dinner time unless a heavier dosage became necessary. Chris and I followed the doctor's advice. Peter found that he didn't like his body's reaction to the medication and opted not to take it unless it becomes absolutely necessary.

Diamox has a number of potential side effects, such as ringing in the ears. It also changes taste. Fortunately, I didn't experience either of these effects. However, there was one that I *did* experience. Without any warning, my fingers, toes or lips would start to tingle and vibrate. It was the strangest sensation! I had forgotten about this particular symptom until I felt a weird buzzing sensation in my boot. Later, I felt the same feeling in my fingers. It took some time to figure out what was going on, but eventually I remembered this side effect and just waited until it passed. Chris commented that he had the same experience. It doesn't hurt; it's just surprising when suddenly the inside of your boot starts to vibrate — and it is even stranger when you realize it's your foot doing the vibrating!

One of the effects of altitude is that it causes the body to need its water supply replenished. It's a good sign if lots of water is being ingested, but it also means that lots of water must go out. Altitude causes frequent urination. As a result, I found myself getting up frequently during the night. I would no sooner get back into my sleeping bag and fall asleep when the call of nature would wake me up again, over . . . and over . . . and over. It didn't seem to affect Chris as much as it did me. Chris was kind enough not to point out that it may have been an age-related thing. I like to think of it as some people reacting differently to altitude than others.

I don't think there is anything noisier than the sound a tent zipper makes in the middle of a frosty silent night on the side of a mountain! Oh, and did I mention our tents had TWO zippers?!! We had to keep them both closed to keep any creatures out. (The only critter we ever saw near our tent was the four-striped grass mouse, but we didn't really want those in the tent, either.)

So every night about the time a peaceful quiet had fallen over the campsite, save for the odd muffled snoring sound, here I would come, trying to stealthily unzip the flap. ZIPPPPPP!!!! ZIPPPP!!!! The zippers on their metal tracks sounded deafening in the silence. I was always afraid it would rouse everyone in the campsite (if not the first zipper, then certainly the second one). Then back into the tent I'd go and a few minutes later the process would start all over again. ZIPPPPP!!! ZIPPPP!!!!! After a while, I finally decided to just leave my coat and pants on in the night, knowing eventually I'd have to venture out again into the frigid night air.

If there was a benefit to all this, it was that I saw more stars and constellations than anyone else in our group. And how magnificent they were! The sky was brilliantly clear and completely unobstructed. With no artificial lighting to dim the brilliance of the stars and moon, I felt like I could reach out and touch the heavens. But enough of that. Back into the sleeping bag! It is much too cold out there for protracted star gazing!

Oh, if you're curious, yes, hikers often use a "pee bottle" device at night. The bottle has a very wide neck, but I wasn't sure if Chris would have appreciated me using that in our tent. (And obviously it wouldn't work for females in the same situation.)

While on this subject, I will address the issue of bathrooms on the mountain itself. This question always came up when Chris and I did presentations following our climb. Well, potential fellow climbers, there aren't any — or there is one big one, depending on your point of view. We had our little private facility at the campsites: it was a small tent with a pail and seat that required the balance and agility of one of the legendary Flying Wallendas just to remain upright on it. And you had to be able to ignore the freezing cold around you. Having grown up on the Canadian prairies, I was accustomed to using similar facilities, so I adapted without much difficulty. On the trail, the only facility for males and females alike is the mountain itself. Dignity and modern-day "facilities" just had to wait for our return to civilization at the bottom of the mountain!

Now back to our climb. It is a brisk morning as we go about getting ourselves ready for today's climb. The sun is just starting to rise over Kibo as we look out the flap of our tent. It is a fantastic site. There are a few glaciers visible, but it's still hard from this vantage point to figure out precisely where we are going in the next few days. We still have to hike over to the east side of the mountain, where we will make our final ascent to the very top. We are nestled in a valley here. It had turned even colder during the night, so we are all wearing fleece garments, and Chris has finally put long pants on.

Chris: I remember this feeling from the time I spent backpacking through Northern Alaska. Anybody who has had the experience of waking up in a tent pitched in a valley surrounded by higher ground will understand the feeling you have when the sun is up, but not yet up over the hills. You stand outside of your tent and jump around to keep warm while you wait for the glorious sunshine to creep over the surrounding hills and its warming rays to hit you full on. From here on, this is what we will experience every day until we reach the top of the mountain. Those first few minutes are hard, but once that sunshine finally hits you, you remember why you love camping.

This particular morning, my handy thermometer tells me it's only 30 degrees F (-1 degree C) as we wake up. I actually spent the night sleeping in long johns, wearing a toque and using my liner within my sleeping bag. None of us are wearing gloves yet, but we are going to need to dig them out soon. Once we finally get hiking, the temperature has risen to 45 degrees F (7 degrees C) and by 9:30 in the morning it's 61 degrees FC (13 degrees C).

Breakfast is corn, scrambled eggs, brown toast, sausage and fruit, with peanut butter and jam for the toast if we want it. Our morning stats show that my heart rate is up to 91bpm from the first day when it was 77bpm and Dad's has hit the century mark from 91bpm on the first day. Our oxygen concentration levels are both below 90%. I begin to notice the pattern that our heart rates are more elevated every morning from the previous evening, and wonder if it's because of anticipation for the day ahead.

As we start hiking, it is quite flat, which makes for easy going. It is a nice way to wake up! There are tufts of grass making up the vegetation, but they are pretty sparse. We trudge along over the fairly flat ground for about three hours when we break for a snack and water. We have a spectacular view of Mount Meru in the distance. Our guides tell us that Mount Meru is often used as a warm-up trek for those about to climb Mount Kilimanjaro. It is about 70 miles from Kilimanjaro and is located in Arusha National Park. What an unbelievable view!

After our break, we are picking our way through much rockier territory. There is a sobering moment as we make our way through the rocks. Before us, we see a cross planted in the rocks, much like you would see at the scene of a traffic accident where there has been a fatality. Our guides tell us that someone lost their life here trying to follow their dream of climbing Mount Kilimanjaro, and once again we are reminded just how serious this adventure can be. We stop for a few minutes and I'm sure I'm not the only one thinking about the person who died in this very spot, and what lies ahead of us as we continue on.

Our guides constantly encourage us to eat and drink. We are now drinking up to four liters of water a day. It isn't difficult. We all have energy bars to snack on. I wish I had brought a little more variety. They are starting to taste like cold sawdust. I get a little grief from Francis for setting my camera down while we are stopped for our break. He's afraid I'm going to leave it behind or that it will get broken or kicked while it's on the ground. I get the message that he has seen more than a few very disappointed hikers as they realize their camera is sitting somewhere on the mountainside where it will do them absolutely no good. The good thing is that digital technology has made the cameras much more durable and able to withstand the altitude and cold temperatures (or so we think).

Chris: I have been keeping track of my water intake as well and realize that I'm drinking more than 5 liters a day! It's a lot for me, but I need it on the mountain to keep from becoming dehydrated. Interestingly enough, even though I am drinking this much water, I find that I'm not expelling nearly as much water as you would think. The fluids are all being used just to keep me going, apparently.

We continue on through rocks and boulders. It is very treacherous as we literally have to pick our way through, balancing ourselves on both sides with our hands. Our eyes are glued on the boots in front of us so we don't catch our foot in a crack. Then we come to a flat section where we can see the trail unfold for what seems like miles (and it probably is) ahead of us. We make good time as we cross the flat section. We cross a stream that is frozen. I am quite sure it has frozen at night and thawed during the day nearly every 24-hour period since the beginning of time. We see unusual shapes in the rocks, with five- or six-foot columns about two feet around with a large round rock balancing on the top. It is pock-marked volcanic rock that we are looking at. Then once again we are on a severe slope. I'm getting excited as we are coming up on Lava Tower, although the descriptions I've read have left me a little confused as to exactly what we will be seeing. Our guides point out that trekkers used to climb Lava Tower until recently. Recent earthquakes have left the tower unstable, so Tusker does not allow their clients to climb it now.

As we draw closer, we are swallowed by the clouds. It is disappointing as it is very difficult to see any of the tower in the distance with the clouds swirling around it, and when we finally arrive, we can't even see the top at all. The tower consists of remnants of the lava flow that occurred during the eruption of Kilimanjaro. The flow formed a craggy, vertical protuberance. The tower is a mixture of rusty brown and orange colors. We have been hiking for about three hours, and the porters have erected our mess tent at the foot of the tower so we can have lunch and get fresh water in comfort. With a lunch of minestrone soup (with a hint of curry), fried chicken, cheese and veggie sandwiches and mango with some banana pieces fried up that were referred to as banana fritters, we are prepared for whatever Francis and Shabaan decide we should do. From time to time, the clouds disperse and we can catch glimpses of the top. There are boulders taller than we are at the foot of the tower, and we can see cracks that have occurred during the earthquakes.

Chris: When I ask our guides about the tower and the numbers of people who climb up, they point to the boulders at the base and remind us that up until the last few years, these boulders sat at the top of the tower and were part of it. Any thoughts of scaling the tower quickly leave my head. Of course, the energy required to scale that tower was probably nowhere to be found either, but I'm just going to blame the safety of the scaling rather than admit that I might have been tired.

We are now at 15,000 feet. Chris mentions he has a slight headache. I have one as well. In my case, it just feels like a tightening around the head and is certainly not unbearable, although I sense it's something we need to keep track of.

Our guides seem to be concerned about the weather. I gather a storm may be approaching the area where we now are, and they ask us if we think we can continue hiking to the Barranco Wall to set up camp there. Our porters have already set up our tents here at Lava Tower, and I am sure they aren't thrilled about tearing everything down again and moving. But our guides tell us curtly, "That's their job." The life of a porter is not to make decisions, only to obey the ones that are made.

It's good to stop and replenish our water supply. We haven't been able to do much of this on the climb to date, and I don't think we will be able to again. Most days, the water we started with is what we have to see us through the day, and we are drinking a lot of water. One of the many things I've learned on this hike is that I should have brought a larger water containment system. My Camelbak is 1.5 liters, which was the right size for my 24-liter backpack. But Tusker recommends a backpack of between 17 and 49 liters, so mine is at the lower end of the range. My pack is just big enough for my clothes, but it needs to be bigger to hold a sufficient water supply for me. There's a fine line between big enough and too big. Remembering that I would be carrying it on my back for nine days or so, I had decided that bigger was not necessarily better. Now I realize I should have considered all the water I should have been carrying as well.

After lunch, we start out again. We are totally in the clouds now, and it is cold! We have put on another layer of clothing as we hike into an area that looks like we've somehow stumbled onto another planet. We are in a valley full of giant senecio trees. They are quite short but with huge well-weathered trunks that are topped with thick palm-like leaves. The leaves have the appearance of cabbage and capture and retain water for their survival. There are hundreds of these strange trees. Some have two or three branches topped by the palm-like leaves. With the clouds all around us, the landscape becomes a surreal sight as the closest trees are clearly visible but within a few feet the clouds thicken and the trees eerily fade away. We hate to leave — it's not likely we will see anything like this again.

As we are observing the senecios, a group of hikers pass us. Later on, we cross a stream and see these same hikers drinking and filling their water bottles. Our guides remind us that the water is not fit to drink. Our water is purified by the porters using proper equipment, and we conclude that these hapless tourists are being led by a less-than-reputable tour company. We do not see them again, and we are very glad we are with a reputable company.

Our headaches subside as we wind our way through the

rocks back down to about 13,000 feet. We glimpse an incredible waterfall through the clouds, and are glad our guides allow us to wait about 20 minutes for the clouds to clear long enough that we can take pictures. (The pictures will ultimately turn out to be a bit disappointing, as it is very difficult to capture the splendor of nature on film, at least for amateur photographers like ourselves. Peter manages to get some vivid pictures with more color on his camera.) Fortunately, we encounter none of the serious weather our guides were concerned about, and we continue on for another two hours to the camp at Barranco.

Chris: Today was a particularly tough day for me. Before starting the trip, I had spent time with a specialist getting fitted with a brace for my knee to enable me to complete the climb. The very first day we hiked on the mountain (after six hours of driving), I'd opted not to use it just to see how the leg held up without any assistance. But after hiking for two or three hours that day, I was convinced it would be the last day I spent without a knee brace. My dad has already described my choice of hiking apparel being shorts and gaiters, but the truth of the matter is anyone who has a knee brace needs to adjust it on occasion. You can lose a fair amount of feeling and cause all kinds of soreness if you don't have it positioned just right, and sometimes that takes a few tries. And I don't think my legs were colder than anyone else's on our hike.

On today's trek, I started to experience the pain of walking downhill, confirming that I too should have spent more time on this during my training. On this particular day, we hiked up about 2,000 feet (610 meters) of elevation, then back down about 1,500 feet (457 meters). Since you use different parts of your body to brace yourself when you walk downhill, it puts a lot more strain on the knees. While the knee brace undoubtedly helped, I was very happy when the walking stopped on this day!

It was also much colder today on the mountain. When we stopped for lunch, I checked my thermometer and noted that the temperature was only 41°F (5°C). My gloves were in my pack that the porters were carrying and I couldn't get to them, but fortunately, Shabaan found some gloves that would fit me. Overall, I guess you could say this wasn't one of my favorite days, though I did appreciate the other-worldly vegetation as we were passing by the giant senecio trees.

A lot of people use hiking poles for climbs. In the past, I've made fun of them in my mind, but this was the day I finally broke down and started using poles myself. As I described above, the strain on a knee can be tremendous as you walk down the mountain, but by using a hiking pole, I was able to use it as a cane to alleviate a lot of the weight on my bad knee in areas where we had to descend. Also, sometimes we had to drop down several feet and being able to use the pole eliminated my having to jump down using both legs and jarring my knee. I became a convert to hiking poles and promise from now on never to make fun of them! In fact, I plan to use a hiking pole in the future for any hiking excursion that isn't across the flat prairies.

When we finally get to camp today, we are all worn out. I have to admit Dad's age is becoming a motivating factor for me during the climb. I have to keep my complaints in check, as I am 30 years his junior and can't allow myself to show any weakness around a 60 year old fellow climber. His constant march up the hill is inspiring me to do the same. There have already been a few points during the climb that I find myself wondering why on earth we undertook such an activity, but when Dad got up to keep going, I did the same. I've always heard in my years of being in gyms how much better it is to work out with a friend, and I can now say from firsthand experience how true that is. Having him here has kept me from complaining and kept me going. I'm sure with the guides' help, I would have been able to keep going if I were there on my own, but having that help in the form of someone close to me is making it all the more impactful.

Once again our "trail chef" serves us a feast consisting of zucchini soup with rice, and beef stew with a hint of curry. We feel much better after food. Oxygen concentrations in the *evening are in the mid 80s for both of us; and the pattern I noticed in the morning continues as our heart rates have dropped a bit. We are still producing good numbers, and by this point, I feel pretty good about how low I'm managing to keep mine. Did I mention my dad and I have a bit of a competitive edge on occasion?*

Yes, there is a bit of friendly competition and razzing when the pulse rates and oxygen levels are announced, as our family does with almost everything. It is a fun thing we have developed, even applying to the size of our respective television sets. I think I am losing on pretty well every count now, but I take comfort in the knowledge that our children are doing very well at what they do. As for the medical stats, I am just glad I haven't been sent back down the mountain. I am nervous every time they are taken that something will have happened during the day or night that worsened my cold or that the altitude is affecting me enough that I will have to end this dream. I am quite happy to lose the competition of the stats to Chris, provided I am allowed to stay on the mountain. I will never let him know that, of course.

Everyone has been pretty quiet today. I, for one, am totally bagged as we sit in our mess tent, having our usual cup of tea. In fact, I hear Chris say, "Hey, no sleeping in the mess tent!" as I drift off for what seemed to be only a few seconds. Shabaan visits with us for a while, and once again his sense of humor comes through. We had just finished talking about how nice it was that there are only three of us on the climb and how well we all get along when Shabaan joins us. We tell him what we were talking about, and he tells us with a perfectly straight face that there will be eight climbers joining us at the next campsite. As if that isn't bad enough, we think he's said "80" climbers because people who speak Swahili add a vowel to every English word that ends with a consonant, so "eight" becomes"80," Chris becomes Chrissy, and so on. Once we figured out Shabaan only means eight new hikers, we decide we can live with that number. Then he grins and tells us he's kidding. We ask him if he spends so much time in our mess tent because no one else will allow him in their tent. We also strongly suggest that he won't be allowed in our tent again either. It is a light moment, and we all enjoy it. Shabaan has a little boy about the same age as Chris' daughter, so they share stories about their families, their children, education and living conditions.

Chris: Shabaan and I spent a good deal of time comparing and contrasting the education systems in particular. Much of a girl's upbringing in some parts of Tanzania depend on how early on in life she gets pregnant; he had some choice words for his sister who had gotten pregnant before she could finish school. At that point, it becomes her role to raise the children, and school is forgotten. In Shabaan's case, he and his wife are very careful about this, as they cannot afford to send more than one child to school within a certain time frame. In Tanzania, if you want your child to have a good education and to have a chance to go on to further education, you must pay to send them to the right schools from a very young age. Once your child is in a stream, they remain there. As such, Shabaan and his wife will be waiting for quite some time before they can consider having a second child – they have no means to provide for another child in school.

The porters play a raucous card game every night called "Last Card." One of the porters has a really high-pitched voice and when he gets excited, his voice carries throughout the campsite. It is fun sitting and listening to them. They don't play too late into the night as everyone has to get some sleep. It certainly sounds like they enjoy the game!

We are camped at Barranco Wall at about 13,000 feet, beside a nice mountain stream. Again today, following the mountaineering axiom, we have climbed high and are sleeping low. Francis is in the mess tent with us, giggling about tomorrow, but he won't tell us exactly what we will be facing. He just says it will be a challenge. It is a crisp evening, so we walk outside to face the wall. It is a sheer face, but we can't figure out exactly where we will be going. Surely we won't be going straight up!? Yet there doesn't seem to be an easy way around it. We take a few photos in front of the wall. Everyone is all smiles in preparation for tomorrow. We have a good view of Kibo from here, and we sense that we are getting closer. Everyone is feeling good. Our headaches have vanished. We are ready for whatever we will face tomorrow.

Onward and upward!

CHAPTER 14

Day Five - Karanga Camp

IT WAS COLD last night! There is frost on the tent with the temperature sitting at 28 degrees F (-2 degrees C). Good thing we have warm sleeping bags! The guides have told us to prepare for a wet day. I have found that layering clothing as everyone tells you to do is the best way to dress for the day. I have been warm enough when we're hiking but it does get cold during the breaks. The key is to stay out of the wind as much as possible, although it seems to be swirling everywhere. I put on my wool shirt, fleece jacket and rain jacket with rain pants over my hiking pants. I can remove layers if I get too warm. Tomorrow will probably be the day to break out the winter coat and possibly balaclava, but we will see.

As I rummage through my belongings, I realize that I've inadvertently brought the wrong gloves. I'd bought windproof gloves with grips on the palm for climbing and placed them side by side with some cotton gloves of the same color on the shelf at home. My climbing gloves are apparently still sitting there. There is a brief moment of panic coursing through me as I consider the impact of this omission. There isn't much I can do about it. I do have some mitts that are not as windproof, but I can curl my fingers up as we hike so that my hands are warmed by my own body heat. It is not ideal as I had intended on wearing my windproof gloves inside my mitts and my hands will get extremely cold over the coming days as the wind whips through the material.

Everyone is anxious to get going to see what this wall is all about. We had the usual solid breakfast with porridge and omelets, and our stats are around 90 for both oxygen and heart rates. The latter is a bit surprising considering we are about to face the unknown, otherwise known as the Barranco Wall. Francis and Shabaan have a different "breakfast" in mind as that is how they refer to the wall. They tell us it is called "breakfast" because we are going to be doing it first thing this morning, but I later heard another popular theory that the reason it has the nickname is because many people lose their breakfast while they are climbing the wall.

"Twende!" says Francis at 8:30 a.m. as we step from rock to rock across the stream to the foot of the Barranco Wall. Much to our chagrin, the wall turns out to be a 600-foot vertical climb. At least we think it's 600 feet. Others have said 800 feet. We start out on the first of many switchbacks we'll undergo today. The first section of the trail is a relatively steady incline, but we are climbing over and around huge boulders and rocks. The rocks are roughly shaped and sharp, as if gouged out of the mountainside, but we welcome the handholds they offer us as we haul ourselves from one to another. They are slippery because of the frost, adding another dimension of difficulty and yes, fear. The trail is well travelled and firm, but not very wide. It is almost impossible to pass or be passed on the trail in most places, and it is fortunate that climbers use another route to descend.

Peter announces a fear of heights. It is a little ironic that he and I are on the highest mountain in Africa as my own fear of ladders keeps rising to the surface. This is clearly the biggest challenge we have faced on the mountain so far, and I have to admit to some nervousness as I don't know how difficult this is going to be, either emotionally or physically. As long as I have something solid underneath me, I think I'll be okay, but my mind keeps wondering what if we come to a point where I *can* see straight down? In some bizarre way, Peter's announcement comforts me. I know Chris will handle it okay, but having someone there who has similar fears to mine helps. This is the exact situation that was in my mind back when I first started to think about the climb and had asked people questions about it.

You're probably wondering why anyone with a fear of heights would even consider climbing a mountain! I guess part of the challenge was to face my fear and prove to myself that I could do it. However, I also knew I wouldn't be walking along a solitary beam hundreds of feet above the ground as I challenged my fear. Mountain climbing is a different kind of height sensation. At least on Kilimanjaro, the climber is usually surrounded by "comforting" rocks, and everyone I'd talked to who had made this climb before me said it wasn't likely I would ever need to look over any sheer ledges to stare at the ground far below, so I felt I could handle my fear.

Yet in spite of the assurances I had received, I have to admit to low-key concern developing into full-blown concern when we reach the "Kissing Rock" at 300 feet up the wall. The kissing rock is a huge boulder imbedded in the side of the Barranco Wall and is much wider and taller than any of us. As promised, there are no ropes involved here, and we don't have to shimmy up the steep slope. In fact, we actually have to plant our faces against the rock in order to get around it. Francis is standing on a ledge below to catch us if we fall. Not very reassuring! Shabaan has gone ahead to pull us along (or to encourage us if we freeze). As he goes, he demonstrates the technique we are to use, which is to squeeze our faces against the rock and hold on with both arms reaching as far as they can on either side. Slowly, we are to move our right foot to a small ledge on the right side of the Kissing Rock. Then we are to shift our weight onto that foot so our left leg can swing between our right leg and the rock onto a slightly higher spot on the rock. This will turn our bodies slightly to the right, but with both arms still wrapped around the rock, we should be able to do it. At this point, Shabaan will grab our hand and pull us up. He goes around the rock with ease and makes it look simple, but inside I can't help wondering: *but how many times has he done this again?*

Peter goes first, and we can tell he's nervous. He is muttering that he won't be able to do it. I'm getting nervous just watching Peter and wish I'd gone first to get it over with. It takes Peter a few minutes to navigate around the rock. Peter's face, with sweat dripping down, is planted firmly against the rock and he seems reluctant to move when Shabaan tells him to kiss the rock. Peter complies and later says it was that moment that took his mind off what he was doing and helped him get through it. He would also say later that he was "scared shitless and he didn't care who knew it."

Now it is my turn, and I am nervously pulling myself around the rock, but I keep telling myself that this is just one more step in the process to reach the peak. I need a few minutes to compose myself when I get to the other side. I certainly didn't need the extra layer of clothing at that point. The combination of exertion and fear leaves us all dripping with sweat. Chris slides around the rock next with a big grin on his face, and then Ignace follows behind with no problem, carrying the huge bundle of safety equipment on his head. As we recover and enjoy our morning break about half way up the wall, we think about what we've just done. Peter and I agree that if we don't go any further, we have already done something really special. We agree that we really enjoyed it… after the fact. Chris, on the other hand, insists he enjoyed the whole experience while he was doing it, although he did admit that his legs felt rubbery. Peter conquered a fear and felt tremendous satisfaction. I don't know that I conquered a fear. I am hugely satisfied with myself and feel a lot of relief when Francis tells us we will not face anything like that again. I know I did something I had to do if I am going to complete this journey. But you know what!? I still don't like ladders and never will!

Chris: As much as I truly did enjoy the thrill of passing that spot, it wasn't lost on me that a backwards misstep of a few inches would be enough to land me back down at the bottom of the Barranco Wall, 300 feet below. In order to make it up the wall, I'd actually needed to remove my knee brace as the amount of flexibility required in certain spots was more than the knee brace would have allowed me. I also had to abandon the poles as I needed my hands for gripping the rocks. It was an invigorating experience! I wouldn't say that it was beyond my comfort *zone, but it was certainly right on the cusp of it which is what made that part of the trip so exhilarating!*

Francis relates a couple of stories while we are on our break. He mentions that the porters also have to climb the wall, and he reminds us that they do it with their bundles on their heads as Ignace had done. Occasionally, they will lose their bundle at the Kissing Rock and they will have to go down the entire 300 feet to retrieve it from the stream below and start over again. I am not sure how the water would affect the bundles, but I can only assume it would make them that much heavier as they resumed their attempt at scaling the wall. This story represents one more reason why they are overworked and underpaid. Francis is in a storytelling mood today, and he also tells us of a woman on one of his climbs who took forever to navigate around the kissing rock. She expressed irritation about having to climb up a rock face to get to the top, to which Francis replied, "Lady, this IS a mountain."

The ascent up the wall is an incredible challenge and very tiring, but it is also very satisfying to complete it. There are many false plateaus where climbers can hope they are finished, only to realize they must keep climbing again. We all feel the strenuous pressure on our knees, thighs and calves as we struggle to get up the remainder of the wall, but none more than Chris and Peter. There aren't the jagged rocks for the rest of the climb to the top of the wall, but it is steep. When we finally reach the top of the wall, Peter takes a picture of Chris and me near the ledge. I wish to emphasize the word "near" because I wasn't about to go too close to see where we had been! The view was spectacular enough from where I was standing.

As I later looked through our photos, I realized that I had taken one picture as we were actually scaling the wall and Peter had taken none. I think that is a good indication of our concentration level as we were climbing. I am amazed at the wherewithal of the mountaineers who take photos and video as they are climbing steep inclines using ropes!

We aren't done for the day by any stretch of the imagination. We hike down into a valley and then across. It is a difficult vertical climb again on the other side. Once we are at the top, it is down into the Karanga Valley and across, followed by another very steep climb. Incredibly, the whole trek from the Barranco campsite only takes four hours to complete so we arrive at lunch time, but it seems to be much longer. Mentally and physically, we have been through a lot. We are ready for a restful afternoon to let our bodies recover.

We have a huge lunch of cucumber soup, pasta, French toast, beans and vegetables, followed by a large dinner: cream of vegetable soup, lots of potatoes, chicken, watermelon and bananas. We are all quite certain we have earned it. The meals are designed for the climb (and always lightly seasoned with curry). In the beginning, they were heavy on protein, but now we are eating a lot more carbohydrates and starchy foods. In spite of the warnings about losing our appetites as we gain altitude, it certainly doesn't seem to be happening to us!

Our campsite is at about 13,000 feet today. It has been cloudy all day, and it hails at one point as we're sitting in our mess tent. Not a lot of hail, but enough to remind us how unpredictable the weather can be on the mountain.

For the "Mr. Gadgets" among you, I should mention that email reception has been pretty good on my Blackberry, with the exception of Moir Camp. It seems to take forever to send a message, but messages arrive okay. I just picked them up again today. I have no idea what the roaming charges will be, but I imagine they will be substantial, which encourages me to leave my Blackberry in my pocket throughout most of the hike. It is amazing that it will work at all in these conditions.

As we reflect on our day, we think about the rocky promontories and craggy cliffs we have scaled. We have hiked past thickets of the cactus-like lobelia and other worldly senecio plants. We have seen crevasses in the rock formations and witnessed various colors of nature, including rusty browns and reds in the cliffs as we passed by. Once we left the valley of the giant senecios, the vegetation had become very sparse. When the clouds clear occasionally throughout the day, we were able to make out Kibo where we are hoping to be in a few days, although we can't see the Uhuru peak which is our final destination. Our campsite at Karanga is so desolate that it could just as well be on the moon. Chris spent some time sitting on a rock enshrouded in cloud, updating his journal. It was a meditative moment. I preferred to stay in the tent out of the wind, as I am still coughing.

Chris: This was surprisingly one of the most tiring days of the climb, as it was also one of the shortest in terms of duration. I think we were all thankful for some rest time at camp afterwards.

We are reminded again how fortunate we are that we hired a reputable company for our climb. Peter was talking to a couple who flew from Germany to climb Kilimanjaro. They contracted a local tour company for $1,000 apiece (we paid more than triple that). Now the woman has a headache, but her guides are not prepared to treat it and won't allow her to continue the climb in spite of her protestations. She is being forced to descend, much to her chagrin. She will lose her money and her chance to reach the top of Mount Kilimanjaro.

We feel sorry for the German couple, but it is a case of getting what you pay for. It is a difficult and sad lesson to learn at this point on the mountain. We easily see that we are treated as well as mountain conditions will allow. We are eating very well and have our own toilet (such as it is). There are definitely other groups at the camp that are not allowed to acclimatize the way we are because they are travelling faster or are being pushed harder. We aren't cocky, because there's a lot ahead of us yet to face. But we feel pretty good at this point. We have been told by other climbers that they haven't been receiving medical tests. We have been assured by our guides that they can treat headaches as long as they don't become too bad, and that they know how to handle more severe symptoms of AMS. Francis is a First Responder and takes a three-week refresher course each year. Knowing this makes us feel much safer in the case of an emergency.

Francis comes into the mess tent and briefly describes the plan. He says things are going well and we all seem to be in good shape, so he will assess our condition when we get to Stella Point, which is about 18,886 feet in elevation, only about 450 vertical feet from our destination. If everyone is still feeling fine, we will summit that day. If we are too weak or ill to summit, we will take a different route to Crater Camp. Apparently, people can develop enormous headaches or other severe symptoms of altitude sickness by staying at the altitude of Crater Camp (18,800 feet), so it is better to keep going. There is also the Ash Pit, which is the active volcano that we hope to reach after Uhuru Peak. It will all depend on how we feel. Chris is anxious to see the volcano. It sounds like either we all go to the Ash Pit or none of us will go. There is an interesting quote in Henry Stedman's book, *Kilimanjaro – The Trekking Guide to Africa's Highest Mountain.* He is referring to climbers who reach the summit first with the intention of visiting the crater later. He says in part, "…by the time trekkers get there (the peak)…they're usually too knackered or in too much pain to spend the two hours-plus necessary to explore the crater".

Chris: Many people who climb Kilimanjaro seem to believe that if you don't go to the Ash Pit, you haven't climbed the mountain. That is not my feeling on the matter. For me, it is simply an opportunity to stand on the rim of an active but dormant volcano – one of the items on my "bucket list."

Later that evening as we sit chatting in the mess tent, Francis and Shabaan come in to check our medical statistics. We have had a great afternoon of relaxation, so we expect the results to be good. And they are not horrible. Our oxygen concentrations have been steadily declining as expected, and my stats show a 90% figure while Dad's is at 86%. As for our heart rates, mine is sitting at 82bpm while my father's is at 95bpm.

It seems strange to think that careful as we're being, we may be plodding deliberately and inexorably towards the worst headache of our lives and maybe worse. Our breathing has been shallow at times, and we've had symptoms of AMS in relatively minor form, but now it seems that in a couple of days, odds are that we will feel much worse. But we don't dwell on this. We are more excited about the prospect of making the summit than we are concerned about feeling ill. We will deal with whatever illness besets us if the time comes.

One of the reasons we are doing this becomes very apparent in the next few minutes. For me, it is one of the highlights of the climb. We had been enshrouded in clouds most of the day as we hiked. We have scaled some 13,000 vertical feet since we first started our trek and from time to time, we've caught brief glimpses of Kibo, but these sightings have been rare. Now this evening, it's still cloudy as we enter our mess tent. After we finish our dinner, I step out of the tent. And there it is. It's as if God isn't completely satisfied that we are fully comprehending the immensity of Africa's King of the Mountains or that we understand that there are another 6,000 feet to the top. So He redid the picture and thrust it right in front of our faces!

There in all its glory is a dominating, stark, predominantly grey masterpiece with distinct jagged edges and folds highlighted by the sun. The depths of the edges are outlined by the shadows behind them, and the mountain's starkness is interrupted by dots of snow and sunlit streams that have been temporarily frozen in time. The portrait is painted against the backdrop of a clear blue sky, framed in front and on either side by lower rock faces that lead to the top, one side of which we will be navigating come morning. The glaciers are clearly visible as they attempt to run down the mountainside and the winds are shaving off small layers at the tips, creating swirling white frozen crystals that vanish into the atmosphere. There are a just a few wispy clouds drifting by, momentarily blocking the view or creating a diaphanous veil over parts of the mountain, which tones down the vibrancy of the colors we are seeing but which also serves to accent the intensity of the colors on the rest of the mountain. It is humbling. It's as if Mount Kilimanjaro is literally flexing its muscles in front of us, taunting us yet beckoning us to give it a try.

In that instant, it all comes together for me. This is why we are here, summarized in a single moment in time. I call Chris and Peter to come out and see, and we all stare in absolute awe at the scene before us. It has taken some very hard work in preparation for this moment and we are thousands of miles from home. Much still lies ahead, but everything else is forgotten. Once again, if it had all ended there and we had not been able to go any further, I am convinced that the awesome sight of Mount Kilimanjaro as I left the tent that day will forever be burned in my mind's eye. And I could be satisfied with that.

We go to sleep that night thinking that the end is almost in sight. It makes for another fitful night.

Barry with his BB gun 1958

Barry in front of the Lava Tower

Chris and Peter on the Barranco Wall

Peter, Chris and Barry among the giant senicios

A meditative moment

Magical view of our destination

Resting at Stella Point – decision time

Barry and Chris with the flag

Peter, Ignace, Chris, Barry, Shabaan, Francis (kneeling)

Furtwangler Glacier

Reusch Crater and Ash Pit

Well deserved refreshment

CHAPTER 15

Day Six – Barafu

MOUNT KILIMANJARO IS in full majestic view again this morning when we awaken and stumble out of our tents. It was cold again last night and we are moving rather slowly as the generally insufficient quantity of air is taking its toll. My heart rate is up again this morning as it is 105bpm. This is *resting* heart rate, remember! I started the climb with a rate in the mid eighties and at home it is normally in the mid sixties. Francis says they will continue to monitor it but I shouldn't be concerned at this time. Our oxygen levels and Chris' heart rate remained relatively stable from yesterday.

Chris: I awake early in the morning to discover that my video camera froze during the night. I thought that digital technology might have prevented this from happening, but obviously not. I am really worried that I have lost everything I had recorded so far and that there may have been damage to the camera. Maybe it is damaged beyond repair. But that is not what really concerns me – the camera is replaceable. I am disappointed that I will not be able to record the historic event of us reaching the top, assuming that we will. The camera had given me a few fits on previous days. As my mental capacity seemed to diminish as we got higher in altitude, I found myself doing things like leaving the lens cap on while trying to record. Even though it had been frustrating on occasion, I still hope it *will thaw out once we start hiking in the sun...if there is any sun today.*

I had some weird dreams last night. You know the kind — you remember in the morning that you had some but can't recall what they were. All I can remember is that I didn't get much sleep. This could be a very long day ahead although we are promised that the hike will be short.

In the hopes of preventing the situation that has arisen with Chris' camera, we have been putting nearly everything in our sleeping bag that we will need for the next day to try to keep it warm. There is barely room for me in my bag as I have the next day's clothing, water bottle, camera, energy bars and whatever else I need to keep warm in it with me.

Chris: To anyone thinking of employing this method of keeping things warm and operational, it is probably important to note that the things you put in your sleeping bag with you will also retain a fair bit of condensation. While putting my video camera in my sleeping bag probably would have helped, there is a good chance that the condensation could have been too much for it to handle.

Our hike today is very challenging since there is a lot of shale and stratified rock, and we deal with a lot of slippage as we take a step only to slide back a little. There are many cliffs and overhangs, and it is very treacherous. We don't want to twist an ankle now. Or worse. There are times, however, when there are very few rocks sprinkled across the landscape and we can see the trail ahead with porters at various stages leading up to the horizon. It is a desolate area with the wind whipping up dirt and small stones. I have no concept of the direction we are heading, how far we have to go, how far we have come or when we might get there. I am putting one foot in front of the other, slipping occasionally, but trudging relentlessly forward on our quest.

After about two hours of hiking, we stop for our break. That has been the normal routine. We have breakfast, head out, hike for two hours or so and have an energy bar. We stop quite often for a drink of water, to take pictures or just to allow ourselves a bit of rest. During our break this morning, Chris stands on a rock and gazes off at the top of Kilimanjaro. The view is spectacular with the glaciers running off the peak. It looks as if Chris is contemplating whether or not we can really do this — or maybe he is silently responding to the challenge that Mount Kili seemed to be issuing to us the previous night. I am not sure. It is one of the countless moments when one of us gets lost in our thoughts.

We continue to trudge uphill after the break with more desolation surrounding us. It is a tough ascent as we gain about 2,000 feet in three hours to arrive at Barafu Camp at just over 16,000 feet. "Barafu" means" ice" in Swahili and the camp is a converging point for several trails, so there are a number of other hikers mingling about. Breathing is steady when we're sitting still, but it doesn't take much to lose our breath. We are probably breathing somewhere between two-thirds and half of our normal oxygen intake at this altitude. We still don't have any major symptoms of altitude sickness, which is good.

Chris: The Barafu Camp also has no water at it. If all the porters arrived at Barafu with us, some of them would have to either descend to the last campsite in order to obtain water from the stream to purify for us, or they would have to head farther up the mountain to collect pieces of the glacier to melt down and make drinkable. At the speed we have been walking, this would mean that water is at least three hours away in any direction. Then they'd have to return. They obviously move much quicker than we do at altitude, but they would be carrying large containers of water when they come back again. Some are tasked to gather water as they pass by the stream and carry the containers to our campsite at Barafu, once again illustrating just how difficult a job they have. Water collected from the stream will, of course, be treated in order to make *it drinkable for us, unlike those poor hikers we mentioned previously who were drinking directly from the stream.*

The weather here is sunny, but the wind is relentless! My climbing mates tell me that my face has become wind–burned, and I can feel it. I'd put on sunscreen earlier but I lather more on. The porters try to find a spot for the tents where they won't blow down the mountain. Our tents end up on a ledge, and sometimes it feels like we'll end up halfway down the mountainside before the night is finished. The porters have difficulty finding a solid place to put up the ever-present Tusker flag, but it's obvious they have worked in these conditions before. They build a nice little supporting mound of rocks so the Tusker flag will stay securely in place.

Chris: They also worked very hard to clear large rocks away from where the tents will be pitched, so that we are comfortable as we sleep.

We have wonderful views of Mount Mawenzi on one side and our final destination, Kibo, on the other. The landscape at our campsite has a few flat areas, but it is a sea of boulders. It's as if the volcano erupted and spewed boulders everywhere and I guess that is what happened. Shortly after we arrive at Barafu, Peter nestles down in the rocks and boulders for a little nap. He looks so peaceful with a bed of solid rock. It looks like he could have napped on a bed of nails and it wouldn't have bothered him. I think we all feel like that. It has been a difficult few days but the most difficult part lies ahead with the elevation we are facing combined with the lack of oxygen. I am just sitting and resting on a rock, watching the clouds. They roll along the ground pushed by the wind, but they only come so far and then veer off behind a promontory. It is fascinating to watch as they creep towards us and then, as if they don't want to disturb us at our campsite, go in a different direction. The first is replaced by a second cluster of clouds, which is replaced by a third. I think I sit there for more than half an hour, just watching and enjoying the solitude and the scene that is unfolding before me. However, everything changes as we go into the tent for lunch. The clouds managed to make it past the promontory and it is starting to snow. It is not snowing a lot but combined with the howling wind and low temperatures, it is starting to get uncomfortable.

We have the usual wonderful lunch. We are supposed to lose our appetite at this elevation, but there is no sign of it here among our little group! If I ate like this at home, I would be seriously overindulging, but here we're just replacing the calories we've burned throughout the day. Even so, I am sure I have still lost a few pounds.

While we thought we had earned an afternoon off, instead after lunch we are taken on an altitude hike, going up another 1,000 feet. We gain altitude very quickly, and it serves a number of purposes. It helps us acclimatize, it tests the state of our health, and it demonstrates what we will be up against tomorrow. And it will determine how we would fare hiking in the snow, as it is still snowing. I am certainly glad I have my mitts, but I haven't changed my outerwear from what I have been wearing all the way. The only difference is that the long underwear is on now.

We are a pretty unenthusiastic lot as we do this acclimatization hike. Everyone is tired and cold, and for us, there is no real goal ahead of us this afternoon. We realize the importance of this activity, but it's an effort for all of us. I silently wonder if this is a better idea than resting for a big day tomorrow, but we defer to our guide who has been doing this for 11 years. Francis knows best. During our acclimatization hike, he surprises us when he points out that, in addition to the twice-daily litany of questions, we have all been additionally tested every day without suspecting it. We had noticed the occasional odd question coming apparently from nowhere from either Francis or Shabaan. They would ask if we had noticed something previously or raise some topic that didn't appear to have any relevance to anything. Now we're told they have been testing our mental capacity to make sure we are adjusting adequately. These guys are good!

Francis tells us that Eddie Frank, the founder of Tusker Trail, is leading a group down from the summit and is going to drop in to meet us. Chris, Peter and I are all impressed that he will take the time to stop in. While we are waiting, we talk to a few people who have either just reached the summit or were not able to make it. A woman tells us that she got as far as Stella Point (about 450 vertical feet from the summit) and had to turn back because of fatigue and illness. Her daughter continued on. For those who haven't tried this climb, it probably seems impossible that someone would get that close and then turn back. However, 450 feet is a bit misleading. It is an increase of 450 feet in altitude, so it is vertical feet. At Stella Point, if you could measure from the middle of the *inside* of the mountain straight up to the top, you would arrive at the correct number of 450. The number of feet we had to hike, however, was a far different story. You must also remember that most of the people on the mountain are people just like us. They have never climbed before; some have not trained properly; have never endured consecutive days of long hikes over treacherous terrain; or experienced the feeling that there is a cloth over their face as they try to draw a breath.

Chris: Our guides had estimated that it would take at least 90 minutes to go from Stella Point to the summit, even though the altitude gain is only 450 feet. Imagine feeling completely spent with nothing left in the tank and then being asked to continue for another 90 seconds. 90 seconds would be tough. Now imagine 90 minutes.

On the "Right to Play" website (www.righttoplay.com.), the Boston Bruins' towering 6'9" defenseman and one of the National Hockey League's best-conditioned players, Zdeno Chara, describes the final ascent this way: "It's the most difficult thing I've ever done. I've done a lot of hard training, many kinds, but nothing compares. You're baby-stepping behind one another, climbing, zig-zagging, losing balance. It's dark, you're tired, your feet are slipping on loose gravel. We must have stopped to rest 15 times." I think this puts it into perspective nicely.

Hearing about the woman's decision to abandon the final last steps of her climb to the top of Mount Kili scares me a bit. It would be such a disappointment to have come this far and then fail to make it that last few hundred feet. I feel in my heart that I won't be back here again. If I am unsuccessful, I will not try again. Chris has vowed that he will be back if he doesn't make it. He has age on his side.

Eddie Frank shows up and spends about 15 minutes with us, wishing us well and congratulating us on our fund-raising project. He is aware of our project to raise money for clean water and educational facilities in Mwanza. He has been climbing for 33 years and has climbed Kilimanjaro more than 40 times. His guides have nicknamed him "Nondo," which means "Steel Bar." Eddie is very personable, and we really appreciate the time he spends with us. It gives us a much-needed psychological lift after some of the other stories we have heard.

Chris: Eddie was also kind enough to comment on the speed with which we made the trip from Karanga to Barafu, a hike that took us three hours. He pointed out that he usually takes a full four hours to do the same trek.

Our dinner on the pre-summit day was very heavy in pastas, potatoes and other carbohydrates designed to provide the energy and stamina that we will need to continue on. Not surprisingly, our oxygen levels were continuing to diminish. Mine was down to 85% from 95% the first day, with my father's at 81% compared to 93% on Day One. My heart rate was surprisingly low when it was taken at a mere 74bpm (I had gotten some rest that day) while my dad's may have been affected by his anticipation of the next day as his continues to be up at 100bpm at the time of the test.

After dinner, we receive our final briefing from Francis in preparation for approaching the summit from the east side of the mountain. There are two factors that will affect what happens tomorrow. One will be the state of our health, and the second will be the weather. We will be leaving around 6:00 am and heading for Stella Point. That is where the decision will be made. If we are still performing well, pass all the questions thrown at us and if the weather is clear, we will continue on to the summit. If one of the factors is not good, we will go to Crater Camp where we will spend the night and attempt the summit the next day.

As I mentioned, going to Crater Camp is not preferable because we will have to sleep overnight at 18,800 feet, which can lead to serious altitude sickness problems. That would make the final ascent the following day that much more difficult and it could also jeopardize a side hike to the Ash Pit.

Chris: There is definitely the prospect hovering of not making it to the mountaintop and it has me half-weighing the pros and cons of trying to fake all the tests they give us, in order to hit the summit as planned. But I had also considered the worst-case scenarios of lying and realized that the end point could quite possibly be death. My stubbornness has started to subside as a result, and I am coming to terms with the prospect of either not making it to the Ash Pit or even not summiting and having to return to Tanzania another time to try again. I spend some time dealing with the fact that I might not make it. Little did I know that this mental exercise was foreshadowing some real events that almost prevented the achievement of my goal.

So, we have come this far and in some ways, the final result will be determined by luck. Here's hoping we have luck on our side! As I am falling asleep, I try to convince myself again that nothing will take away from what we have already done. It is a tough sell. The end is tantalizingly close, only a few more hours ahead of us. But it will be a treacherous climb at best.

CHAPTER 16

Day Seven - Summit Day and Crater Camp

IT FEELS LIKE I have just fallen asleep when there is the sound of shouting coming from another area of the campsite. My first irrational thought is that marauders have come to pillage and plunder. Then I realize that we are at 16,000 feet, and it's unlikely marauders would come this high to do that. It would be too much work when there are tourists down below who are easier prey. When I am groggily awake enough to understand what is going on, I realize that the noise will be the group that's leaving at midnight to summit at sunrise. I don't think the yelling is coming from the hikers (who are probably having as much difficulty breathing as we are). It must be coming from the porters who are tearing down their campsite. Our porters will not be following us to the peak. It will only be our guides Francis, Shabaan and, of course, Ignace who will join us. Our porters will go directly to our next campsite — and even then, only some of them will go. The rest will stay at this site and wait for us to return the next day.

It is still dark when the sound of Shabaan's footsteps echo in the stillness of the early morning as he shuffles from his tent to ours to tell us it is time to get up. It's 5 a.m. and when we exit the tent, we see that the sun is not up yet and there is a slight dusting of snow on the ground. This is exciting, but we know we have a long day ahead of us. Tying our shoelaces is an effort, and going about our morning ritual is a slow process that leaves us breathing hard. Still, nothing can reduce the anticipation of this day. It is cold and windy, so the order of clothing is long underwear, hiking and rain pants, Merino wool shirt to wick the moisture away from our bodies, then fleece and a waterproof jacket. My waterproof jacket that I had taken to wearing a few days before is also windproof and has definitely helped to keep me warm. The guides said they will carry anything extra for us on this final ascent, so I give Francis my microfiber winter jacket just in case it's really cold at the top. My balaclava is in my backpack should I need to cover my face from the biting cold of the wind.

I had read about the certain special things that people carry with them when they go on exotic adventures like this, and I was no different. There was one other piece of clothing that I'd promised myself I was going to wear if I made it to the summit, and I am glad I was lucid enough to remember to put it in my backpack. When I was 30, I had decided on a whim that I was going to train for the New York City Marathon and had launched into a rigorous running schedule. I had a favorite blue cotton t-shirt and pair of shorts that I wore when I was running. I had high hopes of success in the New York City Marathon, but back pain and a doctor's diagnosis of degenerative disc disease soon sidelined me permanently. (The threat of disc stress put a very quick end to my short running career. I did manage to complete a 5 km run and was amazed at how fast some of those crazy people run!)

Because they were favorites, the shirt and shorts remained in the bottom of my drawer for another three decades, much to Evelyn's dismay. Then Evelyn's second cousin Louise and her husband George moved to Ottawa years after my ill-fated running career, and Louise started running. She had designs on running the New York City Marathon, so I thought it would be pretty cool if she could wear the shirt and shorts to complete what I wanted to do. I gave them to her, and she started to train with them.

As it turned out, though, Louise found out that she and George were expecting a baby and that put a temporary hold on her plans to run the Marathon, so the shirt and shorts went to the bottom of a drawer again. I was surprised when Evelyn and I went to visit Louise and George a few months before my departure for Kilimanjaro, and Louise presented me with my decades-old t-shirt. (She mercifully didn't bother giving me the shorts back. I think she sensed that my body shape had changed somewhat over the years.)

There were a few people who would not have been happy with me if they had known I put on the t-shirt this morning for our summit ascent. I'd told the story to Peter and Chris one night after dinner in our mess tent, and they both saw it as an omen of something threatening and unfinished yet to happen. Both of the owners of the shirt had failed to accomplish their goals — albeit for significantly different reasons -- and I am quite sure they would have preferred that I hadn't even brought it, let alone slipped it on. I also kept it hidden from Francis and Shabaan because there was a strict "no cotton" rule in place due to the material's tendency to retain moisture. Normally I would be the last one to go against the advice of the guides, but I thought I would be okay with a Merino shirt between me and the t-shirt. It was just something I had to do.

Chris: This early in the morning and without the normal flow of oxygen to my brain, the last thing on my mind is recording what we were eating for breakfast. It was tough getting the strength and determination to write anything, and as I look back at my journal, I can see this just in the way my words are written. Everything is very succinct and to the point, and my handwriting has gone from not-so-good on the best of days to barely legible on this day. In a lot of ways, trying to write that day reminded me less of writing and more of drawing the letters. It is a subtle difference, but it is a difference. However, I'm trying to remain diligent in maintaining our oxygen and heart rate statistics. Our oxygen levels for both of us are around 15 percentage points less than they were early in the climb. My heart rate is now 26bpm more than when we started, and Dad's is 24bpm more.

We start out around 6:15 a.m. and it is surprising how bright it is, even though the sun is not up. The little bit of snow on the ground combined with the moonlight makes for pretty good vision for hiking. It is definitely "*pole, pole*" this morning as we struggle for each breath, just putting one foot in front of the other. We hike like this for about six hours, climbing over and around rocks and pulling ourselves upwards using whatever we can grab as a handhold. As has happened at other times throughout the climb, there is a sound in our ears as if they're being covered by some giant seashell – but it isn't the sound of the ocean we are hearing, it's the sound of the blood pounding through our veins, our hearts trying to deal with the exertion and lack of air. We are on our way to Stella Point.

At one point, I have to ask everyone to stop because I just can't catch my breath. It's like my breath has completely abandoned me. I am gulping and gasping, digging deeper and deeper to try to find just a hint of oxygen. For a few seconds, my breath just isn't there. I feel (and probably look) like a fish does when it is out of the water. As I thought about it later, I realized I had surprised myself a little as I didn't panic. Previous experience at lower levels had prepared us for moments like this, and I knew if I just stopped for a few seconds, my breath would return. Sure enough, it doesn't take long for it to return to what is considered normal at this height and under these strenuous circumstances. Still, I have to take slow laborious breaths, and each requires tremendous effort when I move.

It is a long, arduous climb with times when we have to lift one leg, followed by the other, up to a rock at a higher elevation. It is a supreme effort. We reach for the next rock or whatever we can grab onto to haul ourselves up barely a few feet, expending whatever precious breath we have in our lungs with the exertion. Although we are moving very slowly, each time we move one foot forward, our back foot slips a little in the shale. The surface beneath us feels tenuous, as if it might give way at any moment. We take numerous breaks along the way to catch our breath. Fatigue is definitely playing a part, but there is no way anyone is going to stop now. The end is definitely in sight, though we all know that the decision point called Stella still lies ahead.

Off to our right, poking its top through the clouds is Mount Mawenzi, one of the peaks of Kilimanjaro. It is a fairytale picture. It reminds me of a jagged turret castle enshrouded in clouds.

Chris: Mount Mawenzi reminds me of Mount Doom in J.R.R. Tolkien's Lord of the Rings. All it lacks is the all-seeing eye. I wouldn't say it was a frightening thing, but it was jagged and imposing as it popped up over the clouds.

To our left are the glaciers we've been seeing off and on during the previous few days. It's almost hard to believe we are actually beside them now. Then the clouds clear, and as we look back at Mawenzi, it is another moment when it feels like we can reach out and touch something that is obviously miles away. Unlike the part of the mountain we are struggling so hard to climb, which actually has some definition to its appearance, Mawenzi's jagged edges are totally random from our vantage point and appear in the light and shadows to be a much darker charcoal grey. A few shale falls are visible, along with some snow and ice. It is quite a contrast to the glaciers to our left, which are pristine for the most part with only a few layers of dirt interrupting their glistening white beauty.

The next magical moment arrives when we reach a level above the clouds and can see them touch the glacier. Above the clouds is blue sky. It's like looking down from an airplane, and I can't help but remember my thoughts just a few days ago when Chris and I flew over these peaks on our way into Tanzania, and I had wondered what we were about to embark on. Now here we are, standing on those peaks, our feet on ground that is actually higher than the altitude of that plane's flight path!

Finally we reach Stella Point. We'd been given box lunches at Barafu Camp to carry with us. Peter, Chris and I sit together, each with our backs against a rock and with the chill coming from Rebmann Glacier that sits a few feet behind us. Every movement causes us to dig deep for the next breath, so we stay as still as we can and there is little conversation. It just takes too much effort to talk. No one has headaches, at least not headaches that the three of us are admitting to each other about. (Keep reading). The sky is clear where we are sitting; the clouds are below us. We can actually see the sign that denotes the roof of Africa as Uhuru is referred to, off in the distance. We think about all those before us who had reached this stage and then had to turn back, because of illness or fatigue or the belief that they just could not take one more step toward the top. In the end, our decision here at Stella Point is a silent one. No one speaks about doing anything. Francis and Shabaan do not question us about how we feel. I guess they see determination and steadfastness in our eyes and in our actions. There is silent agreement among us to continue on. So that is what we do.

Chris: In truth, I had developed a headache within a couple hours of starting to walk that day. The headache had begun lightly, but as we climbed it continued to worsen. Fearing that this was an early warning sign of altitude sickness, I told our head guide. He took my sunglasses and angled them differently so that the arms of my glasses were no longer pressing in the same spot. When he asked me if I thought that helped, I'd just nodded my head (talking was difficult). By the time we reached Stella Point, my appetite had evaporated, my head was throbbing, and I knew that the only relief for me was going to be getting to the summit. Physically, it was not likely going to make me feel better, but at least I might be able to forget about how I was feeling for a bit.

The last few hundred feet are incredibly steep. We are fighting terrible exhaustion, it's bitterly cold and we are moving like automatons, slowly putting one foot in front of the other. I feel like this is the most physically-demanding ordeal I've ever undertaken in my entire 60 years. It's also incredibly windy, but fortunately we have the wind at our back. I turn to Chris and through teeth clenched by wind and fatigue, I mutter, "Do you feel that wind? I think it's the force of the 200 people whose names are on our Canadian flag pushing us to the top."

I wasn't kidding. Early in the climb, I realized that those people were innocently putting pressure on me to be successful because I wanted so badly to complete this journey for them.

They were reading Evelyn's account of our progress every day and sending their good wishes to us as we climbed. They had cared enough about what we were doing to contribute money for our cause to provide access to clean water and education for the children. But their silent presence had become a positive pressure, as if over 400 hands were pushing us and encouraging us along. I know with their help, we are going to make it.

Chris: It's funny to look back at the sources of motivation you pull from in times of severe adversity. This subject will be explored in more depth later on. But for now, I remember how my daughter had taken a liking to Disney's animated movie, Finding Nemo, and in my mind, I kept hearing the character Dory, repeating over and over again, "Just keep swimming, just keep swimming."

Then a startling thing happens. Without any warning, Chris begins running toward the summit. With a preternatural effort, he somehow turns inertia into energy, and takes off as if shot out of a cannon. I have no idea how many feet remain between us and Mount Kili's summit, but in that moment, Chris forgets his bad knee, his exhaustion, his headache (which I didn't know about then), his lack of oxygen and everything else. He's almost bounding up the steep incline, and Shabaan has to pick up his own pace to keep up with Chris. Peter and I are still trudging along inch by inch. It might be my imagination, but there appears to be a cloud of dust arising from Chris' boots as he blazes ahead. I can't help but smile. Just before he arrives at the sign signifying that the journey has been completed, Chris steps aside and waits for us to arrive. Out of respect for my age, I think, Chris and Peter both allow me to be the first to touch the sign.

Anyone who knows us knows that Chris and I are not an emotional pair. The women in our lives are always giving us Finlay men a hard time about remaining unemotional and keeping our emotions tight to our chests. All I can say is, they should have seen us then as we took our last few steps to the top of this magnificent and monstrous mountain. Everything that had gone into our journey came flooding out. For my son, it was the completion of his decade-long dream. For Peter, it was a true return full-circle. He'd been born in Nairobi, Kenya and moved to Canada at the age of 12, and he well remembered sitting on his grandfather's back porch, staring at the snow-covered peaks of Kilimanjaro. In his words, "I used to sit on his knee and he would tell me that if I listened close enough, I would hear Father Christmas coming over the mountain. So Kilimanjaro has always had a very special place in my heart. As I grew older, the desire to go back and touch African soil, and the possibility of doing a climb, has always been a thing of mine. So, turning 50, I said to myself: 'Enough is enough.'" It was the culmination of a lifelong dream." Peter's "impossible dream" had finally become reality. He had come home.

Chris: Climbing Kilimanjaro had been put on my list of things to do since my trip to South Africa, so finally reaching the summit and having the opportunity to do that with my father was a truly life-changing experience. When I started to run to the top of the mountain, the feelings coursing through my body were a combination of fear — that the altitude sickness was going to prevent me from finishing— exhaustion that needed to be fought, and adrenaline and excitement that needed to be released. I'm a goal-oriented person so being able to see the sign 100 feet away was enough of a magnet to power me to it at a pace that might have impressed even the most veteran hiker.

Being the type of person that people refer to as "unemotional," it surprised even me myself that being on that summit forced me to choke back tears of joy. It is truly the most incredible experience to achieve something after 10 years that you fight so hard to do with training and determination. It is easily one of the most difficult challenges I have ever faced, and one of the most joyous occasions (ranking up there with the birth of my daughters and my wedding day) I have ever *experienced. The extreme difficulty and corresponding extreme joy are completely overwhelming.*

For me, there are so many things that have gone into getting here to the top of Mount Kilimanjaro: two years of hard physical training, the family and friends who supported us, the fact that I completed this amazing journey with one of my sons, the fatigue from climbing for so many days, the new friendship Chris and I have forged with Peter and our mutual camaraderie, the opportunity to unfurl our Canadian flag with the signatures of over 200 supporters, many of whom we don't even know, and thoughts of my brother, Keith, lying in the hospital back home. He's been in my thoughts since we left. Everything combined makes our success an overwhelming, incredibly emotional moment.

I step aside and call home with the satellite phone. "Evelyn, I have something to tell you." My voice is cracking with emotion. It may not have been the best choice of words. It is 1 p.m. local time, but only 5 a.m. in Ottawa and to someone still asleep, those words could be alarming. "What!??" she says warily. "We made it," I reply, my voice still choked with feeling. "We are standing at the summit." On the other end of the phone line, Evelyn cheers and offers some congratulatory comments. But I am spent, and I really can't talk anymore.

Evelyn later recounted her feelings, "While he was on the trip, I worried. I will not forget that aspect of the trip, but I knew Barry was challenging himself and it was something he really wanted to do in his life. The family around me tried to reduce the worry by insisting that I write the daily blog, which was hosted on a local web site. I made sure that Barry's brother Keith, who was so ill, was kept informed of Barry's progress, and the rest of our family and good friends stayed in close contact with me and followed the progress on the blog after each call Barry made from Africa. They have all told me how much they looked forward to hearing about the trip daily."

However, there is one thing that dampens our enthusiasm: Chris is unable to reach his wife Laura to share his emotions at that amazing moment. Laura and his little daughter Annika had flown to France to be with her family after Chris and I left for

Africa, so he didn't have a phone number for them until Laura sent it to us in the midst of our climb. And for some reason, we had never been able to get that phone number to work on the satellite phone. Chris is unable to express to his wife what he was feeling at that moment. I know Chris is disappointed, and I feel bad for him.

We hug and congratulate each other and take a few pictures at the sign. We all have an agenda to complete. Peter does a little commercial for the Australian friends he met in Moshi and holds up a couple of signs that he had brought with him to advertise businesses back home. Chris and I have two golf balls that were given to us by a friend who suggested we take golf clubs along and hit them off the top of the mountain. We didn't think we would be able to do that because we wouldn't have room to carry golf clubs in our back packs – or the energy to tee off once we reached the mountain top. Also, we didn't want to start a war in Kenya. Who knew how far the balls might travel in thin air, even with our questionable golf swings? So we simply take pictures of us holding the golf balls that we can present to our friend. Then there is also the "New York Marathon" t-shirt that I've carried all this way. I make sure that I get pictures to show Louise when we return to Canada.

(I later returned the t-shirt to Louise as a friendly reminder about her commitment to finish the race, to which she sent the following reply, "I know that not everyone understands the importance of the shirt, but it represents a way of life. You have embraced that way of life and have motivated me to continue on with my running and just living a healthy life.")

We stay about 20 minutes at the top. We have time for photos, and Francis and Shabaan make sure we see everything we want to see. We take our time, but other people are coming, so it is time to go. Chris' thermometer indicates that the temperature is an incredible 60 degrees Fahrenheit (16 degrees Centigrade) at the top, although with the wind chill, it's probably more like 35 degrees Fahrenheit (close to zero in Celsius). I have a really hard time believing it was actually 60 degrees on the peak but we all saw the thermometer. Maybe the altitude was affecting it.

By the way, the sign at the top says: "Congratulations - you are now at Uhuru Peak Tanzania 5895 AMSL – Africa's Highest Point – World's Highest Free Standing Mountain." From Uhuru, we could see the Southern Ice field and, also the Ash Pit, although we didn't know what it was at the time.

The next part of the plan calls for us to descend to Crater Camp. We are actually hoping not to stop there. We'd like to get to a lower altitude and avoid the increased probability of altitude sickness. We do the 500-foot drop to Crater Camp in about 45 minutes, quite a contrast to our slow, arduous climb to the summit. You might say we pretty much ski down as we slide in the loose rock. In our exhausted state, we had to be careful we didn't pitch forward and roll to the bottom. A misstep could have resulted in some major damage, so we had to be aware enough to be careful where we placed our feet.

Crater Camp is an unbelievably beautiful location, situated beside the Furtwangler Glacier. While the glacier looks huge at first glance, it is a tiny reminder of its former size. At one time, this glacier was a gigantic ice field that covered the entire top of Mount Kilimanjaro. We arrive at the camp and set up chairs to relax and enjoy the view of the glacier. It is getting colder as the clouds start rolling in. It looks as if we may not be leaving as we'd planned. Francis brings out his medical kit. My head is aching – not a splitting headache but more of a dull, throbbing tightening around my head. Chris says his head is really aching to the point of making him nauseous.

Since my chair is first in line, Francis slips the pulse oximeter onto my finger first so he can measure the percentage of oxygen in my bloodstream. When the body is deprived of oxygen, it leads to a condition called hypoxia, or a deficiency in the amount of oxygen reaching the tissues of the body. I can hear some muttering and shuffling behind me. Then, without warning and before I realize what's happening, there are tubes up my nose and oxygen is being pumped into my system. Ignace springs into action and hustles out the oxygen tanks. Apparently, the oxygen in my bloodstream has dipped to 68% and is cause for some alarm. The normal reading should be between 95%-100% (mine was around 98% a few days previously at the bottom of the mountain). I didn't know I was *that* low on oxygen. I felt really tired and I had a headache — but I just assumed that was the way I was supposed to feel at such high altitude. I subsequently learned that levels below 70% can ultimately lead to severe AMS, including loss of consciousness or even coma. Once again, I am very glad we chose tour guides who know what they are doing.

Shabaan asks me to count off the numbers on the oximeter as they rise, but I guess I am a little confused because the numbers I'm reading are going down, not up as they are supposed to. I didn't know I'm reading off my *pulse*, which is going down, rather than my oxygen levels, which are supposed to be going up. Finally, Shabaan takes over and starts to read the numbers off. Now they make more sense. It seems to me in my hazy condition that Chris and Peter enjoy watching me get oxygen, after the initial shock wears off and it becomes apparent I'm going to be fine.

Once my exciting little oxygen replenishing episode is over, we go into the mess tent. The weather is getting much colder. Now it's time for Chris and Peter to get tested, and sure enough, they too require a "hit" of oxygen to improve their levels. Chris sits, tea in hand and oxygen tubes up his nose, with Francis holding the oxygen bottle and laughing. We understand that the situation could have been serious, but now that we're all out of danger, we decide to have fun with it to lighten the mood.

Lunch is good, but Chris wants to lie down to try and get rid of his headache. We decide to attempt the hike to the Ash Pit, which isn't that far away but it will take us another hour or two to get there. Chris was the one who desperately wanted to see the Ash Pit, only now it's questionable whether he will be well enough to go. I had already taken off my gaiters, and it takes me everything I have to put them back on. I wonder if I really want to do this. But the saying that you haven't really conquered the mountain until you see the Ash Pit makes me decide to start hiking again.

As Francis, Shabaan, Peter and I walk past the tent that Chris and I have shared for the last few nights, I call out to let Chris know we're going. He asks us to wait a minute and comes out, dressed and ready to continue the journey.

Chris: This was the most difficult decision I had to make on the entire trip. My body just wanted to curl up and die at that moment. My headache was absolutely crippling with the extreme nausea just making it worse, and the thought of walking anywhere, even to the Ash Pit, was about as enticing right then as jumping in front of a moving train. Yet ultimately I knew that the trip wasn't over until I saw the Ash Pit, and I'd made my decision long before that moment. Now it became a question of mustering up the strength to walk for another couple of hours to do it. In order to accomplish this, I knew I would have to rely heavily on those around me to provide me with the motivation I would need to keep going. Having my father there to follow up the hill to the Ash Pit was one of the factors that helped me make sure I was able to do it, and for that I was very thankful.

It occurs to me that Ignace is not with us for the first time. I assume he's not far away should something happen. I am quite sure he can run up to us if he has to. We pass through the middle of the Furtwangler Glacier, and it makes us sad to think that at one time, it was a magnificent mass of ice. Even in its diminished state, it's still beautiful to see, with the sun glistening off the ice crystals that form the glaciers. There are some stunning formations of ice created as it routinely thaws and reforms. Perhaps the saddest sight of all is the puddles of water lying at the foot of the glacier, which are constant reminders that the glaciers are dying. Through the eyes of someone who is uneducated about glaciers, the process seems to be irreversible: the smaller the ice field, the more dirt that's exposed to the sun's rays to capture the heat that will melt the ice. This is borne out by experts, although not in such simplistic terms. The *Proceedings of the National Academy of Sciences* journal points out that 85% of the ice that covered Mount Kilimanjaro in 1912 had disappeared completely by 2007, and 26% of the ice there as late as the year 2000 is now also gone. Shockingly, experts predict all of the ice will be gone within the next two decades. We are glad that we have seen what is left.

We trudge upwards to the Reusch Crater and, once again, we are fighting to keep one foot in front of the other. I am not sure I have ever been this tired. However, when we arrive, it is definitely worth seeing just as we've been told. The Ash Pit sits in the middle of the crater and is said to be one of the most perfect formations of its kind on the planet. It appears to be a perfectly-symmetrical inverted cone with rounded edges that rise up a few feet, only to drop down some 400 feet into the bowels of the mountain. We aren't allowed to get too close as there is danger of falling in. We are told that the Pit was formed about 200 years ago by volcanic activity and the gases and sulfur rising out of it are indications that it's indeed still active, though dormant. The heat generated by whatever is going on inside the crater is enough to ensure that no snow will gather around the Ash Pit itself. It's a good thing for us that the sulfur arising from the pit is blowing in the opposite direction because it sure wouldn't do much for our headaches! Shabaan recognizes how tired I am and has taken over my camera. I am glad, as he gets some great shots of us standing at the Ash Pit.

Slowly we make our way back down. There is no hurry. We have nowhere to go. Our big climb is behind us now, and we are left with a resonating feeling of achievement mixed in with total body-numbing exhaustion. The clouds are moving in. We are definitely going to spend the night at Crater Camp, whether we want to or not. I think we are all thankful for that. In spite of the thought of worsening headaches and possibly illness, I know *I* am. We have been hiking today for about nine hours, breathing half the oxygen we normally do, on some of the most severe slopes we have encountered during the entire trek. It has been a tremendously emotional experience and now I am really looking forward to crawling into my sleeping bag.

Chris: Even before the sleeping bags, there is still dinner to get through. Just like at Stella Point, I am noticing one of the other symptoms of altitude sickness— a disappearing appetite. Trying to force down our dinner of pasta, curry potatoes and veggies that evening was difficult to do. Deep down,

I know that I need to eat, but the act of eating isn't an easy undertaking. Much like walking at this altitude and staring at the boots of the person in front of you while you methodically keep pulling one foot in front of the other, I keep staring at my plate and methodically putting one mouthful of food in my mouth, chewing it, then another. After dinner we have our oxygen measured, and there are no more oxygen depletion scares this time. I am at 72% and Dad is up to 75%, which still isn't very good but I think it is considered a success. Our hearts are struggling to keep up, and our heart rates are 102bpm for me and 108bpm for my father.

We are taking medication for our headaches given to us by the guides, and doing it willingly now. Chris is really having a tough time with his headache. We have to take dosages every four hours. Shabaan will wake us up at 10 p.m. for the last dose. He will also take our pulse and oxygen readings again at that time. We go to bed at 7 p.m. that night, and it turns out to be the best sleep I've had since we got here! (Except for having to get up about six times during the night to go to the bathroom.) Once when I am up, I notice that the sky is clear, the stars are shining and the moon is out. It's not a full moon, but close to it. The scene is spectacular. The stars, constellations and moon are shining brilliantly down on the glaciers, creating muted but dazzling ice sculptures that would make any ice carver envious. Cliffs leading over to Uhuru on one side and the Ash Pit on the other cast eerie indigo shadows. The smaller boulders and rocks scattered across the valley floor cast their own little shadows on the sides not highlighted by the celestial light show above me. It's such a different scene from what I experienced growing up on the prairies, but it's the same solitude and a reminder of the open spaces I grew up with. It's a scene I wish I could just sit and enjoy, but it is now well below 0 degrees centigrade. No way am I going to stargaze here outside the tent when I could be slipping back into my nice warm (by comparison) sleeping bag!

With so many people attempting to climb Mount Kilimanjaro every year, you might wonder if the mountain is covered in hikers and commercial tour guide companies. No, not really. There were certainly times when we passed other climbers and times when we stepped aside to let others pass. At the campsites, we saw other hikers in varying numbers. But there were more times when we seemed to be the only ones on the mountain. It was quiet and peaceful, and sometimes when we stopped for a break, all we could hear was the wind blowing across the barren landscape and through the tufts of grass. On one of my journeys outside the tent, the wind had died down and there was an eerie silence surrounding the mountain, giving the impression that we were the only ones there. The quiet times were special times. On this particular night after our summit ascent, I did hear a sharp cracking sound as a glacier split, but I think I slept the sleep of the dead (or at least dead tired) when I was in my sleeping bag.

Chris: Interestingly enough, my perspective of the night at Crater Camp was not quite the same. It was a decent sleep except for the interruptions of my father getting out of the tent every hour, but added to that, particularly closer to morning, was the constant shifting and cracking of the glaciers which led to loud cracks and noises, each one of which sounded like a not-too-distant gunshot. Having spent time in South Africa, I'm well aware of what gun shots sound like too, for comparison's sake. I also found that I had woken up at 4 a.m. that night with even more nausea, though I was fairly certain the next morning that it was just hunger. (A good sign that my appetite was coming back again!)

Shabaan follows me into the tent after one of my excursions. It is 10 p.m. We submit to the oximeter one more time and apparently, everyone passes because this is the last we see of him until morning.

Chris: Sorry, everyone, I was unable to record those figures as I was much too tired, much too asleep and much too *nauseous and it was much too dark to even think about finding my notebook!*

During the question and answer ritual in the morning, it is the first time I have been able to answer "no" to "Do you have a cough?" and "yes" to "Did you sleep well?" In the end, all of this worry about the head cold had been for nothing; although I am sure it increased my heart rate and decreased my oxygen levels throughout the climb. But it was a valid concern from everything I'd read leading up to the climb and based on the sign at the park entrance. Evelyn had worried about it since she blamed herself for giving it to me in the first place. (After our son Trevor found out we had reached the summit, he sent Evelyn a message saying, "Now you can quit beating yourself up about Dad's cold." I'm very thankful it never developed into anything more.

Since tonight is our last dosage of our altitude sickness prevention medication, I would like to say one last word about the effectiveness of it. For me, it seemed to work. My only symptom of altitude sickness was a relatively mild headache. Chris' reaction to the altitude was more severe, but neither of us woke up during the night gasping for breath. All in all, in spite of my headache and need to have my oxygen replenished, I think I got off relatively easily with altitude sickness.

Chris: I'm still not necessarily convinced of the merits of taking the altitude-sickness medication, considering the headaches I had towards the end of the climb. On the other hand, maybe it really did make a dramatic improvement, and that's a scary proposition, too. It's possible the side effects would have been much worse had I not taken it. Dad and I had different experiences so, as always, seek the advice of a professional rather than listening to us!

Peter did not take medication, and he seemed to have exactly the same symptoms that I had at exactly the same time. Did Peter's first 11 years in Nairobi make a difference to his ability to adapt to altitude? Maybe. I can only rely on the experience I had, and I would definitely recommend the use of Diamox or something similar. I would not want to chance a climb of this altitude totally unprotected by any altitude-adjustment medication. Based on my experience, I am convinced it made for a more comfortable and enjoyable climb for me.

CHAPTER 17

Day Eight - Millennium Camp

WHAT THE HECK happened to my sunglasses? When I woke up this morning and got ready to go, I realized my sunglasses were missing. I read somewhere that going without sunglasses on the mountain can result in snow blindness because of the intensity of the sun's rays and the close proximity to the glaciers. The glasses can't have gone far but I checked again in the tent and they aren't there. They are prescription Ray Bans, so I doubt that anyone picked them up. If they did and get caught, it would mean losing a job that they can ill afford to lose. It is a day of beautiful sunshine, of course. Shabaan asks me what I am going to do, and I tell him, "Squint a lot, I guess." He has a pair of sunglasses with white frames, which we have kidded him about a lot. He very generously offers them to me. However, they don't quite fit over my regular glasses (they may look stylin' on Shabaan but they look pretty stupid on me), so I set off wearing the glasses I normally wear when it isn't sunny. I certainly don't recommend it, but I will just have to avoid looking toward the glaciers. It doesn't really seem to be that bright.

Chris: Our morning breakfast consisted of millet, toast and sausages (hot dogs). I know what you are saying. The trip is almost over so now they're eating hot dogs. Actually, they tasted pretty good! We didn't mind at all. The temperature registered only 36-37 degrees F (2-3 degrees F). Heart rates had slowed a bit from after dinner the previous night, with mine down to only 99bpm while Dad's was a "mere" 106bpm. Our oxygen percentages had also recovered slightly, with mine now sitting at 75% and Dad's at 81%. Before the final heart rates were taken, I had an interesting experience with the heart rate test. I knew it was getting close to time to have my heart rate measured, but I also knew I had some things to put away in the tent before we could leave. I set out to walk the 10 steps from the mess tent to our sleeping tent to pack up my sleeping bag. Even though I felt better than I had in the previous 24 hours, for some reason, this simple exertion seemed to take more strength and determination than you would believe. When I was done, I just sat there for a few minutes catching my breath before getting up and walking back to the mess tent. Shabaan put the pulse oximeter on my finger and discovered my heart was beating at a rate of 155bpm after only 10 steps! It quickly slowed to the 99bpm that I ended up recording for the day, but this incident offers a good example of how much exertion is required by your body when you are at altitude — even just to walk the 10 steps I needed to walk!

The thought occurs to us that this is our second-to-last day on Kilimanjaro. We have been far from civilization for the past eight days, breathing the rarefied air of Africa's tallest mountain, but now we are about to head back to the real world again. We are going to hike for five hours to reduce the time we have to spend hiking on the final day. We wonder to ourselves whether we are going to be sad to be leaving, or if it will be a feeling of "I can't wait to get this over with." We will find out soon enough. We drop the first 2,500 feet in just over half an hour, managing to "ski" down the loose rock. I find it hard on the calf muscles and a little intense as I'm using my legs to prevent myself from suddenly careening down the mountainside. We drop another 1,000 feet in the next forty minutes or so.

One of the porters suffers an embarrassing and bone-threatening moment. Professional porters are used to pretty much running down the mountain, but this one somehow lost his balance right next to us. There was an awful noise, as everything he was carrying preceded his sprawling body into the dirt. He got up and dusted himself off under the angry glare of the guides, who I can only presume were not happy with him for embarrassing himself in front of the clients. In fact, there didn't seem to be a lot of sympathy for him from anyone but us. Hopefully, the porter didn't have his pay docked for his wild and totally unexpected adventure. The skin removed by the friction of his slide would be painful reminder enough. Fortunately, this porter was not a member of our team.

People always ask us about the effects of suddenly having more oxygen in your lungs as you return to lower altitudes. Some ask us if it is similar to rising to the surface too quickly after a deep sea dive, or if it might be compared to the sensation deep-sea divers get if they surface too quickly and get "the bends." Those of us who are old enough will remember the diving shows on television where the theme often revolved around someone rising to the surface too quickly developing the "bends." I always thought if the divers in any of those shows would just watch shows on diving, they would realize they weren't supposed to surface quickly. But I digress.

My answer is no. Decompression sickness has to do with the amount of nitrogen in the body and pressure on the lungs from being underwater. For me, there wasn't any significant effect from coming down the mountain quickly, other than great relief at being able to breathe without effort again. And in my follow-up research, I have seen no evidence that problems can arise from descending too quickly, other than the stress on the joints.

We spend the entire day after our steep and rapid descent watching every step we take. The footing is stony, and we must pick our way as we go. Then we find ourselves hiking through the middle of a river bed. I can't imagine how people do this in the rainy season, but apparently they do. We deliberately chose the time of year to avoid the rainy season, but according to our guides, people climb in the rainy season as well. We did encounter some mud in the river bed, making for treacherous going. I can't imagine doing it when the water was flowing!

Because of the sharp angle at which we were descending, we also spend the entire five hours today with our toes crammed down into the front of our boots. No wonder they told us to cut our toenails as short as we could before our hike! I'd had no pain as we climbed up Mount Kilimanjaro, but now I am making up for it. My toes, ankles, calves and knees are all burning. I wish I'd spent more time training for this part of our trek, but the thought never really crossed my mind – all I'd concentrated on was going up, not down! Amazingly, I don't recall reading anything in my pre-climb research about the agony of this part of the expedition.

As we arrive at Millennium Camp at about 12,500 feet, every step hurts. Even with lighter shoes at the campsite, it still hurts to walk. I walk gingerly and very, very slowly from our tent to the mess tent. It is amazing to think that this morning we were walking very slowly because it was difficult to draw a breath. Fatigue was also a factor. But I will say this: now we can breathe! Our lungs are probably doing a little jig with every effortless breath we take. After all, it's the way my lungs have been doing it for most of my 60 years. You could say my lungs are used to freedom and never expected to encounter the thin air and difficult breathing of a mountain peak summit

From Millennium Camp, I call Trevor and Josée. Josée is exuberant by nature, and she is absolutely ecstatic and barely able to contain her excitement. She is relieved that we are safe and thrilled that we have successfully completed our journey. Chris' wife Laura and Joseé had both heard from Evelyn that we had scaled Kili's summit, but she is clearly excited to hear it firsthand. Unfortunately, due to the time difference, Trevor is still sleeping and there is no time to wake him as the satellite phone is dying. I know he will be proud and relieved when Josée passes along the message. I am fatigued, and probably don't sound as exuberant over the phone as I feel, but Joseé easily makes up for both of us. Later on, it strikes me that this was our first taste of our supporters' and friends' reactions. Evelyn tells me via the satellite phone that congratulatory messages are pouring in from friends and family everywhere.

As we sit in our mess tent having lunch, the weather is slightly foggy. Millennium Camp is another barren site dotted with a few dead trees. We passed back into the clouds on our way down, although the day had been mostly sunny until a few minutes ago. The temperature is reasonable, but it is damp. Nevertheless, we are able to reduce the numbers of layers we are wearing. There is a whooshing sound and we catch sight of a giant white-necked raven in flight in the fog as it swoops past the entrance to our tent. It is as if it is bidding us farewell and congratulating us for not being their dinner. (Although they aren't really buzzards, we have enjoyed making them out to be.)

Chris: We are a pretty sorry lot throughout the afternoon. We sit quietly in the mess tent, enjoying our success and reading or dozing off and trying not to think about our sore feet, calves, knees, etc. One thing we don't do is walk far. We have an early dinner on our last night on the mountain with pumpkin soup again, which is a special treat. Our oxygen levels had skyrocketed over the course of the day as we descended, so by the time we were tested, my levels had gone from morning's 75% to 93% tonight. My father's oxygen level had jumped from 81% to an impressive 94%. Since our hearts are not working as hard any more, my heart rate had dropped from 99bpm this morning to 77bpm now. My dad's had gone from 106bpm when we started out this morning to 92bpm tonight. I find the rise and fall of our heart rates and oxygen levels as the altitude changed throughout the climb has been fascinating. It is so important for the guides to keep an eye on the rates to see how we are reacting to the various altitude levels.

As we go to bed, I think we probably all allow ourselves the luxury of a similar thought, one that we have deliberately prevented ourselves from picturing over the last eight days.

One more day and we will be able to have a hot shower!

Chris: The shower might have been my dad's luxury image. But for me, the only thing more exciting than a hot shower is, of course, a cold beer.

CHAPTER 18

Day Nine - Mweka Gate

IT IS HARD to believe that this is our last day on the mountain. We have a 6:30 a.m. wake-up call. Francis believes there will be a lot of people arriving at Mweka Gate at the same time, so he wants us to arrive early to sign out. My sunglasses mysteriously appeared the night before when I unrolled my sleeping bag. Somehow they were rolled up in the bag when I readied it for the porters. It is a bright day, and I am glad to have them again. It is a small thing, but important when you are on a mountain three degrees south of the equator.

After we finish our morning ritual and are told that all our vital signs are back to normal (no more questions and no more Diamox – hooray!), Francis, Shabaan and the porters gather us together to commemorate our success. Led by the no-longer-quiet Benson, they sing two songs for us. The first is simply called "Kilimanjaro," and the second is "The Song of Kilimanjaro" which they had tried to teach us our second day on the mountain. The latter turns into a raucous event as one by one, Peter, Chris and I are brought into the circle to participate in the singing, dancing and hand clapping. Chris' camera had fortunately thawed out somewhere along the way so he recorded the event and after looking back at the video, there isn't much visible action from the three of us as our bodies battled between celebration and understandable fatigue. However, it is a touching gesture, and it attracted a bit of a crowd from neighboring campsites. I believe it is a ceremony that is played out for all hikers on their last morning on the mountain but it is special for us nonetheless. At the end, we thank the porters very much for their efforts in making our climb enjoyable and successful. Our tips will be paid to the Tusker coordinator who would divvy them up among the porters and guides.

Chris: To this day, watching my copy of the tape of our porters and guides singing the "Song of Kilimanjaro" never fails to leave me with a huge smile and an overwhelmingly warm feeling. To me, that moment really captures the essence of the people we were travelling with, the joy of having achieved a monumental goal and the celebration that we all felt inside. Having others stand around watching the spectacle makes it all that much sweeter as you can see the recognition in their faces of what we were all feeling at that time.

Shabaan begins leading us out of the campsite when he slyly turns and starts heading *up* the mountain. I think Chris and I would have actually followed him back to Millennium Camp, but Peter catches on to Shabaan's joke and says, "Where are you going?" Shabaan turns around with a huge smile on his face and then heads back down the mountain in the direction we really want to go right now.

The trek down continues to stress our toes and knees. Obviously we are still descending, only this time much of it is on steps. I can't imagine what Chris' and Peter's knees are telling them, but neither complains. I find that I am almost stepping down sideways to avoid the shock on my knees that stepping straight down brings. Chris is setting a pretty quick pace with Shabaan, so it is obvious that the question has been answered for him - he wants to get this over with.

Chris: My knee had had just about all it could handle, and I knew that the sooner we got to the bottom of the mountain, the sooner the knee brace would come off and the sooner things would start to feel better. I will try to delay surgery as long as possible when I get home but it appears to be inevitable at this point. But the journey was worth every iota *of pain. I'm not sure now that I would do it again, but I'll never regret having done it.*

Our hiking lineup this morning is Shabaan, Chris, Peter, me and Ignace. Francis remains farther back, as he had something to do at the campsite. We are all using our hiking poles, just as we've been doing most of the way down. Going up, I'd only used mine on the really steep sections, preferring if possible to keep my hands free to grab anything within reach should I need to. Minutes earlier, while we were still on loose gravel, I'd accidently dropped both my poles. Because of fatigue, rather than turning around to pick them up properly, I just leaned backwards to try to pick them up. Bad move! The weight of my backpack caused me to lose my balance, and I careened off a tree on one side of the trail and started to fall towards the other side. Ignace came running up, said, "Sorry, sorry," grabbed my backpack, hoisted me up with my feet a few inches off the ground, and planted me back down on my feet. I'm not sure what he was sorry about: whether it was because I had fallen or because he had to lift me up to get me on my feet. After getting to know him a little during our time together, even though he didn't seem to speak English, he could well have been sorry because he wasn't there to pick up my poles for me. Obviously picking up my poles was not necessary and hopefully, not part of his job description. Either way, I am glad he was there.

We have found our way into a different part of the rainforest from the one we were in a few days earlier, and we catch another breathtaking view of Mount Kilimanjaro through the fronds. Already it's starting to become difficult to believe we were actually up there. It's surreal to stand here and realize that only two days before, we stood on Kili's peak, atop the roof of Africa.

When we finally arrive at Mweka Gate, there are quite a few people milling around. There are people selling souvenirs, soft drinks and beer, and they are quite happy to show us their wares and offer us the best deal of the century while we wait our turn to sign out. The quality is not bad, and the prices are relatively cheap. You can't help but think, what the heck, how often will these chances come along? We all buy something, but there is one consumable that we will always cherish more than anything else at that moment in time: the nice, cold, celebratory Kilimanjaro beers that we drink in the van as we head back to the hotel.

Chris: Please note that none of us were driving at the time, and we certainly do not condone drinking while in moving vehicles, driving or not! But that bottle of beer was quite possibly one of the best I have ever had in my entire life.

And now – it's over. We wave goodbye to our porters and watch them pile in a truck to be taken to their homes. It is a picture of stark contrasts. We (the tourists) are being taken back to the relative luxury of our hotel, having paid thousands of dollars for this adventure; they are being taken to their simple homes and families to rest up before their next hike at $10 a day. While they are fortunate to have work, it is very, very difficult work. One can only think, "There, but for the grace of God, go I."

Francis and Shabaan give us time at the hotel to shower and shave. My razor was broken on the way over so I get half a shave, but it still feels great to get rid of nine days of dirt and grime. As an aside, I also had some powdered Gatorade in a plastic container in my suitcase that I was planning to mix with water and drink in the evenings. The powder was white, unfortunately, so some exuberant Customs official somewhere, thinking he or she might have stumbled upon something, had opened the container and broke it. I had to empty my suitcase and dump out the powder before we started our climb.

Francis and Shabaan meet us after lunch for a little certificate presentation ceremony and final farewell. They have been absolutely wonderful to us, and we have so much respect for them. They wish us good luck back home and we wish the same for them…and continued safe climbing. That is about all we can say.

Peter, Chris and I head to downtown Moshi in a cab, where we find the Indoitaliano, a restaurant that is highly recommended and order… pizza! Our celebration is heartfelt but short. We are all fatigued, and Chris and I have to get up early the next morning to catch a flight. We will be traveling to Mwanza to visit the schools there. We have finished the first part of our journey, but there is even more to come.

CHAPTER 19

Things I Know I Didn't Know

NOT EVERYONE READING this book will consider climbing a mountain. But we have all said at one time or another, "I think I would like to do _______" (fill in the blank). We're all faced with challenges of varying degrees throughout our lives. Sometimes we accept them, and sometimes we don't. When we do accept challenges and we accomplish our goals, it leaves us with a new feeling of satisfaction. But it's often even more than that. It can leave us with a new feeling of being alive and with renewed strength to take on greater challenges in life.

That is what it was like for me. Climbing Mount Kilimanjaro was an extraordinary experience, one that I will savor for the rest of my life. Chris and I were in the elite percentage that has actually gotten to experience the top of what seemed to us to be a seemingly-insurmountable mountain, and we are very proud of this fact. Most of those who do make it to the summit and beyond to the Ash Pit say that it is the most physically demanding thing they have ever done in their lives. I would certainly fall into that category.

We learned a great deal in the weeks and months leading up to the climb — and on the mountain itself. We had questions before we went. We learned as we went along, as well as from the many people who offered advice and guidance. We learned life lessons: lessons about the preparation required to undertake such an adventure and then about the will and determination to actually do it. The life lessons we learned we will always apply, whether we're climbing mountains literally or figuratively.

In retrospect, I realize that our mountain was a metaphor for all the "mountains" we face on a daily basis. The mountains may be physical or mental challenges or something else entirely. Sometimes we make life's challenges much bigger than they need to be, but they truly seem like mountains to us at the time. I'd like to think that those who followed our quest – and now the readers of this book — will realize that there really isn't much difference between the mountain Chris and I climbed and the challenges we all face in our lives. All challenges require decision-making, along with the forethought and preparation that go into making those decisions. We climb mountains; we come down and move on to the next challenge. We're not always successful, but we gain from the experience and apply it to the next mountain we have to deal with. Our mountain just happened to be a rugged and very tall piece of volcanic rock!

I believe now that our minds set artificial limits for most of us that are, unfortunately, lower than necessary. We see things that we would like to do but our minds tell us that they are beyond our capability or outside our comfort zone. We see other people doing amazing physical activities that we too would like to try, but our inner voice will say that they are somehow beyond our potential. My experience on Mount Kilimanjaro has taught me that we *all* have the capacity to surpass our self-imposed artificial limits. We are *all* capable of facing up to the challenges life puts before us if we only believe in ourselves. The key is maintaining a positive attitude so that when things start to get tougher, we can bear down and keep forging ahead. This was never more evident to me than when my brain was telling me during my months of training that I could not do any more. My brain had apparently reached its artificial limit, established by my lifestyle and conditioned by my previous activities (or lack thereof). My inner self was trying to fool me into deciding I had had enough…yet my body still had more to give. The key was to convince my brain that it could keep going so my body could get the message. I guess what I'm trying to say here is that we can always dig down inside ourselves a little deeper to complete whatever task we are up against.

It also became apparent to me during my time on the mountain that age shouldn't be perceived as a negative factor or allowed to prevent us from doing the things we want to do. Age is only a chronological means of counting where we are in life, nothing more. It is not a measuring stick that tells us how we should *be* in life. Traditionally, there have been stereotypes in life that tell us how we should act at age 60, 70 and 80 or beyond. This is changing now as older people are realizing they have to remain active to truly enjoy their so-called "golden years." No longer should we be looking for someone of the same age just to commiserate with and discuss how we're feeling or moan about things we did or didn't do or that we should or shouldn't have done. Mark Twain once said, "Age is mind over matter: if you don't mind, it doesn't matter!" If we don't mind that we're growing older – in fact, if we can embrace it — nothing else really matters. We're never too old to get up off the couch and undertake some physical or mental activity designed to keep us healthy and our minds alert. Much has been written elsewhere about the virtues of an active lifestyle for people in their 50s, 60s and beyond. And if anyone doubts it, I offer myself as a prime example of what you can achieve as you get older.

Finding something to be passionate about is good for the soul. My passion certainly grew as I went along — but there was always an internal drive that fueled it. Laurie Skreslet's speech, Chris' comments about wanting to climb Kilimanjaro, the doctor's advice to get more active and watch my nutrition — they all led me to become very passionate about what I wanted to do. In fact, my family and friends probably became tired of hearing about it before the climb, but fortunately they were very good about not telling me to talk about something else. I can't really explain it, but there was something inside me all along the way that wanted to climb a mountain. And I firmly believe we *all* have inner passions. We owe it to ourselves and our dreams to find those passions and then pursue them. The late, great country outlaw Waylon Jennings perhaps said it best: “"This is not a dress rehearsal. We are all professionals and this is the big time!" Passion discovered too late can lead to that debilitating time-waster called regret. There's nothing more satisfying than proving you really can accomplish a major goal by giving it your all and making it happen.

For Chris and me, climbing Mount Kilimanjaro made us walk a little taller afterwards. The trip was a microcosm of life packed into nine short days. We have a new appreciation for nature's beauty and a sense of foreboding, having seen what is happening to the glaciers. We have a new appreciation for the way others live and how fortunate we are to live where we do. We developed a new admiration for others who are not as lucky as us but who face their daily challenges and address them. After spending so much time with our guides and porters under difficult circumstances, we learned that we are all the same. The only difference between the guides, porters and us is that, somehow, we drew the lucky straw and live where we have more than enough of everything. We learned in some small way that we can enjoy and make do with the bare essentials, but that we really have no concept of what it would be like to have to do it day in and day out for our entire lives. We learned to laugh when the going got rough and to really appreciate it when someone helped us out.

THE BASICS

There may be some reading this book who are inspired enough to undertake their own climb of Mount Kilimanjaro — or another mountain! For people who actually want to undertake this formidable challenge, there are some practical basics that I learned to do, and there are also some things that I would do differently on the mountain if I were ever to undertake a climb such as this again. Being a first-time climber (and someone who hadn't even camped for longer than I care to remind you of again), I definitely benefited from talking to others beforehand. Most of what I learned has been shared throughout the previous chapters but I will summarize the points here for ease of reference. I am not an instant expert because I climbed one mountain but these are the things that worked for me and I hope they will make your climb more enjoyable. I would not give up the overall experience I had for anything. I recommend the climb and will tell you that if it is even remotely on your "bucket list," give serious consideration to doing it. It is the experience of a lifetime.

Conditioning is important to having a good climb. I've heard of people attempting the climb without having trained prior to their attempt. It can probably be done, but it will be far safer and more enjoyable if you have practiced long hikes and worked on your cardio vascular conditioning. It is difficult enough when you are in decent shape. I can't imagine what it would be like if you were wheezing before you get there.

It is very important to hire a company that is reputable and that has a membership in the Kilimanjaro Porters Assistance Project (or its equivalent, depending on where you are climbing). The guides should have First Responder training and a program of testing for oxygen readings and pulse rates every day. Look into the way the porters are paid by the company to ensure they receive their proper due. If the guides have an understanding of the history and the flora and fauna of the mountain, it will make your climb just that much more enjoyable as well. Confirm their climbing experience before going.

Make sure you have the best equipment you can afford. Undergarments of wicking material are important, as are microfiber and fleece jackets. The tour company should provide a list of the requirements. Any store specializing in trekking equipment can help out as well. Buy boots with an aggressive tread and make sure you put a few miles on them before you go. Blisters would be a major distraction on the mountain and would severely impact the enjoyment of your climb. You should also make sure your backpack and water bottle are the right size, not too small or too large. Wear the backpack on a few outings before you go.

Visit a doctor who's knowledgeable about international travel before you go. Make sure you have the right medicines and all the vaccinations you need for the countries you're going to. While we were fortunate not to have to use a lot of the medication we took with us, we were still well-prepared just in case. Climbing to even higher altitudes is a totally different experience with different requirements and would necessitate talking to high altitude experts.

It's important that you understand what you're getting into from the beginning. Read up. Go online. Talk to people. Be sure you have a basic knowledge of the effects of altitude sickness so you can tell your guide if you start to experience discomfort that could be linked to High Altitude Cerebral Edema or High Altitude Pulmonary Edema. Reaching the summit is important, but it isn't worth your life.

Listen to the guides! They have the experience of many previous climbs. They know what to look for. They know the signs of incoming bad weather or other problems along the trail. We came across one older gentleman who was arguing with his guide about eating a snack. The guides aren't telling you to eat because they own shares in the protein bar company. They are telling you for your own health and survival, and frustrating though it may be at times, it's important to do what they say.

Carry a second water bottle with you that you can keep under your jacket for the summit. One of adventurer Meagan McGrath's most important pieces of advice was to take an extra water bottle to the summit because the Camelbak would likely freeze and, as predicted, it did! The alternative here is to carry an insulated Camelbak as Chris did, which resulted in the tube freezing and not the whole pack.

Savor every second you're on the mountain. Take time to enjoy your surroundings but leave it as you found it. Take all the pictures you want, but respect the mountain. Don't leave debris behind. There are people who are paid to keep it clean but that is no excuse for leaving trash, wrappers or garbage on the mountain. We are fortunate to have the opportunity to make a climb like this. The Tanzanians are benefiting from the tourism, but they do not appreciate tourists defacing their mountain by careless behavior. Leave everything the way you found it, if not cleaner.

Finally, thank your guides and porters as often as possible and take care of them at the end of your excursion. We were told that some people will create any excuse so they don't have to leave a tip. That is just abominable. While the porters and guides are only doing their jobs, remember that they primarily rely on tips for their livelihood. They work brutally hard in difficult conditions to ensure you have the best experience possible, and they will be grateful for your recognition in the form of a gratuity. Remember that your life is in their hands on the mountain at all times. Without them, there would be no climb. Treat them with the respect they deserve, and tip them accordingly.

CHAPTER 20

Life is About Choices

CHRIS AND I made two major choices in the summer and fall of 2008. No one forced us to try to climb Mount Kilimanjaro. We didn't have to do it. It was a willing choice we made. We also made the choice to use our climb as a platform to help children in Africa. We realized that by making the choices we did, we had just given ourselves two chances to be complete failures.

The realization hit us one day when Chris, Laura and I were hiking. It was a Sunday morning. Chris had Annika on his back in a carrier, their dog Tundra had joined us, and the sun was shining. There was not a cloud in the sky, the temperature was perfect, there was no wind, and we were surrounded by greenery and babbling brooks. It was an idyllic day! We were hiking along and chatting, wondering aloud whether the terrain we were hiking on would be similar to parts of Mount Kilimanjaro. Then one of us stepped on the conversational land mine. You know the one - when people are having a great time until someone says something that stops everyone in their tracks and brings the conversation to a sudden halt. Not surprisingly, none of us can remember who actually said it, but we all remember how it went: "Do you realize that, with all those people watching, it's a possibility that we will not accomplish either goal?" We continued on in silence, buried in our own thoughts.

We knew that everything could go south in a hurry. We could fail in our attempt to climb the mountain, and we could fail in raising money to support our cause. In fact, it was possible we might not only fail but fail miserably on both counts, and everyone would know because of the attention we would have to draw to ourselves for fundraising.

Of course there are risks involved in making choices. It goes without saying. Sometimes we make the right choices in life, and sometimes we don't. We just have to hope and trust that we make the right choices more often than not. When we do make the wrong choice, we just have to keep in mind that if we aren't making mistakes, then we aren't doing anything. Chris and I knew that once our choices were made, there would be no turning back. We were comforted by the fact that we would do everything in our power to ensure success on both counts.

Life is all about choices, especially in our part of the world. From the time we get up in the morning until we fall asleep at night, we are making choices. Some are relatively minor, like choosing what to eat for breakfast or what to wear – although the latter can be a difficult choice for some fashion-challenged individuals. Sometimes we are placed in situations where we have to make a choice; other times we create those situations for ourselves. It's not necessarily about whether we can or can't do something; it's about whether we will or won't. Climbing Mount Kilimanjaro was a choice that Chris and I voluntarily made. Our choice undoubtedly paled in comparison to many of the choices we are faced with in life, but it's easy to think the choices we are confronted with at any given moment are the biggest decisions anyone on the planet has ever made.

It has been my experience that we often spend valuable time agonizing over a decision and then exhaust even more time questioning the decision we have made or being jealous of a person who has made a different choice. Some people even take the decision to their death bed in the form of regret. I feel this is just too much wasted effort. Without a doubt, we need to perform a proper analysis of the situation before making the decision. But once the decision is made, it's made! What is done is done. Move on. I refuse to sit and look back and wish I had done something differently. Nothing is gained by it. If we decide the decision we make is the wrong one and it's possible to change it, by all means we should do so. But if the decision has been made and is irreversible, then it's time to stop thinking about it. Worrying, second-guessing and regretting can be debilitating.

If Chris had decided he couldn't go on the trip with me or if my cold had prevented me from making the climb, it would have been very difficult to put the disappointment behind me. But the decision would have been made for a reason, and I would have accepted it and move on. In spite of our deepest fears, we are satisfied that we completed the goal established by the first choice – to reach the peak of Mount Kilimanjaro – and we did it with hundreds of people observing our every move through our daily blogs.

I think delaying a decision can be equally debilitating. Sometimes our decision is to put off a decision for another day. Then another day turns into more days. This indecision can weigh heavily on us as well. Once all factors have been considered make a choice and live with it. All too often at the place where I used to work, I would see decisions postponed by senior executives so that "more study can be undertaken." It is paralysis by analysis. The real question that should be asked is, will postponing really help in this situation or does it only delay the inevitable? Indecision often leads to serious frustration and regret. I always try to make a decision as best I can – and then live with it.

I completely understand and respect those who choose to make the Mount Kili trek and focus only on their climb. Making the climb requires enough preparation, concentration and determination by itself without being distracted by other activities at the same time. The choice we made to use our climb as a platform to raise money meant that we would have to draw attention to what we were doing so that people would want to donate to our cause. Chris and I are relatively private people, so we would once again be outside our comfort zone. It meant that we would be putting our efforts on display for everyone to see, no matter what the outcome. If we didn't make it to Kili's summit, we would have to live with it as friends and supporters looked on. We decided that we wanted to provide daily updates to help publicize what we were doing; this meant that if we failed and had to turn back without reaching the top, people would know immediately in real time. While I didn't realize the extent of it at the time, our choice put added pressure on us because our fundraising would be dependent on people supporting us and cheering us on.

We had concerns, of course, about trying to raise money. We had never done this kind of thing before, and the mountain was our first priority. However, we also realized that we might never have another opportunity like this to help these deserving African children. They have no drinkable water; they have no schools in many cases. Chris and I made the choice to pursue the simultaneous goals of finding a project involving children in Tanzania and raising whatever money we could before our climb. People wondered if any of the money we raised would be used for funding our trip, but that was never the case. The thought never crossed our minds.

With the decision to raise money to help out the children came other choices. How would we go about doing this work? How much money could we raise? What agency would we partner with? Which specific projects would we support? How much effort would we put into them? There were many questions that needed answers, and they're addressed in the next part of this book.

Just before drifting off into much needed sleep in our room in Moshi, I think again about the multitude of choices we are faced with or that we deliberately put in front of us in the western world. For many others, choices are severely limited by virtue of being born in a different part of the world. How many choices do you have if you are a young teen who is the head of the house because your parents have died from HIV/AIDS or there aren't enough schools to provide the education you need or you have to walk over three miles (five kilometers) each way every day to fetch clean water?

Looking back at the last nine days, I have a strong sense that tomorrow my life is about to change once again, and that I'm about to undergo another and possibly even more life-changing adventure. It has been quite a journey thus far. Phase one of this wonderful adventure has been completed and we are now ready to take on the second phase. We are about to meet some unforgettable school children in Mwanza, Africa.

PART III

HOW DO WE TOP A MOUNTAIN (TOP)?

CHAPTER 21

It Was Another Eye-Opener

THERE IS A popular fable that has been making the rounds on the internet. It's so applicable to the second part of our journey that it's worth repeating here. The author is unknown.

A mouse looked through a crack in the wall to see the farmer and his wife opening a package. What food might this contain, the mouse wondered. He was devastated to discover it was a mousetrap. Retreating to the farmyard, the mouse proclaimed the warning: "There is a mousetrap in the house! There is a mousetrap in the house!" The chicken clucked and scratched, raised her head and said, "Mr. Mouse, I can tell this is a grave concern to you, but it is of no consequence to me. I cannot be bothered by it."

The mouse turned to the pig and told him, "There is a mousetrap in the house! There is a mousetrap in the house!" The pig sympathized, but said, "I am so very sorry Mr. Mouse, but there is nothing I can do about it but pray. Be assured you are in my prayers." The mouse turned to the cow and said, "There is a mousetrap in the house! There is a mousetrap in the house!" The cow said, "Wow, Mr. Mouse. I'm sorry for you, but it's no skin off my nose." So the mouse returned to the house, head down and dejected, to face the farmer's mousetrap alone.

That very night a sound was heard throughout the house — like the sound of a mousetrap catching its prey. The farmer's wife rushed to see what was caught. In the darkness, she did not see it was a venomous snake whose tail the trap had caught. The snake bit the farmer's wife. The farmer rushed her to the hospital, and she returned home with a fever. Everyone knows you treat a fever with fresh chicken soup, so the farmer took his hatchet to the farmyard for the soup's main ingredient. But his wife's sickness continued, so friends and neighbors came to sit with her around the clock. To feed them, the farmer butchered the pig.

The farmer's wife did not get well; in fact, she died. So many people came for her funeral that the farmer had the cow slaughtered to provide enough meat for all of them. The mouse looked upon it all from his crack in the wall with great sadness.

The moral of the story is very clear. The next time you hear about someone facing a problem and you think it doesn't concern you, remember — when one of us is threatened, we are all at risk. We're all involved in this journey called life. We must keep an eye out for each other and make an extra effort to encourage and help one another.

When one of us is threatened, we are all at risk. It bears repeating. Everyone is aware of the challenges facing Third World nations. The disparity between what we have in our countries and what they lack in theirs is shocking. And this lack of the necessities we take for granted eventually leads to frustration and despair. It's hard to know what to do or how to get involved. Chris and I realized after we had made our decision to climb Mount Kilimanjaro that we had an immense opportunity to make a difference. Believe me, we didn't know how to help when we started out, either. But we sensed that we could somehow get involved if we made the extra effort.

My son and I were just two ordinary people who were attempting to do something special by climbing a mountain. We thought we could leverage our personal experience into raising money for needy children in Africa, living relatively close to the mountain we would climb, but we had no idea how successful we might ultimately be. There is so much to do there. Could we *really* make a difference? There are lots of celebrities who make good use of their stature to do noteworthy things in the world. One needs to look no further for an example than Bono, lead singer of the rock band U2, who uses his celebrity status to bring attention to world hunger issues. And there's Al Gore former Vice President of the U.S., who uses his political stature to raise awareness of climate change.

Their stories, and many others like theirs, are well chronicled. These stories are motivational and inspirational, but they are beyond where most of us can or will ever go. They are about exceptional people blessed with extraordinary talent or abilities, and financial independence, doing amazing things. But I also realized that many of us gain our inspiration from stories of people we know or can relate to (including our own families), individuals who've done all that they can with the resources they have. Canadian hero Terry Fox, who ran across the country with one prosthetic leg, is a great example of an ordinary person who, even though struck by a fatal cancer, managed to raise awareness through sheer determination and will. But Chris and I didn't fit into these categories. We weren't celebrities. We didn't have social status. And we certainly didn't have unlimited financial resources! We asked ourselves over and over, what can we do as two ordinary people setting out to accomplish a remarkable personal goal halfway around the world? Could we make a difference?? Our answer somehow had to be yes.

In October of 2008, Chris and I brainstormed about what we could do and who it was we wanted to try to help. We both knew that we wanted to try to help children, but which ones and where? We decided that, if we were going to be walking all over their mountain, we should try to give something back specifically to the children of Tanzania. After a little research, it became very clear that even with the big tourism dollars pumped into the Tanzanian economy because of Kilimanjaro, there are still serious issues with orphan children, lack of education and clean water, HIV/AIDS and so on.

Armed with a better sense of where we could help, we sent emails to five agencies that are child centered and that we thought might be interested in partnering with us. Plan International Canada Inc. (Plan Canada) sent a response immediately indicating that they were intrigued by our suggestion. Evelyn and I were familiar with Plan Canada because we had been sponsoring a little boy in Guatemala through them for a number of years.

Plan Canada is part of Plan International. We liked what we read on the Plan International website, which states, "Founded in 1937, we are one of the world's oldest and largest international development agencies, working in partnership with millions of people around the world to end global poverty." They go on to say that "through programs in 66 countries, we give children, families and communities the tools they need to break the cycle of poverty and build sustainable solutions with measurable results for improving their own lives."

We were also impressed by their vision, which is of "a world in which all children realize their full potential in societies that respect people's rights and dignity." Finally, being accountants, we liked the idea that Plan International publishes voluntarily world-wide financial statements that clearly provide their combined financial position, results and cash flows.

Plan Canada's objectives closely matched what we wanted to do as they point out on their website that by investing in grassroots programs we could help local people build schools, train teachers, empower girls, dig wells…and much more. We receive updates from our sponsored child in Guatemala and have been encouraged to visit him so it wasn't difficult to make a phone call to Plan Canada to follow up on their expression of interest. They immediately suggested the idea of raising money towards building a classroom in a town called Mwanza, which was close enough to our home base in Moshi that it was workable for us in the time we had available. We wanted to visit the school where the classroom would be built in conjunction with our climb and Plan Canada's representatives readily agreed that they would arrange that for us as well.

Our overall approach to fundraising will be discussed later, but in short, we spoke to our friends and relatives, sent out a plethora of emails in September and created a web site and Facebook and Twitter pages. The results were beyond anything we expected. Chris and I discussed over and over what we thought we could raise. We decided to set our goal at $5,000 and hoped that we could achieve somewhere close to that. We knew we would be setting ourselves up for the failure we had discussed on the hiking trail a few weeks earlier. The thought was quickly dispelled as we reached our original goal in November!

The goal was then adjusted to $8,000 for the classroom and our donors again blew by that goal by the beginning of December. It became necessary to once again adjust our sights, so further discussion with Plan Canada came up with the goal of raising money to drill a borehole at another school – a preschool near Mwanza. A borehole is a narrow shaft drilled in the ground, in this case to extract water. We liked the idea that we would be providing access to clean water for some kids in the community so we agreed to the new goal. We continued our fundraising activities and by the time we left for Africa, we had raised over $15,000 and inscribed the names of all the donors on the Canadian flag.

So once again, Chris and I are sitting on an airplane but this time we are waiting to take off for Mwanza. It is early in the morning after our little celebration at the Indoitaliano Restaurant in Moshi. The flight from Moshi to Mwanza is only about an hour, and this time we are not filled with the anticipation of seeing a mountain. This time, we are filled with the anticipation of seeing how children in Africa are educated, and how they deal with their often-desperate situations. Frankly, we are once again unsure of what lies ahead of us, but we suspect it will be life-changing for us. Our plane touches down on schedule at what appears to us to be one of the smallest airports in the world. Mwanza is a town of about 500,000 and is a southern port of Lake Victoria. Its name is roughly translated as "lake."

Chris: If you were to look at Mwanza on a map, you would see that it is a city that borders on the edge of Lake Victoria, which is the largest body of water in Africa. Many people then immediately ask us why we would need to provide access to water when they are situated on the edge of the largest body of water on the continent. The answer is quite simple and it relates to what our travel doctor had told us before we left for Tanzania. He had said that we should not even put a finger in the lake! The water is not drinkable out *of that lake. It can be boiled to the point of being drinkable, but our time in Mwanza demonstrated almost immediately that the facilities to boil water in some areas were no more available than the cash to purchase bottled water.*

As we wait patiently for our driver who has been hired to pick us up at the Mwanza Airport, we watch people come and go, and the taxi drivers sitting around outside the airport smoking and waiting for fares. Several times we're approached by drivers hoping they can take us somewhere, but we wave them away, confident that our driver will arrive shortly. One hour turns into two, until finally we realize that something has gone wrong and no one is coming to pick us up. Chris and I decide that we'll go ahead and hire one of the drivers and catch a ride to the Hotel Talapia, which has been booked for us through Tusker Trail. The hotel is presumably named after one of the local fish.

We have no clue where the Hotel Talapia is situated in Mwanza, or how much the fare should be, but when the driver says the fare will be 15,000 Tanzania shillings (about $15), I remember Peter's story on the mountain about the not-so-extravagant meal that he paid for extravagantly. I had also read about bartering being expected, so I suggest the fare should be 12,000 shillings. The driver readily agrees, making me think that I probably should have offered only 10,000. There is a combination of housing along the road to the hotel. Most of it is dilapidated, the streets are dusty and grimy, and, as in Moshi, there are people everywhere going in all directions, all intent on reaching their destination. Most people are walking, though a small percentage of them are riding bicycles, and an even smaller number are riding in ancient vehicles. It is apparent that Mwanza is built on solid rock. In fact, we have been told that the region of Sangabuye, where the schools we will be visiting are located, is named from the words of a local fishing tribe. Its name is "nasangilemo mabuyiila," meaning, "I found only stones."

When we arrive at the hotel, we give the driver 15,000 shillings and, of course, predictably he says he doesn't have the cash to make change. We are out 3,000 shillings. (Why am I not surprised?!) We feign indignation and then check into the hotel. Our luggage consists of our backpacks with a change of clothing for the next day, the Canadian flag that survived the trip up and down Mount Kilimanjaro, two soccer balls and a pump. We are counting on the fact that our backpacks will be even lighter on the way home.

After we check into the hotel, we are picked up by a Plan Tanzania representative and transported to their offices where the schedule for our school visitations is finalized. We will be visiting a primary school within Mwanza the first day and then a preschool on the outskirts of Mwanza the second. Chris and I are both excited by the prospect of meeting the children of the schools in person.

We leave immediately for the primary school, and it isn't a long ride to get there. Once again, we travel through a poor area with run down shacks and bounce over a dirt road to make our way to the school. We come upon a small one-story blue and white painted brick building with a tin roof and a concrete veranda. We can see some eyes peering out at us above the window frame. When the eyes notice that we're looking back, the surrounding edges crinkle and we know that the unseen part of that little person's face below the windowsill has broken out into a big smile.

Although Chris and I are anxious to meet the children, we first meet the teachers, who seem very shy, and then the school administrators who tell us about the school. We spend some time talking with them at a picnic table outside the classroom and we discuss our project and the needs of the school. The numbers are astounding! They tell us that there are 225 Grade Two students and over 300 Grade Three students being educated in just two classrooms housed in that small blue and white building, and that more children are still registering! The students are educated in shifts, so that each can receive at least some education. They tell us that 12 classrooms would be needed to accommodate all the students in the school. The average family size in the area is 11, and the kids walk up to three miles or five kilometers each way to and from school. They mention that the teachers and kids share outdoor toilet facilities. The administrators make the disturbing comment that the "Wazungu" (plural Swahili word for white people) make promises to help, but often nothing happens. I know this is a common refrain throughout Third World countries, and it's one of the questions I had to answer for myself before undertaking fundraising activities. I don't want to be one of the empty promise-makers. I resolve to do everything I can to make sure this doesn't happen with our project.

There is a bit of a lull in the conversation, and Chris and I take the opportunity to make our presentation to the school administrators. It is a moment we've been waiting for since we started on our incredible journey. We explain how more than 200 Canadians felt so strongly about helping these students with their education that they have contributed money to our cause. We point out the names written on the flag that we had brought with us. We tell them how we prepared and succeeded in our quest to climb their mountain, Mount Kilimanjaro, and how we carried the flag with us every step of the way to the summit – and now to their school. We tell them that the only thing we ask in return is that the flag will someday be hung in the new classroom, once it's built. It is another emotional moment for us, and the Africans appear impressed and grateful for what we've done and for our promise to continue. The teachers show great interest in the names on the flag. They say that until the new classrooms are built, the flag will be hung with pride in the existing classroom. (And they are true to their word! A few months later, we receive a photo showing the flag hanging in the classroom.)

Then along comes yet another emotional moment that leaves us surprised and determined to do even more. We had brought two soccer balls with us to present as well. We wished we could have carried more balls, but we just didn't have extra room in our luggage with our hiking equipment. One of the soccer balls was donated by a friend from our local church. The other was given to us by another friend, who also gave us the pump. He had acquired the ball as a promotional giveaway inside a case of beer. I note how he came to have the ball not to diminish our appreciation for receiving it, but just to illustrate the depth of our surprise at what came next during our little presentation ceremony.

We decide to leave the soccer balls and pump with the kids at the primary school so we make the presentation to the Head Teacher. Her reaction is overwhelming. Her eyes glisten as she struggles to find words in English to express how she is feeling. She is unable to find the words and I find my own eyes filling with emotion. I am quickly coming to the conclusion that at age 60, this has become a trip of unbelievable discovery for me. I'd already had many emotional and eye-opening moments along the journey to Kilimanjaro, but this is burning yet another lasting impression into my mind. It is the juxtaposition of two severely-contrasting lifestyles that is the cause of a new awakening for me. It's like starting into my senior years, but looking through the eyes of our two-year-old granddaughter as every day brings her new meaning and new experiences. It is the effect that a simple soccer ball, acquired free of charge simply by buying a case of 24 bottles of beer in Canada, has on a school teacher at a primary school half a world away.

Chris: Seeing the look in the Head Teacher's eyes when she received the soccer ball will be etched into my mind for as long as I'm alive. The fact that we were able to provide so much joy from something so seemingly trivial is really something to behold. I think about all of the toys my daughters have, and how — if they were to receive a soccer ball they wouldn't think twice about it and probably would forget about it within a few minutes once they see another toy. But here in Africa, being able to give the soccer ball and have the Head Teacher on the brink of tears is really amazing. This was just one more moment in a long list of moments that made me stop dead in my tracks and rethink things in my life so I can see more clearly what is really important. I don't consider my children to be spoiled by North American standards but by the *standards of this community, my kids have more toys than all of the children that attend this school in a year put together, I'm sure. It is something to think about at Christmas and birthdays. In fact, my wife and I have discussed the idea of only taking donations instead of toys for our daughters' birthdays.*

The truth of the matter is, we are all equal as human beings, but we don't all start out with a fair and equal playing field. These underprivileged children and their teachers make do with what would be considered unacceptable conditions in our country. The realization that we are forced to value things differently by virtue of where we are born is overwhelming! It is truly a situation in which a person's lot in life is determined solely by circumstance, not by choice. And it makes me vow with even more determination and dedication to do everything in my power to help make a difference.

CHAPTER 22

The Kids Are Alright!

AFTER THE INITIAL shock of seeing the impact that one soccer ball could have, we inflate it with the pump and walk into the classroom. While the teachers had told us about the huge numbers of children being educated at the school, we are still not prepared for what we see. Some of the children are seated two or three to a small desk, but most are seated on the floor. There are well over a hundred Grade Two students crammed shoulder to shoulder in the small room. While it's upsetting to see so many kids in one room, I feel a mixture of admiration and optimism as we stand at the front of the room watching them. I see their strength and courage, and think to myself, "We can *do* something for these kids!"

We don't inquire about the dress code at the time, but there is obviously one in effect as most are wearing white shirts and green skirts or pants. We are aware that Africans view a dress code in schools as a means to imbue a culture of respectability throughout the community and eliminate distinctions among students. We later noted an example of a dress code in a 2009-2010 Secondary School Handbook, which provided the following excerpted dress code expected for students attending International School Moshi:

1. *A smart, collared sleeved shirt or t-shirt (without inappropriate labels or slogans) or sleeved blouse to cover most of the upper torso, i.e. no exposed midriff or chest, no exposed underwear.*

2. *Trousers, shorts or skirt. Pants/trousers must be worn around the waist without exposed underwear.*
3. *Shoes, leather sandals or leather malapas are allowed. No plastic or rubber malapas (flipflops).*

The students welcome us very politely in English. The official language is Kiswahili, which is used for instruction in primary school and is taught as a subject. Students learn English starting in grade three, but the grade two students we are meeting have obviously been primed. English is the language of instruction in secondary schools and other institutions of higher learning. Primary school textbooks are written in Kiswahili.

The conversation which ensues after our welcome is in Kiswahili (translated to English for us), and the teacher mentions to them that we have brought a soccer ball with us. She tosses it out among the kids. They laughingly fight over the ball, but even the kids who are on the outside of the chaos that ensues are smiling broadly. There doesn't appear to be any jealousy that the ball landed among one group and not another. We had also brought a laminated world map with us, and we are asked to say a few words to the children. I am proud to do so, but I'm really not prepared to say anything. I say a few words in English while the teacher translates.

Unfortunately, my Swahili was – and is still — mostly limited to "jambo" (hello) and "pole" (slowly). I had already used the first, and the second is of little use in this conversation. Chris's Swahili vocabulary includes the same two words, plus he now knows the translation for "warm water for washing" and "water for drinking" which he learned and put to good use on the mountain. His understanding of the language is of little help here. With the use of the map, I show the children where we live all the way on the other side of the world, and I explain why we are here. They listen with big smiles and then salute us with the back of their hand facing forward and their thumb to their forehead. We are told the greeting means "Welcome."

Next we are escorted to the second classroom of grade three students, and encounter more of the same. The classroom is severely overcrowded, another indication that more classrooms are desperately required. Clearly, we have made the right decision in our commitment to raise funds for more classrooms at the primary school.

Once we have finished our visit at the school, we are transported through time back to our room at the Hotel Talapia. Situated on the shores of Lake Victoria, it presents the ambiance you get when you arrive at a Caribbean sun destination and drive from the airport through rundown, poverty-stricken areas to an all-inclusive resort. It is a little piece of luxury seated among the poorest of the poor. The owner of the hotel has a Rolls Royce, Saab and a couple of antique cars on display near the office. We are told that they can be rented for weddings, but it is doubtful that any of the locals would be able to afford them. The room is large with a flat screen TV on the wall. Save for the mosquito netting hanging over the bed, we could be in a decent hotel in the West.

As we sit in the open air dining room on this clear, warm evening, overlooking the pool on one side and Lake Victoria on the other, it is difficult to believe that only a few blocks away, life exists just as it is depicted in the rather depressing Academy Award nominated documentary, *Darwin's Nightmare*. In this documentary, Director Hubert Sauper describes the depressing side of life in Mwanza with kids sniffing glue and girls and women supporting their families by selling themselves or putting some sort of food on the table by picking through the leftover carcasses of the fish that are exported to Europe. There are families nearby living in the shadows of our hotel whose eldest teenagers must care for their brothers and sisters because their parents have both died of HIV/AIDs. For Chris and me, as we look out on what appears to be the pristine water of Lake Victoria, it is very hard to imagine that children are dying from waterborne diseases every day, simply because they have no access to clean water. The water situation is clearly supported in a statement by UN Secretary-General Ban Ki-moon coinciding with World Water Day on March 22, 2010, when he said that more people die from unsafe water than from all forms of violence, including war. None of these problems will be solved in a few days, but we become even more acutely aware that the clean water and education projects we are working on will help children of future generations and (dare we hope) create leaders who can lead them out of their current situation.

We arise the next morning ready to meet a younger group of school kids and anxious to drive to the country where their school is located. We haven't seen much of rural Africa yet, and we're looking forward to the opportunity. We realize that our time is too short. It's difficult to absorb everything we are seeing, and we realize this can't be our only visit: a future trip with more time will be necessary. We also realize that we are probably doing ourselves a disservice by visiting the schools so soon after having spent nine days on a mountain. The physical aftermath and resulting fatigue of the climb was probably leaving some questions unasked and some sights unseen, but we would just have to make do.

We jump into the Plan Tanzania vehicle for another bumpy ride; this time 40 minutes to the preschool, the house of learning for some children in the Mwanza region. The trip gives us the opportunity to observe the countryside near Mwanza, although our driver is travelling a little bit faster than the road should allow. Passing is an adventure on the roads, as drivers will take every opportunity to move a car length or two ahead. Often we find ourselves on the wrong side of the road racing towards an oncoming vehicle. No one seems capable of driving without a horn – they're used incessantly to warn oncoming vehicles to get out of our way, even as they barrel directly towards us. We miss cyclists by mere inches along the way. No one seems to mind. All I can assume is that the same scenario is played out every hour of every waking day and night, and that eventually, your nerves just adapt.

Along our drive, we see workers in the fields tending their rice paddies. We pass tiny farm buildings and yards far too small to house the traditionally-large families that we're sure live in them. The buildings we see are made of mud with thatched roofs and often require repair, although we learn that processes are being developed to fire more durable bricks from local clay using agricultural waste. There are gaunt goats and cattle in the yards. On our left as we approach the school is

Lake Victoria. Several million people live within 50 miles of Lake Victoria, making it the most densely populated area in Africa. They survive on fishing and agriculture. The preschool sits within a few hundred yards of the shores of Lake Victoria, the largest lake in Africa with fishing boats dotting its shores. Yet, unbelievably, there is no clean water for the children or the community.

The preschoolers are four to six years old, and what a wonderful group they are! They are all invited out to the playground to pose for pictures, and they gather around behind us, practically shoving us out into the gravel parking lot in their enthusiasm. One little girl can't stop staring at me until her teacher forcibly averts her gaze by turning the little girl's head towards the front. My thought is that either she is amused by the fact I am a Mzungu (white person), or she is interested in my glasses. Or possibly it's because my forehead is still peeling in layers from the windburn I had received on Mount Kilimanjaro. Maybe she had never seen anyone's face fall off before!

We note the teacher's office is one austere room in which a desk and two chairs just fit. After the photo session, the kids are turned loose into the playground, which consists of an open field with razor wire around the outside and one slide and a swing. We are told that the razor wire is to keep out two-legged and four-legged predators. That seems to contrast dramatically with the number of kids we saw walking alone to school – a distance of up to five kilometers. Some of the kids wear the green uniforms, which seem to be hand-me-downs from siblings since they are falling off at the shoulders. Most wear traditional clothing. The majority of the kids have no shoes. But in spite of whatever hardships they endure, they are engaging and melt the heart with a smile. Some smile shyly and others broadly, but they smile. They bump fists with us as we pass by and they hold "thumbs up" for the cameras. We hear the word, "Mzungu" one more time as it is used to generate good natured laughter from the kids during the photo shoot. Hmmm…I wish I could understand Swahili!

The well for which we are raising money will be drilled within the fenced playground and remain locked at certain times of the day, but will be available for use by the local community. It will be administered by a community committee, including youth representation. There have been heated debates worldwide about establishing a global "right to water." As an ordinary citizen of the world, all I know from visiting the kids at the school is that they require clean water and sanitary conditions just as we do. They certainly have access to water — but the key word is "clean." They have no choice but to live with what they have, but to us, watching as outsiders, we see a desperate need. These young children need to know they will have clean water so they can focus on being children, gain an education, and one day help influence their community and country in a positive way in the future. It's pretty difficult to grow up and become a leader of your community if you are worried about where your next drink of water is going to come from.

The kids are happy now as they are only starting to become aware of their surroundings. The grade two and three students are filled with youthful enthusiasm and dreams that they will become doctors, lawyers and teachers when the facts are not optimistic. According to statistics received from Plan Canada, only 6% of children in Tanzania enroll in secondary school and only 76% of these children will reach the fifth grade. The overall statistics for the nation are even more staggering. Almost 58% of the population lives on less than $1 per day and the life expectancy is only 49 years – compared to 80 years in Canada and the United States.

It will be difficult for the children to remain enthusiastic under these circumstances. Put yourself in their situation for a moment. Consider how you would react if it were you or your own children without adequate clean water for daily living. It won't take you long to realize that, given the same circumstances, you would quickly become despondent and frustrated with your lot in life. In my opinion, the deplorable living conditions, coupled with the lack of clean water and education, can only exacerbate the cycle of human suffering and the resultant frustration and anger. And as I wrote earlier in this book, when one of us is threatened, we are all at risk.

CHAPTER 23

Why Should I Care?

WE WERE VERY fortunate to have the opportunity to visit the schools in Tanzania. We learn so much by seeing how others live and react to the situation they have found themselves in. Generally, Westerners are unbelievably fortunate to have the opportunities that we do, as well as the means to change things if they need improvement. That is not to say that our governments necessarily react as quickly or as often as we would like them to, but the resources are available to do so. Seeing the African kids in their native environment and watching them deal with their situation is awe-inspiring.

As a result of our school visits, Chris and I came away with a new perspective about the critical necessity for clean water and education. Chris and I focused on Tanzania because of our Mount Kilimanjaro climb, but of course, the same needs and wants are prevalent in many other countries. There is a severe lack of access to the basics in life throughout many third world nations. But we didn't completely understand how closely our two projects were tied together until we visited the schools. It turned out there is a direct link between clean water and education that may not be obvious at first.

There is no one better to explain the affect that clean water has on education than someone who has lived it. Our friend Richard Tibandebage sums it up this way: "*From the perspective of a Tanzanian like me, Barry and Chris could not have chosen nobler causes to support than education and water supply. Both are among man's most fundamental needs and, for Tanzanians, their significance is best exemplified in two of the most frequently quoted Swahili adages: 'Elimu ni ufunguo wa maisha' (Education is the key to one's life) and 'Maji ni uhai' (Water is life). Yet they are in very short supply for us. In Canada, as in many other western countries, education and water are readily available and, generally, whoever wants to access them can do so. They are there and you take them for granted. Alas, not so in Tanzania. For us, one has to strive, or be lucky, to have ready access to education* ***and*** *water, and in many places the shortage of water has a direct effect on the education and upbringing of children. In urban areas, the huge numbers of people moving to towns are straining the systems of water supply to the breaking point. For example, in our largest city of Dar es Salaam, an estimated 3 million inhabitants rely on a system that was designed to cater for less than half a million. But the situation is worse in rural areas where the majority of people do not have access to clean water. I can vividly relate to the situation in rural areas because I grew up in a village and I return there every year. The situation is as it was 50 years ago, and is similar to villages elsewhere in Tanzania. Water has to be fetched,* **always by women and school-age children**, *from as far away as 5 kilometers or more. Invariably, they have to go down steep hills to the water springs, and then climb up the hills carrying 18-litre (almost 40 pounds) containers of water on the head. For the children, this chore has to be done after school, using time that would have otherwise been devoted to study, home work or more pleasant activities like games and sports. And if they are lucky to avoid going down steep hills because there is a stream flowing nearby, what they fetch is very probably water that has already flowed through other villages with no sanitation, and where cattle, goats and sheep will have had a share of the same stream. In short, what they get is water that is not fit for human use.*

One can therefore understand the significance of what Barry and his family are doing. Thanks to them, some lucky school-age children in Tanzania will have access to clean water and, by having this precious commodity, will have better chances of growing up healthy, and have more time to study or partake in other nourishing activities that children of their age enjoy elsewhere. In other words, clean water is facilitating conditions that will increase the children's chances of growing up as healthy, learned and dependable members of the community. I can't think of a better gift than this!"

Author Greg Mortenson points out in his book, *Stones into Schools* the importance of education for the girls who are spending their time gathering water: "Simply put, young women are the single biggest potential agents of change in the developing world – a phenomenon that is sometimes referred to as the Girl Effect and that echoes an African proverb I often heard during my childhood years in Tanzania: 'If you teach a boy, you educate an individual; but if you teach a girl, you educate a community.' No other factor even comes close to matching the cascade of positive changes triggered by teaching a single girl how to read and write."

The Tanzanians certainly recognize the importance of education. The National Website of the United Republic of Tanzania notes that it "realizes that quality education is the pillar of national development, for it is through education that the nation obtains skilled manpower to serve in various sectors in the nation's economy. It is through quality education Tanzania will be able to create a strong and competitive economy which can effectively cope with the challenges of development and which can also easily and confidently adapt to the changing market and technological conditions in the region and global economy." The evidence of the need is irrefutable. The question is, how do we — as ordinary people at the grassroots level — find a way to address a need that is so huge? Surely it is impossible to accomplish! Or is it?

Crowded classroom (2009)

Presenting the soccer ball (2009)

With the preschoolers (2009)

Purchasing new school books for the primary school (2011)

New classrooms at primary school (2011)

Signing the guestbook (2011)
Shannon Singh (Plan Canada), Evelyn, Barry, Doris Chalambo (Plan Tanzania)

Demonstrating a yo-yo in front of 400 kids can be intimidating (2011)

Tanzanian and Canadian flag side by side in the new classroom (2011)

Planting a tree at the primary school (2011)

A new borehole pumping water (2011)

CHAPTER 24

Myth Understood

WHEN CHRIS AND I made our decision to start actively helping others (and specifically the children of Tanzania), we discovered that there were questions. Boy, were there questions, and not only from others. *We* asked ourselves questions. The fundraising exercise that we undertook and continue to undertake forced me to examine some of the issues that surround fundraising for worthy causes. Although people are incredibly generous by nature and want to donate, they aren't always completely comfortable that their money will do the good it is intended to do. Donating money into a big ambiguous pot and relying on organizations (corporate or otherwise) to disperse it properly is worrisome to many people. They prefer to know the specific purpose to which the money will be directed.

I was able to satisfy myself with most of the answers I came up with. A Fraser Institute's study entitled *Generosity in Canada and the United States: The 2007 Generosity Index*, points out that 30.6 % of U.S. tax filers and 25.1 % of Canadian tax filers donate to charity. When the purpose of the funds is focused, such as the Haitian earthquake disaster, people are inclined to contribute even more. World Vision is a Christian relief, development and advocacy organization dedicated to working with children, families and communities to overcome poverty and injustice. World Vision launched campaigns on Facebook and Twitter during the Haiti relief effort, and one of their spokespersons was quoted as saying that the number of donations that were made following the country's catastrophic earthquake was 10 times greater than usual. Perhaps the late Helen Keller said it best: "Although the world is full of suffering, it is full also of the overcoming of it."

We discovered that one of the keys to fundraising is passion. If the fundraiser is passionate about a project, it's considerably easier to convince others to be passionate as well. It was important to me that I was comfortable enough with what I was doing that I could share my passion and pass it on to others. I knew this would be the only way to generate the funds we would need for our projects. On the other hand, philosopher and inventor Benjamin Franklin also made an important point when he wrote, "If passion drives you, let reason hold the reins."

The only way I could be passionate was to develop confidence that I was doing the right things, so I undertook to answer my own questions about fundraising. Perhaps the answers I was able to come up with will help others when they undertake projects of their own or contribute to projects with the satisfaction that their money is being put to good use.

Let's start with the issue of cynicism. One of the most consistent questions arises from the cynicism generated by certain agencies that have been less than transparent about their activities. People have real concern that the money they contribute doesn't go for its advertised purpose. We found that there are ways to find out about an organization's transparency. With our accounting backgrounds, Chris and I knew we'd want to work with a fundraising agency that publishes worldwide consolidated financial statements, which would help to ensure transparency of expenditures and overall operations. We also expected a reputable child-centered organization to encourage donors to meet the families and to visit the communities that are benefitting from the monies raised to observe the end result of the fundraising activities. We wanted to receive regular progress reports from the agency about our projects. In our case, we also knew we'd be able to get periodic updates on the progress of our projects from the administrators in Tanzania who would be overseeing the projects and could send us photographs and reports. We were satisfied that our money would indeed go towards our designated projects. We understood that donors would be asking us these same questions about how their money was being used, and we felt we were fully prepared to answer them.

The second most commonly-asked question relates to administrative costs. There's a common view that agencies take a substantial proportion of donated funds for their own overhead in the form of salaries, travel, meals, bonuses, and so on for the Executive Director and staff. And unfortunately, whenever an agency does occasionally make headlines for misuse or misapplication of funds, the ensuing controversy fuels the fires of doubt and negative reaction. The fact of the matter is that agencies do require support, so there are always some overhead costs. But what is considered exorbitant? Fortunately, there is a control agency overseeing what charitable organizations do. Tax collection agencies, such as the Canada Revenue Agency (CRA) exert certain controls on charitable organizations so they can maintain their charitable status. Furthermore, anyone contributing money is perfectly within their rights to ask an agency how the decisions are made on how funds are allocated and which causes will be beneficiaries.

In the beginning, one of our main decisions was where to focus our attention. It is not an easy decision. There is no such thing as the "wrong" charity, and there are thousands of worthy causes to choose from. There are also plenty of issues in our own communities that deserve financial support — and people constantly asked Chris and me why we weren't supporting these issues instead of a cause thousands of miles away in Africa. For instance, a Salvation Army report recently announced that approximately one in 10 Canadians live in poverty. There are many more examples of local issues, not to mention all the international issues and natural disaster relief efforts requiring enormous amounts of cash. (As we continued our fundraising activities, catastrophes occurred in Haiti, Chile and Pakistan that received an outpouring of financial support from around the world.)

We were passionate about "our situation in Africa." We knew they lacked the means to improve their future, so we chose to make this our focal fundraising point. But sadly, it's easy to get distracted from a goal, no matter how worthy it is. We were hosting a fundraising event shortly after the earthquake in Haiti struck. I wondered if we should redirect whatever funds we raised at our event to assist in this new disaster. But then I realized there will always be a need somewhere; and just because there's a new disaster somewhere in the world does not remove the importance of the original cause or project. I saw that it was important for us not to take our eye off the ball. We needed to stay focused and on track if we were ever going to be able to raise money for the poor school children of Tanzania whose faces and spirit remained indelibly burned in my mind.

And then there's the question of general corruption where Third World countries and governments are involved. No one specifically directed their concern about donating to our cause toward the Tanzanian government — but our activities did generate the question. Certainly, we have all become aware of corruption in various forms on this side of the ocean so it is not endemic to Third World nations. Martin Luther King once said, "Intelligence plus character - that is the goal of true education." Education is crucial to creating future generations of leaders in Tanzania (and elsewhere) who will have the intelligence plus the character to ensure that the common people are treated with respect. We felt strongly that providing educational opportunities for kids anywhere and everywhere in the world could ultimately play a role in reducing the cycle of corruption, and possibly violence, so for us, the argument that funds should be withheld where corruption might be prevalent was not a valid one.

Then there is the question about whether or not a Third World country can properly care for a school building or a well once it's funded and put in place. This question was supplemented by cynical comments such as: *It's their fault that they are in the situation they're in and it will probably never change.* However, most people welcome education. As Greg Mortenson notes in his book, *Stones Into Schools,* the Afghans welcomed the opportunity to train their children, and especially the girls. In my opinion, it's important that the community is not just "given" a school. Local involvement in the project is essential to a buy-in by the whole community, making long-term success much more likely. I will always remember how much I appreciated my childhood baseball glove because I had to earn it. It still would have meant a lot to me had I been given it, but I would have had more of a sense of entitlement. I'm a strong believer in working for what you receive. And ironically, that's what made scaling the summit of Mount Kilimanjaro so special. Had we been magically placed there by helicopter, the views would still have been great — but there would have been no feeling of satisfaction. By the same token, I felt it was important that the local people in Tanzania have a hand in the projects we were undertaking. We were encouraged that part of the plan for drilling the borehole was to "train a water committee" and that construction of the school would involve a "community awareness program." We felt this would make people take more pride in the project and that they would be more inclined to care for what *they* had built.

It was also important to me that the agency we were going to work with not force Western values and attitudes on a Third World country. Who is to say that our ways are necessarily better than any others, or that most long-standing Tanzanian social traditions shouldn't be encouraged? In my opinion, westernized countries should share their advancements to help others develop and improve, not change or eradicate their cultures completely. Our role, as I see it, is to offer assistance and to ensure that the recipients are pro-actively involved in any projects we undertake for them.

Then there is the question of addressing only the symptoms rather than solving the underlying problem. For example, with our well-drilling project, the comment was made that drilling a bunch of holes in the ground does not solve the overall problem of water contamination. Well, I certainly can't argue with that. It would be great to be able to address *that* problem. But let's take Africa's Lake Victoria as an example. The preschool and community we visited sits on the edge of Lake Victoria, yet they cannot use it as a source of clean water. It is polluted by discharge of raw sewage into the lake, the dumping of domestic and industrial waste, and infiltration of fertilizer and chemicals from farms. The lake is bordered by three countries - Tanzania, Uganda and Kenya. It's the largest lake in Africa and the largest tropical lake in the world. Yet it is beset by problems. Invasive plants clog lake waterways. There is a floating maze of shoulder-high reeds along the shores, making them difficult to navigate. Millions of farmers use the lake as a source of water, thereby reducing water supplies. Dams are being constructed, causing changes in water flow and water reductions in certain areas and erosion caused by reforestation is changing the nature of the water. According to the movie *Darwin's Nightmare* the introduction of the Nile Perch into the lake in the 1960s resulted in a reduction in the native species of fish and created a situation whereby perch are exported to western countries in exchange for arms to fuel wars on the continent!

The problems with Lake Victoria are huge. They are still not insurmountable but they are not solvable by you or me. In the meantime, children sicken and die from waterborne diseases. American short-story writer, poet and novelist Charles Bukowski wrote, "You begin saving the world by saving one person at a time; all else is grandiose romanticism or politics." It's romantic to think that we can save everyone in Tanzania, Uganda and Kenya, but the situation with Lake Victoria requires the political will of the three nations (and possibly with huge financial assistance from the West). It's surely out of our league at the grassroots level. But what we *can* focus on, contribute to and be proud of, is saving or at least changing the lives of a handful of people by providing the clean water they require.

Things do happen very slowly in Third World nations, and donors will sometimes get the impression that nothing is being done. With technology has come the expectation that everything should happen immediately. Our experience was not that way in Africa. Things *do* happen; they just take longer. Patience is requisite when dealing with an African nation!

The final question Chris and I asked ourselves was whether or not we should establish a foundation for our fundraising activities. A foundation may become necessary at some point in the future, but I still struggle a little with the number of fundraising agencies that seem to be doing similar things.

Creating another foundation would lead to another layer of administrative costs. For now, I believe I can accomplish the same goals by directing the funds generated by our activities to the particular project we are passionate about at the time. And just as we expect an agency to be, we will be very transparent as to where the money will be going.

It is true there seem to be a number of child-centered agencies doing work in the field. I pick on them only because that is our area of interest but the potential duplication is never more apparent than when a natural disaster strikes. The media plays up delays in reaction time at the beginning as a "Keystone Cops" scenario, with everyone running around trying to figure out who should be doing what. For example, there are stories of aid packages piling up at airports while workers are getting frustrated and people are dying. But the logistics of hitting the ground running and moving people and supplies when there is a natural disaster all of a sudden in a distant, and often remote part of the world, are massive. While it appears there is duplication among agencies, they all apparently assist in their own way. I am sure the same can be said of child-centered organizations as there can never be too much help for those in need. Would consolidation of agencies reduce overhead and the time it takes to deliver aid where it needs to go? I haven't sorted out an answer to the question in my own mind yet and probably never will. It is something that should be under constant scrutiny so that the help is getting to its intended purpose as quickly and efficiently as possible and so that the reaction time is just that much better each time a disaster occurs.

We satisfied ourselves that we were doing what we were comfortable with and that we could explain it to everyone who asked. The results were astonishing to me as I never expected to accomplish what we did. It is work in progress for me as I continue to learn every day about the world of fundraising and what it takes to help those so desperately in need. In the next chapter I will explore what worked and what didn't. I am just thankful that most things we tried did work and some children in Tanzania will be that much better off as a result.

CHAPTER 25

Okay, How Can I Help?

THE MASSIVE DONATIONS and the overwhelming contributions of time and resources to the many natural disasters that have occurred over the last several years demonstrate that people will really step up, particularly when the need is focused. Based on what has transpired, it's easy to see that in times of disaster people want to contribute, but they're much more inclined to do so when they can see a direct need that's identifiable. With a little more effort and when one feels strongly enough about a cause, it is possible to step beyond strictly donating into the world of philanthropy.

Philanthropy is a planned strategic approach to giving. It requires the identification of a cause that one feels strongly about and the establishment of a plan to address that goal, coupled with ongoing monitoring and follow-up. Philanthropy implies a long-term commitment, vision and continuous effort, but it's also extremely rewarding. While I didn't realize it until recently, Chris and I have somehow slipped into the world of philanthropy as our approach has become a strategic effort requiring commitment, monitoring and all the other terms in the definition. It has also become very rewarding!

Two things happened during our visit to the schools in Mwanza that left me with the feeling of unfinished work that had to be completed. The first was the feeling of optimism that came over me there. The second was the comment that people often make promises but rarely deliver. I wanted to be the exception to that comment! I felt that there was cautious enthusiasm for our projects among the school administrators and maybe some skepticism from the teachers in Mwanza. I can visualize visitors being invited to the schools and being swept up in the same enthusiasm and desire to help that we were. I can hear promises being made with the best of intentions and I completely understand that people fully believe that they will do something when they get home. Then on the flight back, reality sets in and when they disembark from the plane, daily responsibilities and family obligations once again take over their lives. Maybe they do make contributions, but nowhere near the promises that were made. It is human nature to want to help, but the reality is that many people don't have that luxury to do as much as they want – or as is needed. We've all been in situations where promises have been made to us and broken. We can remember how disappointed we were. Imagine if it were the possibility of clean water or improved education at stake. I'll just say that I would caution visitors to communities requiring assistance to make only promises that can be kept, or better yet, to make small promises and then surprise the recipients with more. To do anything less than this causes dashed hopes and genuine disappointment.

Once we returned to Canada, Chris and I were happily surprised by the number of people who wanted to be involved in our project. Initially, we'd been given an idea by a member of Plan Canada's staff who had climbed Mount Kilimanjaro herself, carrying a Canadian flag to the peak with the names of donors on it. We'd hoped the idea would work for us and with her permission, we borrowed the idea and adapted it for our climb. In the beginning, we thought our success might have been driven by the prospect of people having their name placed on a Canadian flag on its way to the peak of Mount Kilimanjaro and then hung afterwards in a school in Africa. And I am sure that was part of it. But it was much more than that.

When we returned and continued with our fundraising efforts, people remained interested. They asked us for updates and kept on donating. The real answer to our support, we believe, is that we had *been* to the project site, *met* the kids and *told* our story. In doing so, we saw firsthand how inadequate the children's school was, and how desperate their need and dependence upon fresh water truly was. We could describe a tangible need, share our conviction and passion, and light a fire under those with whom we spoke. We told people about each new progress report we'd receive, and let them know we would be going back to see the results. People were reassured that their money would be put to its intended purpose. (Admittedly, some people are probably getting tired of hearing about our story, but most are very receptive.)

Fundraising is not a competitive sport, but there are a lot of organizations competing for the same resources of press, time and money. It can be frustrating at times, and both Chris and I have had moments of discouragement along the way, wanting to do so much but not knowing how much we could actually accomplish. Still, in the end, we always managed to overcome any disappointments that have arisen along the way.

Some things we tried worked; others didn't. Chris and I approached mainstream newspapers to try to draw some attention to our project in the early stages, before we left for our trip, and had an interesting conversation with one reporter in a conference call. The reporter started by asking what our storyline was. We said that we would be climbing Mount Kilimanjaro and that we were raising money to build a classroom and drill a well at schools in Tanzania. He asked what else there was. We said, "Well, we are a father and son team working together to accomplish our goals. The reporter said, "Oh good, are you bonding?" We told him that if he meant did we have problems previously and were we going to sort them out on the mountain, the answer was "no." We weren't climbing Mount Kilimanjaro in a last-ditch attempt to salvage a rocky father/son relationship. We told him we'd had had typical father and son issues over the years and would probably have more on the mountain, but we would not be bonding in the "reconciliation" sense of the word. The reporter said, "Okay, what else can I use as a storyline?" By this time, we were getting a little frustrated, but I said, "I will be turning 60 just before the climb. How about this?" He replied, "Well, that's interesting, but older people have done things like this. Anything else? What do you do for a living?" We said,

"We're accountants." He said, "Oh." And that was pretty much the end of the conversation.

Chris: My recollection of that conversation was that the fact we were accountants was the most exciting part of the trip from his perspective – and that is a scary thought.

In my opinion, this reporter completely missed the point. We were ordinary people attempting to do something extraordinary with our own lives and those of others. Unfortunately, there aren't enough stories about how ordinary people can make a difference, because it's the people working at the grassroots level who can collectively accomplish the most. But that doesn't always make for glamorous or exciting storylines in the newspapers.

Chris and I undertook to raise money with a very modest goal of contributing to a classroom. Our modest goal quickly developed into something much bigger; as money started to come in we found fundraising activities that worked for us. We continued to get wonderful support from Plan Canada: they've been supportive in everything we've asked of them. Obviously, it's to their benefit to be supportive since *anything* we raise benefits their programs but their staff has been incredibly easy to work with and very capable. Perhaps I'm a bit jaded by my many years of working in the federal bureaucracy, but having someone get back to me immediately with answers to my questions was a luxury I wasn't accustomed to!

In the early stages of our mission, it was important to draw attention to the fundraising projects; today, it continues to be important. It was obvious from our conversation with the disinterested reporter that attracting the attention of the mainstream news wasn't going to be easy. However, every city usually has at least one community television station that covers local initiatives, and we found that they welcome the opportunity to present "feel good" stories from ordinary people. I learned just how many people actually watch local programming on community stations. It's a shame that under-funding is always an issue for local stations, and many struggle to survive on limited budgets. These community outlets play an incredibly vital role in getting the message out about local initiatives, and it would be a sad day indeed for local communities if they do disappear.

Chris and I quickly learned that a radio or television interview often seemed to last mere seconds when we were actually talking to the interviewer for two or three minutes. We found it was really important to have our message clearly in our minds, so viewers and listeners would care, and we also learned that sometimes we needed to take control of the interview in order to get our message across when the questioning wasn't going in that direction. In our case, interviewers were always interested in hearing about the dramatic parts of our climb, asking if we were ever in real danger, whether we had to take oxygen or, believe it or not, where we went to the bathroom on the mountain. What we wanted to get across is that we were preparing to hold a fundraiser in the coming months. As interviewees, we had to learn how to steer the conversation in the direction we wanted in a very short period of time, so that our message and information got delivered before the end of the interview. It wasn't always easy!

Keeping our friend the "couldn't-care-less" reporter in mind, we relied on smaller community newspapers for our print coverage. Once again, we were amazed at the press we received, and the number of comments from people who had actually read the articles. Community newspapers are always looking for interesting stories to cover; besides local politics, charitable events seem to be their bread and butter. I contacted each one in our area, and we received excellent coverage from every one. They always like to include photos with their stories, so we made sure to provide them with pictures both from our climb and from the fundraising events we held. What's that they say . . . a picture is worth a thousand words? We sure found that to be true!

To augment the coverage we received from the community radio, TV and print media, we also took advantage of the social media outlets on the internet. Through the help of a volunteer, we immediately created a web page for our fundraising project, and then found someone who was able to host our site at a reasonable rate. We utilized both Facebook and Twitter as heavily as possible. Hundreds of people became fans and followers of our project, and event pages were created to inform people of our activities. We sent out brief reminders on Twitter to keep people updated on our activities and to stoke their interest. Twitter can be a bit limiting, not because of posting size restrictions but because so many people are using it. The posts are only available for a few minutes at most before they are replaced by more current posts. But we found we could also use social media to express our thanks to donors, participants and volunteers after an event was over.

I also have a blog that I use liberally to make people aware of our fundraising activities. Blogs require some work to maintain, because you have to continually update content as people visit your site online. But I like the fact that I have complete control of the blog. It's fast, it's current, and it's personal. There's no waiting around on someone to update your website. Pictures and video can be added to help ensure that people will keep coming back. I've been fortunate to link my blog to Plan Canada, so that secure donations can be made directly through them, and tickets for our various events can be purchased securely online. Any email I send out has my blog address as part of the signature block as a constant reminder to friends and family to view the blog. And I never forget to send thanks to those who are supporting our initiative.

Thanking people is so important. When people are willing to give up some of their precious time to help out, it's so important that they feel appreciated. We have had many people involved in our projects. I'm sure if they didn't feel appreciated for their efforts, they would soon become disappointed and move on. In fact, I had one volunteer and friend who didn't feel I was appreciative enough and she did, in fact, move on. Sometimes there can never be enough thanks and that is something to keep in the back of your mind. With so many projects clamoring for attention and money these days, it's humbling that people have chosen to ally themselves with our project. We should never take this for granted.

Since we returned from Mount Kilimanjaro, I have held a number of events that proved to be popular. We have done things like a "Clean Water for Africa Day" for kids, with inflatable and water games, an annual 'Kilimanjaro Golf Fore Kids" tournament to raise money for the education project and various social events such as cocktail parties. The first annual golf tournament, organized by a very passionate and committed volunteer, Debbie Harbridge, turned out to be a big success, in spite of some of the heaviest deluge of rain I've ever experienced on a golf course. Every time someone putted a ball, a rooster tail of water sprayed up as the ball attempted to roll towards the cup. Golfers are famous for making excuses for inept play, but this was ridiculous! Nevertheless, we had more golfers for the second tournament and they seem to be prepared to continue to come back. (Hopefully, with sunshine each time!)

We always keep our eyes and ears open for creative fundraising ideas. The ideas usually come from talking and listening to people, as well as seeing what others are doing. Once an idea surfaces that appeals to us, we talk about it with friends and family to get a sense of whether or not it might work. It also gives us an idea of who might be interested in helping out if we decide to proceed. Not every idea is going to work. If we think an idea has a chance for success, we try to identify two or three issues that could be "showstoppers" and address them. Then and only then do we approach the people that we think might be interested in participating on a planning committee.

We've found that people like to have fun while contributing, and it's a bonus when they receive something in return. An event works better if it has an element of fun for the donors and volunteers. Before we left for Tanzania, we organized a "Welcome Back Party" at a local club called Tucson's in Ottawa. Admission was free, but we asked for and received a number of silent auction items from vendors in the city. We also arranged for a number of door prizes for the attendees. Chris and I showed our photos from our trip, and a representative from Plan Canada explained the organization's activities and how our projects fit in. The event was very well attended, and we raised over $4,000 that night for our projects.

I have made numerous presentations about our time on the mountain and our visits to the schools. It's immensely enjoyable for me every time I have the chance to relive the adventure. Each presentation has become a fundraiser in itself. I even made a presentation in my home town of Rapid City. About 25% of the area's population showed up for the presentation, and they were very generous towards the project. While the obvious benefit of the presentations is to generate more cash for our cause, I hope in some small way that people are encouraged by the presentations to undertake their own projects and become involved with a cause they care about.

Shannon Singh, Development Coordinator for Plan Canada, summarizes the value of volunteers and the need to get the word out. Shannon generously focuses on the work my family and I have done (for which I am very grateful), but anyone with a passion for helping can have the same impact. "Having worked with dozens of fundraisers over the past few years, it is always extremely heartening for me to see their dedication towards our cause," she says. "The commitment that volunteers put into their efforts is extraordinary, and ultimately, the key to their success. Not everyone reaches their monetary goals, has as many event attendees as anticipated or can secure large scale sponsorship, but that doesn't stop them. Even when their task appears insurmountable, I always tell organizers not to get discouraged. The impact of even a few dollars to the types of projects that Plan implements in developing communities is astounding."

Shannon goes on to say, "Even more than the dollars raised however, is the tremendous impact of getting our message out to fellow Canadians and raising awareness about global poverty issues. The efforts of Barry Finlay and his family have provided not only the obvious benefits of clean water and improved education to the people of Mwanza, Tanzania, they have also brought the story of Mwanza to hundreds of Canadians. In a short few months, Barry, along with support from friends and family members, is making a real and lasting difference in the lives of hundreds of children an ocean away."

How big or small should a fundraiser be? A larger event can potentially raise more money, garner more attention from the mainstream press, and help spread the word about the cause among a greater number of people. But there can also be significant cash outlay at the front end, (such as hall rental), which can reduce overall profits for the charity. There's more likelihood of financial risk if attendance isn't what was projected. The larger the event, the more risk undertaken by the fundraiser. Conversely, smaller events raise less money and don't attract the same attention a larger one would. But the amounts raised do not have to be huge to have a successful event. All of our events have had minimal risk attached to them as the upfront costs have been next to nothing or, at least small enough that we could ask for donations to cover them. And we have been fortunate enough to raise substantial amounts of money by staging a few smaller events.

At our events, silent auctions have been very successful for us. Guests feel they are getting a bargain as they put in their bids, and they're contributing to a worthy cause at the same time. I've also learned a very valuable lesson. It never hurts to ask vendors for contributions! Suppliers receive countless requests every day from various organizations, so it's understandable if they say no. But my experience has been that they will do whatever they can within the budget they have available. A polite request by letter or email with a complete explanation of the cause and description of the event, followed up by a polite phone call, will often generate a positive response and a donated item for the auction. I always try to follow up with an acknowledgement of the donation, an invitation to the event and a thank you note afterwards describing the amount raised for the charity. To my surprise, using this strategy has led to vendors asking us if we will need a contribution for an event the following year! As I am writing this, I just received an offer for an item for next year!

Regarding donated items, we've found we're most successful when we approach owner-operated stores rather than corporate mega stores. The larger stores and chains usually have an approved list of charitable organizations to which they contribute annually, and many are not allowed to deviate from that, even within their own local community. Or you'll be asked to submit a formal request donation form, which will then make its way through the chain's bureaucracy to someone who can make a decision. Smaller organizations, though, can decide on the spot whether they are in a position to make a contribution – and they appreciate the personal contact and chance to participate in a local area event as well as the promotion that their contribution may bring.

Our most significant event to date was held on May 18, 2010 at a small venue known as Petit Bill's Bistro in a trendy section of Ottawa. We decided to make a final push to finish raising money for the borehole at the Preschool. Once again, thanks to some very dedicated and focused volunteers, people came forward with donations and over 90 people attended the event. With the help of ticket sales, silent auction purchases and a 50/50 draw, we raised over $8,000, which was more than enough to complete the borehole. Why was this event more significant than the others? Because it meant that very soon 830 school children and 50 households (and countless more in the future) will benefit from having access to clean water. It is hard to fathom the impact that this will have on their lives! I am thrilled that we've been able to complete the project. It's impossible to thank all those that helped; some helped financially, others with their time and still others offered moral support and encouragement. No matter what their contribution, everyone involved should be proud and satisfied that they participated in an activity that will forever change (and potentially save) lives.

I was a neophyte when it came to raising money for a cause. When I began, I had no experience, no knowledge, no how-to maps or instructions. It's been a step by step learning curve for me all the way. Exhausting at times, stressful at others, but always – *always* – rewarding and thrilling.

For anyone reading this book that has felt their own passion and wants to jump in, you'll find many websites on the internet that will outline ideas for fundraising events and tell you how to go about them. Of course, there are countless other ways to get involved. Ours is one approach.

Chris and I went into our project knowing it wouldn't be easy. Yet we've succeeded beyond our wildest dreams. And we're not done. At the time of this writing, we remain two ordinary people who, with the help of countless friends and volunteers, have raised approximately $38,000 towards drilling the borehole and providing a building that will house new classrooms for the primary school. I hope the lesson you'll take from our story is that once you find a cause that inspires you, raising money for it is entirely within the realm of reality! And guess what? It's even fun.

CHAPTER 26

Finding Your Inspiration

AS WE ARE waiting in the airport in Mwanza, it dawns on me that this part of our incredible journey is nearly complete. We have had two life-altering experiences, and now we just have to go home (via Moshi) to continue with the next phase of our lives.

However, as we are about to leave the tarmac at Mwanza, it feels like we are going to have a third life-altering (or life-ending) experience on our flight back to Moshi The airline shall remain unnamed; the plane looks fine from the outside. Once we are inside, the first thing we notice is that the door to the overhead compartment won't stay closed. It gets worse. Our seat belts don't work, the seat tray won't stay locked in position, the door to the cockpit is swinging back and forth, and our seats won't stay upright. The stewardess isn't bothering to check whether we have our seatbelts done up and chairs and tables in the upright position. There is no point. Nothing works! The last straw for Chris is when he turns on the overhead light so he can read and forget about everything we have seen on the plane. Nothing! With a groan, his head sags forward and he closes his eyes. I am not sure if he is praying or trying to sleep, hoping that against all odds he will wake up at the end of the journey. Fortunately, the ground crew must have spent some time maintaining the engine, because the fact that we survived and are writing these words is evidence that we did make it to our destination successfully.

I tend to take a fatalist view to flying. Once I am on the plane, there is nothing I can do about it, so I think about other things to distract me. I spend some time thinking about the inspiration or motivation it takes to accomplish a goal and where that comes from – for me, anyway. Webster's Dictionary describes motivation as "the goal or mental image of a goal that creates a motivation." In our case, the image of standing on top of Mount Kilimanjaro, and then the image of the children at the school in Tanzania was my motivation. But if that was all that was needed, it would have been simple enough. We would just have to focus on our end goal and do it. We're motivated by the goal of not being hungry, so we eat. We're motivated by the goal of being rested, so we sleep. We're motivated by the image of standing on a mountain, so we climb it. Uh, no…it doesn't quite work that way.

Inspiration is similar. As we moved along on the journey to our end goal, there were times when it would have been easier to just say, "Well that was fun…it was a good try…now let's get back to reading a book." Accomplishing something outside my comfort zone required inspiration from time to time. I didn't have to seek it out. I was surrounded by it. I just had to realize it was there and use it to my best advantage.

For me, there are two types of inspiration. First, there is the inspiration that comes from more distant sources. I find stories about seniors or people with disabilities doing amazing things with what they have to be inspirational. It makes me realize that even though I have reached the "sixty plateau," I am healthy so there is no reason why I can't attempt to do the things I want to do. We have all attended funerals of friends and relatives who have died much too young and have not been given the opportunity to accomplish everything they wanted to do. I realized that if you want to do something, you can't wait. Tomorrow may not be there for you. In a sad way, that is inspirational. It's not in my nature to think about things I should have done and I don't intend to do it on my death bed either!

There is always inspiration to be found from various books about people that you admire. One such source for me is author Greg Mortenson, who wrote the books *Three Cups of Tea* and

Stones into Schools. Mortenson made a disastrous attempt at climbing K2, the second-highest mountain in the world with the second-highest climber fatality rate, in 1993. When he visited a village in Pakistan, he was so impressed by the generosity of the locals that he promised to come back and build a school for them. As his website describes it, "By replacing guns with pencils, rhetoric with reading, Mortenson combines his unique background with his intimate knowledge of the developing world to promote peace with books, not bombs, and successfully bring education and hope to remote communities in central Asia. *Three Cups of Tea* is at once an unforgettable adventure and the inspiring true story of how one man really is changing the world—one school at a time." The second part of our journey involved helping others and *Three Cups of Tea* and its author were certainly inspiring to me in our quest to help out some kids in Tanzania.

However, one can look much closer for sources of inspiration and in my experience, one need look no further than family. My family is my second source of inspiration. Every family has inspirational stories. My brother Keith struggled long and hard with his disease and never once did his wife, son or daughter hear him complain. In fact, they often commented that even on his worst days, if Keith was asked how he was, he would respond, "I'm fine."

Keith lost his battle in August 2009. I'm convinced that he chose his time to go because he knew his family would be taken care of and he was satisfied that he had fought as hard as he could for as long as he could. In the end, he didn't win the war but he won a tremendous number of skirmishes, and he was satisfied with the effort he had given. He will always be an inspiration to me, but the moment that stands out most in my mind was a phone call I had with him in the early stages of deciding whether I was crazy to even think about climbing Mount Kilimanjaro. I was telling him about my plans and my trepidation about undertaking such an adventure, and his response, without hesitation, was, "If it is something you want to do, you should do it." I will never forget those words. They were inspirational to me.

Evelyn has also been an inspiration to me, as she has been dealing with osteoarthritis for a number of years. Osteoarthritis is a degenerative disorder of the joints caused by gradual loss of cartilage. Bony spurs develop at the edges of the joints, causing severe pain. It has resulted in both of her knees being replaced. Yet, Evelyn soldiers on. She is taking Aquafit sessions three times a week and, while her issues have limited her activities, they have not stopped her, and I never hear her complain. In fact, her motto is that you can be *in* pain but you don't have to *be* one.

Both of our daughters-in-law are determined and assertive career women who will knock down walls to achieve their goals. They are both an inspiration.

Benefitting from our own upbringing and the lessons learned along the way, we have tried to instill in our own sons the will to work for everything they get, to appreciate everything they receive and to be tough enough to realize that, while there will be setbacks in reaching goals, the fight should continue if it is something worth fighting for. Somehow, that has happened beyond our wildest dreams. They have chosen career paths at opposite ends of the spectrum, but both have made us very proud while we watch their progress as the years go by. Chris is self-motivated in pursuing knowledge. He is decisive and has a dogged determination to chase down his goals. His decisiveness became apparent at a gigantic yard sale we took him to at age two when he spied a basket selling for 10 cents that he immediately decided he preferred over anything else within his $1 budget at the sale — and there were a number of items within his budget. His determination was in evidence early when he would attempt to negotiate the number of peas he had to eat on his plate, starting around age six. Chris was a tremendous inspiration to me leading up to and during our trek up Mount Kilimanjaro by training and climbing with two rips in the meniscus of his right knee. (What is it with knees in our family!!??) He was obviously in pain, but he persevered.

Our other son Trevor has chosen a career path that is wrought with extreme highs and lows, disappointment and satisfaction, adulation and criticism. He is a professional musician and performer. He chose the entertainment business knowing full well that he would be reviewed, critiqued, praised and criticized, and that he might never enjoy a steady, reliable income like Chris.

Trevor has been pursuing his dream to be a professional musician since the age of six. Since we recognized his interest in music at a very early age, we suggested to him that if he saved his money to buy a guitar, we would then buy an amplifier. It didn't take long for him to save his money from his newspaper route, his allowance, birthday and Christmas money, and the money his sympathetic grandmother was slipping him under the table. Trevor managed to buy his first guitar, and we found ourselves having to come up with the money for the amplifier. (We didn't really complain.)

Evelyn and I are not musically inclined, other than having a deep love for music. The boys grew up listening to the Rolling Stones, The Who and others from that era. I took Trevor and his buddies to see Motley Crue and Whitesnake at a very early age, so I suppose we are somewhat responsible for the path that he has followed.

Trevor reached one of his first milestones when he began playing professionally around age 15. I would take him to open mic sessions, and he easily fit into the local music scene with much older musicians. He was so in love with his guitar that his peers at school threatened to put a picture of him with his guitar in the "Couples" section of the year book.

Chris: Ultimately that picture did make it into the yearbook in the "Couples" section, much to the chagrin of his girlfriend at the time, as I understand it.

His mom and I had lengthy discussions with him about perhaps wanting to find a second career *just in case the music business didn't pan out*. We soon discovered that the discussion was going nowhere, so we backed off so that he could pursue his dream for a "little while." I managed Trevor and his band in the early years, and although I didn't really know what I was doing, I tried to find them gigs and teach them something about money.

I can remember one particular discussion with the owner of a bar who said, "How much beer will they sell?" I said, "Well, they're 16 years old, so their friends either won't be able to attend or if they do get to attend, they won't be able to drink." The bar owner promptly said he wouldn't be able to hire them then. He was upfront about it: it wasn't about their talent; it was about the beer sales. To which I replied, "I guess by the time they are old enough to sell beer with their performances, you won't be able to afford them." While that discussion didn't accomplish anything, it *was* very satisfying.

That was the beginning of the limited understanding I have of the music business. I don't profess to fully understand it, and probably never will. In most businesses, talent equates with success. In the music business, having talent might take you a long way, but then again, it won't necessarily. The corollary is that you don't necessarily have to be that talented to become a star. Stars can be created. I consider the music business to be like professional sports – up to a point. There are a number of baseball players in the major leagues who command enormous salaries for their skills. Then there is everyone else at various levels in the minor leagues where you'll find players who are barely making enough to live on; some have to work two jobs to support their family. Yet, in baseball, there is usually an explanation as to why an individual is in the minors, such as the speed of the fastball a pitcher is able to deliver or the ability of a hitter to hit a curve. The music business is a whole lot more unpredictable than baseball. Apparently, I am not the only one confused by what it takes to make it in the music business. In his autobiography, *Clapton*, Eric Clapton, who is widely acknowledged to be one of the greatest rock guitarists of all time, admits that he didn't think the song "I Shot the Sheriff" was good enough to include on his album. He says upon the record company releasing it as a single, "…to my utter astonishment it went straight to number one."

Which brings me back to how Trevor motivates me. He has now been in the business some 20 years without flinching. That is what has impressed me the most and has inspired me to reach my goals, no matter how lofty they may be. My view of the music business is that it can be very cruel. There are many people arriving at the Nashville airport every day of the year with guitar in hand and visions of stardom dancing in their heads. And there are just as many leaving Music City every day with the knowledge that their dream has evaporated but not really understanding why. Yet Trevor has persevered.

In 2008, Trevor and Josée Déschênes, his manager and fiancé moved to Nashville to continue to pursue the dream. Evelyn and I are fortunate to have had many opportunities to see Trevor in action onstage, and we've shared many proud moments. In December 2009, we had the opportunity to see Trevor perform in a private setting with some of Nashville's top songwriters, and he fit right in. I felt that moment was vindication for his hard work and dedication. It wasn't the end goal by any means, but it certainly was a satisfying milestone.

Trevor has never wavered from his goal of success in the music business, in spite of the setbacks he has endured over the years. It is difficult to define success, particularly in the music business. There are those who are obviously successful based on hits and stardom, but even stars seem to crash and burn sometimes. Maybe the definition is more esoteric for musicians. Perhaps success is defined as having the nerve to follow your passion and being happy with what you are doing. And maybe more of us should be doing that, at least on some level.

Using a more concrete measurement, Trevor has released five albums and has the adulation of his fans and recognition by his peers, but he is not satisfied with that. He inspires me through his perseverance and he reminds me that the pursuit of goals and following a passion should never end. You can see him at (www.trevorfinlay.com) or if you get a chance, go see him live. You will see for yourself how well he is doing in a very difficult field.

Chris: Certainly watching my brother struggle through decades of hard work and keep at it for as long as he has, has been a huge source of inspiration for me.

The point I want to leave you with in this chapter is that inspiration is all around us! I have learned not to underestimate the inspiration that my own family can provide. As parents, we try to mold our children into our own images, so if we are satisfied with the job we've done raising them, our kids will provide inspiration for us right back. If we pay attention, we will learn things, like the determination with which they try to accomplish their goals as they undertake their own career objectives, and it is a gentle reminder of what we were trying to accomplish when we were younger. When we weaken in pursuing a goal, we just have to look at what they are doing for the renewed initiative to continue the pursuit. Stories about people we don't know can be inspirational, but I have learned that it is also important to allow ourselves to be inspired by our offspring and the family around us.

What is that sound? It is the comforting sound of the wheels coming down on the aircraft as we begin our approach to Moshi. Looks like we will make it after all!

Trevor rocking the stage

CHAPTER 27

So . . . What's Next?

ON OUR LAST day in Moshi, we meet with Peter again to find the souvenirs we want to take back to Canada. We are to meet an African acquaintance who has agreed to act as our guide at a rendezvous location. As it turns out, he is a no-show but as we are awaiting his arrival, we soon find ourselves surrounded by a number of local young entrepreneurs. They are a non-threatening, ambitious and pleasant enough group but they have a great deal of difficulty taking no for an answer. There are some policemen watching nearby with amusement, and I surmise they would step in if things get ugly. It seems more likely that they are there to enjoy the entertainment value.

The young gentlemen have handmade bracelets, necklaces and earrings, wooden carvings, paintings, t-shirts, beaded and carved artifacts, and Maasai clubs. The Maasai are a nomadic people living in Tanzania and Kenya who follow their cattle and sheep as the animals look for food in different seasons. I supposed the Maasai warriors use the clubs as weapons. I don't ask any questions. Our young entrepreneurs seem to be familiar with Canada and certainly with the value of Canadian currency. They want no part of the latter since they know it doesn't have the same value as American currency at the time. We finally buy some necklaces for a few American dollars, thinking the pushy young men will be happy with that and go away. One does for a few minutes, only to return with a four-foot square sheet of plywood absolutely laden with colorful necklaces of all shapes and sizes. We can't blame him for seeing an opportunity: us!

One is pestering me to buy a Maasai club for $35 U.S. I finally convince him that I have no use for a club, so he goes off to talk to someone else. A few minutes later, he notices my heart monitor watch. He comes back and asks how much my watch is worth. I tell him I have had it for awhile and have forgotten the value and he says, "$300?" Just to end the conversation, I say, "Sure." He says, "Okay, I will trade the Maasai club (worth $35 a few minutes ago) and 10 bracelets (worth no more than a dollar or two each) for your watch." I tell him I could have bought all that for $40 a few minutes ago. He smiles slyly and says, "Oh yeah," and goes away to find someone else to pester. I guess he had forgotten our previous conversation.

We have a lot of fun with those young men while we are waiting. Their English is pretty good, and they're only trying to make a living any way they can. We see them again off and on during the day and they wave, but never really bother us again. We learn that the entrepreneurial spirit is alive and well in Moshi.

That night we keep the agreement we had with the Australians to have a celebratory drink, and we all enjoy the outdoor patio at the Keys Hotel one last time. They are a wonderful group, and we wish them much success with the orphanage they are working on.

And then it's our time to go. Back to our homeland, back to our families and friends, and back to reality. One big adventure lies behind us, but another one lies ahead. We have pledged ourselves to an enormous effort, and we have a long way to go to realize that goal.

Chris and I deplane at the Ottawa airport on January 22 after the long, quiet flight home. It is difficult to explain the feeling I have as we walk toward the arrival area after clearing Customs. I feel like I'm standing taller and am much, much lighter, as if transported by some invisible cloud of euphoria. It is a feeling that can only be achieved, I think, by reaching a previously-unthinkable goal. We are exhausted from the 30-hour flight, the time zone changes and the effects of everything we have been through in the previous two weeks. But the fatigue can't remove the huge grins on our faces as my son and I walk through the door into the arrival area where Evelyn is waiting for us along with a group of friends holding up a "Welcome Back" banner and balloons. I was a little surprised but very pleased to see the people waiting. I knew we had accomplished something that some people can only dream about. But to have it recognized by friends was something special.

There's one more surprise waiting for Chris and me when we turn on our respective computers the next day. Trevor and Nashville co-writer Leslie Satcher have written and recorded a song called "Top of the World" with lyrics inspired by our climb. "I'll be calling from the top of the world/walking on clouds with my flags unfurled/when it's time one thing's for sure/ I'll be calling from the top of the world." I have to admit that it still makes me misty-eyed when I think that he took the time to write the song based on our journey.

Two years later, the magical feeling I had as I walked to the waiting area at the Ottawa airport has still not left me, and I doubt that it ever will. It has left me with the feeling that I can accomplish anything if I want it badly enough. The last two years have not been uneventful.

I am still fascinated by mountains and volcanoes. I recently had the opportunity to trek as high as tourists are allowed to go on Mount Vesuvius in Naples, Italy. While it is a day hike with an elevation of 4,200 feet or 1,281 meters, we were guided by a volcanologist who explained the history and inner workings of the volcano. It was a fascinating trip.

I recognize that no matter how exciting another mountain might be for me, the feeling I got the first time atop Kili will never be duplicated. It would be satisfying, but the exhilaration you get from doing something the first time can never be re-created. I think it would be a lot like the first time I ever saw the Rolling Stones. The Stones were my all-time favorite rock band, and they came to Toronto in 1989 during their "Steel Wheels/Urban Jungle Tour." Evelyn and I took Trevor and Chris to the concert, and sat so far away from the stage that the sound was out of synch with the images we were seeing up on the big video screens. But for me, it was still a huge thrill watching the Stones walk out onstage as I had been a huge fan for years. Since then, I've seen the band perform three more times and while I always enjoy their performances, I haven't been able to match the thrill I got from seeing them live the first time. I think that another climb would leave me with the same feeling. It would still be a huge thrill, but it would not be the same as our successful climb of Mount Kilimanjaro. (I guess there is something to the adage that you can't put your foot in the same river twice!)

My experience with my trainer and the subsequent training regimen required to prepare for the climb at the age of 60 resulted in a lifestyle change that I believe will stay with me forever. I am starting to realize that I have to work much harder as I get older; but it gives me a lot of pleasure to be able to debunk some of the useless stereotypes about people in their senior years. I have had two such situations happen to me since returning from our climb. In the first, I was inquiring about a boot camp that my local gym was holding. The young man I was asking warned me with a smirk that the class was for much younger people and that I would have a difficult time keeping up. Whether I would or wouldn't have had trouble was never tested. I opted not to join, but I went home muttering under my breath. In the second incident I asked a young Information Guide at Mont Tremblant in Quebec about the hiking trails on the mountain. Mont Tremblant has an elevation of 2,871 feet or 875 meters. She told me that there was a nice trail to the top that winds around the mountain and takes two hours and 20 minutes to complete. I asked about the one that goes straight up the mountain. She said, "Well, it takes me two hours to do it and I'm much…" The last part was left unsaid, but I deduced that had she finished the sentence, she would have said "fitter" or "younger." I hiked the trail in one hour and 48 minutes. It's comforting to know that age and gravity catches up to everyone eventually. Of course, stereotyping is not the sole domain of the young. As we get older, we also tend to stereotype younger people. Maybe I just did …

I still enjoy going to the gym, staying current about fitness and diet techniques and watching what I eat. I have become somewhat annoying to my wife, since I will check every can and box to see what the nutritional facts are. But this is because I want my body to continue benefitting from the gains I made during the preparation for the climb. I want to watch my granddaughters grow up through the eyes of someone who is healthy enough to enjoy them. My dad never got to know his grandkids, and I want to do everything I can to make sure that I have the opportunity he didn't have.

I continue with the fundraising efforts. We've learned as ordinary people at the grassroots level that we are the ones who can make a difference in the lives of kids around the world. The amounts we have raised are small in comparison to the need, but we continue to chip away. It is the collective that can make the difference. If even half of the 40,000 people who attempt to climb Mount Kilimanjaro every year raised $2,000 each, there would be another $40 million dollars per year to contribute to whatever cause the climbers are passionate about!

I humbly present the views of Plan Canada President and CEO Rosemary McCarney as she sums up the contribution of one ordinary person and his family: "Margaret Mead famously said, 'Never doubt that a small group of thoughtful, committed citizens can change the world.' Barry Finlay exemplifies the point. His passion-driven fundraising with family, friends and colleagues has multiplied the impact of his efforts many times over, making a profound and lasting difference on the lives of children in Mwanza, Tanzania. With better access to clean water and education, these children, and their families and communities, are getting the tools they need to help break the cycle of poverty for themselves and for their country. And while the challenge of tackling global poverty can seem overwhelming at times, it is the small but impactful actions of individuals like Barry that are fuelling a global movement for change. Thanks to people like Barry, we are steps closer to realizing that long term goal to create a better world for children everywhere."

So, where do Chris and I go from here? I will let Chris go first:

One of the things I am now most looking forward to in life, having now accomplished the goals as lofty as we set out to accomplish, is to take a trip back to the schools in the Mwanza region about 10 years after our climb. As we were visiting the schools and seeing how much good we can achieve with so little money from a North American perspective, I couldn't help but stop and reflect on how different life there was compared to the opportunities and privileges that my kids are going to be raised with. By that time, I would hope that my kids (who will be 11 and 9 then) will be old enough to recognize the differences and have their eyes opened to a different way of life and begin to see just how fortunate they are and how much good can be accomplished. The whole time we were on the mountain with the flag nearby, I just kept imagining how my daughters would one day hopefully be able to see the flag hanging in the school and see how much their father and grandfather achieved with some determination and hard work. I truly hope it will serve as inspiration to them and ultimately to their children, and their children's children, long after I'm gone. Hopefully, it will be inspiration and motivation to show that you really can do amazing things if you put your mind to it. Who needs to live forever when you can do some good that will impact generations to come.

Yes, the Africa we saw is a poor, hot, dry, dusty and mostly barren place. *But I also will go back.* It has a charm like no other. We were only there for a few days and most of what we saw of the country was from the perspective of thousands of feet above sea level. Africa has much more to offer. I want to observe firsthand the results of our fundraising efforts. I want to see the water flowing from the borehole that we are sure will tremendously enhance the lives of the preschool kids and their families and I want to see a school where the kids are still smiling, but where they don't have to sit on the floor or shoulder to shoulder. The reward from what we are doing is the satisfaction of knowing that one day there will be a doctor or lawyer or politician helping his or her fellow Africans as a result of what we ordinary people have done.

I will continue to address my fundraising efforts to Africa. Certainly, Tanzania is not alone in requiring whatever assistance we can provide. On a recent visit to Cairo we saw kids fishing in a canal where dead animals lay a hundred yards away. The chances of children achieving their potential in Africa are minimal given that the International Labour Organization estimates there are at least 10 million working children on that continent alone.

Because of the Kilimanjaro trek and what it did for me, I will continue to focus on Tanzania. I am very excited about having committed to another project with Plan Canada, which will address economic insecurity throughout Tanzania by training women and youth, helping them to acquire the vocational skills they need to secure livelihood opportunities so they can support themselves and their families. Savings and Loan Association groups will be formed so participants can access small loans and savings facilities to start businesses and manage household cash flow. Representatives from groups who show exemplary results will be enlisted as trainers for new groups in other communities, making the project a truly sustainable solution to a common issue in Tanzania. The Canadian Government of Canada will match gifts 3:1, stretching the value of donations. This five-year initiative will benefit 11,000 women and youth directly and ultimately touch the lives of tens of thousands of people across Tanzania, as entire communities are led on a path to self sufficiency. You can read more on my blog at www.plankilimnajaro.blogspot.com.

I haven't ruled out the possibility of another major trek, this time to Everest Base Camp. Some have asked why I wouldn't attempt to reach the top of Mount Everest. I think readers will be able to unanimously answer that question from what I have said previously but it comes down to three words. All together now: ropes and ladders!

Good health, conditioning, time and money will be the determining factors in whether or not I undertake another major trek. I know that there would be no guarantees of being successful on another trek at high altitude, but I also know now that

I would have a good chance of success, and thanks to my experience on Mount Kilimanjaro, I am not afraid to try.

As I look back now over the last two years and realize where I was, where I am, and where I'm going, it's almost hard to believe. I started out as a man staring at 60, with health concerns and normal fears. But all that changed suddenly when I reached out for the golden ring of impossibility, worked harder and longer and with more focus than I've ever worked before to achieve a dream, and somehow – I did it. My son and I did it. How many other fathers and sons can say that they have stood together atop Africa's tallest mountains, felt the chill of the wind across their faces, slept on the hard ground in below-freezing temperatures, and achieved the ultimate satisfaction of turning impossibility into reality together?

I am a lucky man. I have much to be thankful for. Yet, indelibly stamped in my mind, seared in my brain, are the images that came afterwards. Images of those children crammed into their tiny schoolhouse, striving for an education that could mean the difference between hope and despair in their lives . . . images of the little girls walking long distances to get water to drink, missing out on their learning . . . images of their dangerously polluted water sources and their meager living conditions.

I'm only one person, yet the effort I spend each year on raising money and trying to inspire others to become involved is the most worthwhile and lasting thing I could ever do. But there is still much more to be done.

After careful consideration, I entitled this book *Kilimanjaro and Beyond – A Life-Changing Journey*. It doesn't just apply to my life. I know now that I can make a difference in my life *and in the lives of others*. You and I can make a difference in our lives and the lives of others! It's a matter of putting one foot in front of the other with our eyes firmly on the summit. Fueled by hope and passion and dedication, you just keep going.

It's exciting!

It's realizable!

But most of all — it's very, very satisfying!

EPILOGUE

I Feel Like a Rock Star

YES, WE ARE going back! Touching down again on African soil on January 31, 2011 brings back a flood of memories, but not as much as the sight of Mount Kilimanjaro poking its majestic peak up through the clouds as we fly from Dar es Salaam to Mwanza. While my story started before Mount Kilimanjaro, it was the climb that was the highlight of the first part of the journey. Now we are back to see the fruit of the labor that was the second part. This time Evelyn has accompanied me to Africa and we are joined by Shannon Singh from Plan Canada.

The first order of business in our jam-packed itinerary, after we meet with the Plan Tanzania officials, is to meet with the District Commissioner so that he is aware of our presence in his district and notified of the schools we will be visiting. He will also beef up security at the hotel where we are staying. Then we buy 62 textbooks with money donated by some supporters before we left.

The next morning we all pile into the Plan Tanzania vehicle to go back to the primary school that Chris and I visited two years ago. I am a little apprehensive and very excited, not knowing what to expect. I mentioned at the end of the last chapter that this work can be very, very satisfying. I couldn't even begin to imagine how the changes we are about to see will make it even more satisfying!

There is the gleaming new school with four new classrooms, painted in the same color combination as the original. A number of tables and chairs are set up for a variety of government officials, school administrators, teachers and…us. Facing us are about four hundred primary-aged children. I think they are probably most excited about having some time out of the classroom. At least that is how I remember being when visitors arrived.

After we sign the guest book, the show begins. Nearly every adult present gives a speech, thanking us for the work we have done, and the children sing songs of thanks with words in English, such as, "We are family, we are happy…" There is immense pride in knowing that the sentiments are directed our way, but we are also representing over 600 people who have participated in our various fund raising events. We had brought a number of items with us for the children, including the textbooks, three soccer balls, candy, skipping ropes, yo-yos, Canadian stick flags, etc. Each one elicits cheers from the kids, but the soccer balls and the candy bring them to their feet.

Then we head off to visit the classrooms. On the way, Evelyn starts something by shaking a number of hands before disappearing into the classroom. As Shannon and I follow, all of the other students realize that some hands have been shaken and each one of the 400 or so want theirs shaken too, prompting Shannon to remark that she feels like a rock star. I have to admit that we are all reveling in our celebrity just a little.

Upon entering one of the new classrooms, the first thing that catches my eye is the Canadian flag Chris and I had carried to Kili's peak hanging proudly beside a Tanzanian flag. There was always the concern that the flag would somehow disappear, but there it is with all 200+ names of the donors who contributed to this moment prior to our climb. It would have been special if Chris had been here to see this, so I hope he can come back with his family one day. Behind the flag is the laminated world map that we brought last time. Obviously, the teachers have taken excellent care of what they have been given!

The second thing we notice is a sign that reads in part, "Thank you! Thank you! This is to certify that we are happy and glad to see you today. We are praying God for you proceeding with that good heart to help us." I have a lump in my throat and I notice a tear welling up in Evelyn's eye. I have to keep reminding myself that we only provided funding for one of the four classrooms because we are being treated as if we had provided an entire school.

We hand over some letters that the Youth Group at our church had written to some Tanzanian students who have been handpicked to write back, plant some trees and start a small stampede when the Canadian stick flags are handed out. Rulers suddenly appear in the hands of some of the teachers, quickly settling down the riotous group.

It is so enjoyable in the company of some very dedicated teachers and some very eager children that the time flies by way too fast. It is time for us to leave. It was many of those very teachers and students who convinced me two years ago that this project was worth finishing. It wasn't as much what they said as the dedication and enthusiasm they demonstrated. And here it is again. Only it has grown. One thing that really strikes me is the change in the atmosphere at the school. The teachers are far more confident this time and have no problem making eye contact. They are warm and welcoming. I don't know what to attribute this to but I would like to think that it is, at least in part, because we have gained their respect by delivering on our promise. It was a fantastic few hours but we have much more to do. I asked the Plan Tanzanian officials earlier if they considered the project to be complete and the response was heartening. They said that they will be monitoring the educational system at the school as the children progress through the grades. That was an important issue for me and an answer I wanted to hear.

There is one big concern as we leave. We are told the potential enrolment has grown to over 900 students compared to 525 when we were here two years previous. That's an increase of nearly 400 students in two years! We discuss this at lunch with two senior government officials. One of the officials says that a large family is well respected, especially in rural communities. The average family size is still about 6 and can be as many as 18. We shake our heads. We tell them that the average family size in Canada is something like 3 and shrinking. We tell them that some young families in Canada are foregoing children for the sake of their careers or because of the cost, and that schools are closing. They shake *their* heads. While we don't hold up

Canada's average family size as being necessarily ideal, family planning is still an issue in Tanzania. Large families may not be the only reason for the increase in potential enrolment as more girls are going to school – but it *is* one reason.

The next stop is 40 kilometers away at the preschool where the borehole is to be drilled. I have to admit to a little disappointment when I find out that it had not been completed. However, we are told that there are very few reputable drilling companies in Tanzania and Plan Tanzania uses one they have found to be trustworthy. Given the options, I would rather have that choice than see a well drilled that would not meet the needs or would not produce drinkable water at all. We see the drill at a site about five kilometers away and speak with the drillers. They assure us that the preschool is next. The borehole will be a deep well of about 60 meters (about 200 feet) to ensure the quality of the water. We also meet the Water Committee who will be in charge of the well and allocation of the water. They are a serious group and I am convinced that the borehole will be pumping water by the time this book is published and that it will be in good hands when it is done.

The third and final stop is a visit to a nearly completed residence for teenage girls at a secondary school, and it is an unexpected treat. We anticipate a nice quiet tour of the accommodations and then we will be on our way, but it isn't to be. When we arrive there is a sea of over 900 blue and white clad teenagers awaiting our arrival. The procedure is the same – a number of dignitaries, speeches and thank yous. We feel a little guilty, as we had nothing to do with this project but we are still made to feel like we were part of it. When the speeches are done, a number of girls split up so that some are with Shannon, some with Evelyn and the rest with me and they give us an excellent tour of the new facility. We plant more trees and we get to interact with the girls for a few minutes. Evelyn and I are talking with seven girls and one shyly points out that our skin is a different color and we think she is trying to say that in spite of that we are the same. She just can't find the words. Evelyn helps her out and the girls all readily and happily agree that we are not different in spite of differences in our skin tone.

Of the more than 900 students at the school, 400 are girls and sadly, almost all of the students are orphans. A residence is desperately needed, as the girls walk up to 10 kilometers to school in the dark so they are very vulnerable. They are also hungry and tired when they arrive. As there is only room for 100 in the residence, some difficult choices will have to be made as to who gets to live there. Criteria will be established based on issues such as disabilities, distance walked to school, etc. to determine who gets in.

At each location we have visited, someone has isolated me to lobby about something. At the primary school it was teachers' rooms, at the preschool it was more boreholes and here the girls are asking for more residences and a laboratory for conducting science experiments. They are not talking about an elaborate lab – just somewhere to mix two test tubes together. It isn't that they are ungrateful. There is just such a huge need and they see an opportunity to ask for a little bit more. Who can blame them?

As we talk with the girls, they tell us that two want to be pilots, two want to be lawyers, two more would like to be doctors and one a nurse. They are noble aspirations, but with the challenges they must face every day for the most basic things, it will certainly be an uphill battle for these girls to accomplish their goals. We were talking with an African friend about this later and he said that all Africans have dreams like everyone else, but at some point many realize that reality will not allow them to reach their goals so they settle for what they can be and accept their lot in life. The euphoria of whatever we have accomplished is dampened somewhat by this discussion but we have to remember that we have given some a chance to further their education and others the clean water they so desperately require to change their lives. Maybe some children will be able to achieve their goals as a result.

It is an incredible day! It is one that will stay with us for the rest of our lives and it will encourage us to keep working. Evelyn says as we are leaving, "I will never forget the children putting their hands out to be shaken as we walked to see the classroom. I took that to be their way of saying thank you. We were treated like royalty and you could tell that they really appreciated the 'Mzungu' coming through with their promise. I was very touched to be part of it all."

I can't resist one more comment about the rhythmic chaos that is the traffic in Tanzania. Similar to the last time we were there, as we drive along the highway there are people everywhere along the roadside. Some of the women carry large buckets of water or bundles on their heads. Some of the men are riding bicycles with six feet of sugarcane balanced sideways on the back of their bike. Others are struggling with carts full of bricks or who knows what else. Children herd goats or cattle when they probably should be in school. And they are all on the edge of the road or within inches of the side of the road.

Buses go by on the road, crammed with people hanging off the sides or out the window. Scooters are everywhere. Most of the vehicles are belching blue or black smoke with every gear change and even if the road is paved, there is dust raised by the constant motion on the roadside.

Now throw all of this into a confined space, add a few hundred thousand of each, all vying for very few parking spots, and you have the chaos of Dar es Salaam. But the amazing thing is that there is a rhythm to it all, a synchronicity that is created by a pecking order at play that everyone understands and adheres to. It basically comes down to smaller means of transport being trumped by anything that is bigger. The sound of a horn or flashing headlights encourages smaller means of conveyance to temporarily move to the side, albeit grudgingly sometimes. And it seems to work. In fact, I am sure if you could look down on it all from above, it would seem like a symphony is in progress with the crescendo occurring at rush hour. Evelyn often rode in the front next to the driver and she said she wasn't afraid. I think my driving bothers her more in Canada. But in spite of the rhythm, I would expect that if there is a list somewhere of the "Worst Things That Can Happen to People", being involved in a traffic accident in downtown Dar es Salaam is probably on it.

There was one more site visit that occurred while we were there. I mentioned in the previous chapter that we have a new project related to providing women and youth with savings and loan programs so they can start sustainable businesses to support their families. In Dar es Salaam we were taken to a ramshackle part of town where the houses are built of anything the inhabitants could scrounge: corrugated metal, Coca Cola signs, cardboard. We were led into a small room where a number of benches were set up. It was 35 degrees Celsius outside (95 degrees Fahrenheit) and it was humid. Inside the room, it felt like twice that. One meeting was just finishing and another was about to start. We were about to see the project in action. Those in attendance were mostly women. They had to shuffle over to make room for us. Most ignored us, some stole a glance and one or two outright stared. At the front were an accountant and a no-nonsense woman who chaired the meeting. The participants were there to request loans or to make payments on those they had received earlier. In order to receive a loan they need five guarantors who are responsible to pay if the person with the loan fails to do so. If they don't show up for the weekly meeting, or do not have a really good excuse for being absent, they are fined. One man earned a stern shake of the pen and a dirty look from Madame Chairman. The interest rate on the loan is up to 35%, depending on the length of time before repayment. But this is the savings part of the program and the money is eventually returned in the form of dividends. Being an accountant, I am reassured that there are controls in place on the financial transactions that would make any auditor proud.

Does the program work? After a lot of encouragement the participants start to tell us their stories. One woman tells us that she walks to the fish market, takes the fish home, cooks and resells them and makes $20 profit a day. That will help her pay the rent and buy food or pay for education for her children. A tailor buys cloth and makes suits, a woman buys clothes outside the city and sells them in the city, a woman buys soft drinks and resells them and a loan will allow her to buy them in bulk. And these are people with little or no education! It is changing their lives!! After hearing their stories and seeing the satisfaction in their eyes as they tell their stories, I *know* it works! While they barely cracked a smile while we were there, they nearly burst with pride when we congratulated them. It not only gives the participants a livelihood but it gives them a feeling of empowerment and self esteem and that is worth its weight in gold.

So I am convinced more than ever after our visit that we ordinary people can make a difference in the lives of others. It is just a matter of figuring out the way we want to do it. There are any number of ways. Ours is just one. And after having had the opportunity to see how others make do with what they have, I am more convinced than ever that we should take the time to make a difference in our own lives so that we can enjoy everything we have for a long, long time. We just have to take action. I hope you can agree that the rewards for helping ourselves and others are immeasurable.

We had the good fortune to do a small safari after our school visits, something Chris and I weren't able to do the first time due to time constraints. We visited the Serengeti, Ngorongoro Crater and Lake Manyara Park and it was tremendous. As we left Ngorongoro Crater, we stopped at two plaques commemorating a father and son team who had committed their lives to caring for wild animals and their place on the planet. They had a passion and they did something about it. Rather than sit idly by or complain about something that is or isn't happening, they must have found it far more rewarding to take action. For as it is says on Professor Bernard Grzimek's plaque, "It is better to light a candle than to curse the darkness."

The opinions expressed in this book are based on the personal observations of the authors and are not the result of extensive research.

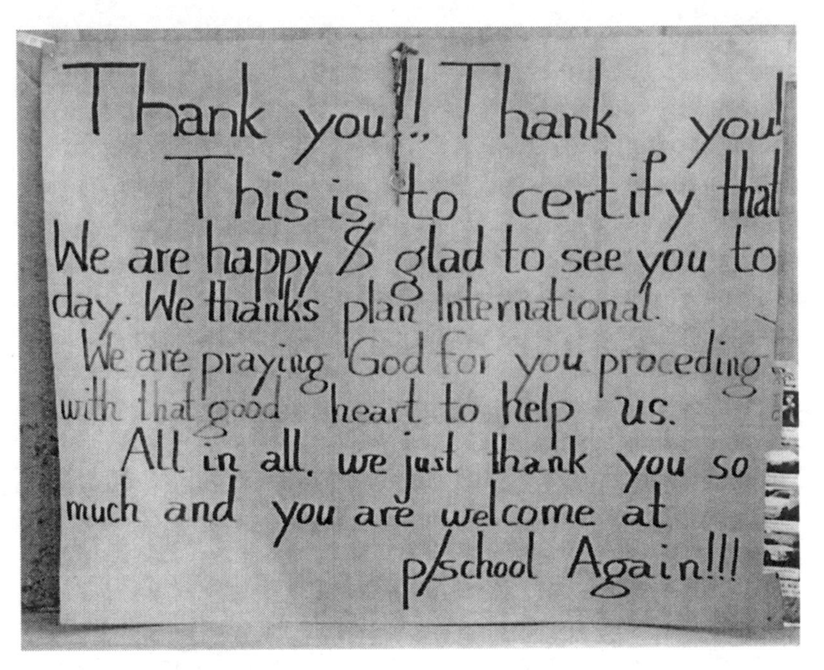

For everyone who has contributed in any way to our projects - we thank you too!